Presented

YORK COLLEGE LIBRARY

By

MRS. H. R. BOMHOFF

Ten Epochs of Church History

❧

Edited by

John Fulton, D.D., LL.D.

❧

Vol. VIII.

Ten Epochs of Church History

edited by

JOHN FULTON, D.D., LL.D.

A series of hand-books, giving a popular, comprehensive and authoritative church history. Price, $2.00 each, net.

Arrangement of Volumes

1. The Apostolic Age. By J. Vernon Bartlet, M.A.

2. The Post-Apostolic Age. By Lucius Waterman, D.D., with an introduction by Rt. Rev. H. C. Potter, D.D., LL.D.

3. The Ecumenical Councils. By Prof. W. P. Du Bose, with an introduction by Rt. Rev. T. F. Gailor, D.D.

4. The Age of Charlemagne. By Prof. Charles L. Wells, Ph.D.

5. The Age of Hildebrand. By Prof. Marvin R. Vincent, D.D.

6. The Age of the Crusades. By J. M. Ludlow, D.D.

7. The Age of the Renaissance. By Paul van Dyke, with an introduction by Henry van Dyke, D.D.

8. The Age of the Great Western Schism. By Clinton Locke, D.D.

9. The Reformation. By Prof. Williston Walker, Ph.D., D.D.

10. The Anglican Reformation. By Prof. William Clark, M.A., LL.D., D.C.L.

THE AGE OF THE GREAT WESTERN SCHISM

BY

CLINTON LOCKE, D.D.

❀

28168

New York
Charles Scribner's Sons

1901

YORK COLLEGE
Library No. 22908

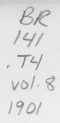

BR
141
.T4
vol. 8
1901

Copyright, 1896, by
THE CHRISTIAN LITERATURE CO.

THE CAXTON PRESS
NEW YORK.

270.5
L814w

PREFACE.

ENAN, in the preface to one of his books, says, "When I read over what I have written, the matter appears to me very poor, and I perceive that I have put in a multitude of things of which I am not certain." Every writer of history must feel the force of those words. Personal likes and dislikes, race, language, religion, environment, so color testimony that the absolute certainty of even the smallest item seems doubtful. In this account of the great schism, a period particularly marked by fierce passions and violent religious hatreds, the writer has often felt entirely at sea amid the conflicting witnesses.

Of course in working over material as often used as the events of the fourteenth century there could not be much originality; everything has been said and resaid a hundred times; but an attempt has been made to give a coherent, concise, and yet interesting recital of a period full of stirring events and rich in glorious promise.

It was determined not to have any notes. These volumes are, as the prospectus states, " popular monographs, giving a bird's-eye view of the most important events in the life of the church," and in that light notes are more confusing than helpful. The writer is very much indebted to many historians. He would mention especially Creighton, Milman, Robertson, Jahr, Hecker, Försteman, Gieseler, Renan, Von der Hardt, Dietrich von Niem, Hefele, Kurz, Gregorovius, Gibbon, Sargent, Wratislaw, Eneas, Sylvius, and Hallam. Sometimes credit is given in the text, sometimes not, but especial thanks are due for the aid afforded by Creighton's "History of the Papacy" and Milman's "Latin Christianity" in the preparation of this volume. The writer regrets that the publication of parts of the immense collection of documents in the Vatican archives relating to the Avignon popes, which is now being favored by the present enlightened pontiff, was not available.

The preparation of this volume has been a delightful task, and it was with regret that the closing chapter was written. The wonderful vitality of the Christian religion and its supernatural origin can be by no other argument more forcibly impressed upon the mind than by the fact that it survived the degradations and wickednesses within its own exponent, the Christian church of the fourteenth century.

CLINTON LOCKE.

CHICAGO, August, 1896.

CONTENTS.

CHAPTER I.

THE FOURTEENTH CENTURY.

HE fourteenth century of the Christian era was no dull and stagnant period of the world's history. It glows with life and power. The stage is filled constantly with men and scenes which stir the blood and fix the attention. Consequences which we feel now in religious and in political life had their causes then, and blows struck then for religious and social liberty cut so deeply that in this very hour we note their effects. There were dark tragedies and amusing comedies. There were splendid gatherings of clerics and of nobles, and there were battles where the cross of the merciful Saviour, Prince of Peace, was borne before the armies of either side, and was held to sanction causes in principle and practice directly opposed to the genius of Christianity.

In a book of this size many minor incidents must be omitted, many interesting episodes passed over. The political history will be considered only so far as it is interwoven with the history of the church, and it was only in the century we are considering that men began seriously to think that the two things could be at all separated and such a thing exist as a church and state untrammelled by each other. We have to consider in this volume: the tremendous blow that the papal pretensions received; the prestige which the Papacy lost by the transference of the seat of its power to Avignon; the vast consequences of the great Western schism; the noble efforts of the councils of Basel and Pisa and Constance to reform the church; the lives of Wyclif and of Huss; and with these great questions others of less importance, such as the mysterious episode of the ruin of the Templars, the terrors of the Black Death, the story of the Flagellants, the career of Rienzi, and the victory of national languages over the Latin tongue.

When the curtain rises on the fourteenth century, the stage is occupied by two figures which dwarf all the rest, the Pope of Rome, Boniface VIII., and the King of France, Philip IV., surnamed "the Fair" on account of his personal beauty. Boniface had succeeded that weak pontiff Celestine, whom Dante with infinite scorn places in the mouth of hell among the

> " Melancholy souls of those
> Who lived withouten infamy or praise,"

and stamps him forever with the bitter words:

> " The shade of him
> Who made, thro' cowardice, the grand refusal,"

referring to his cowardly resignation of the papal throne.

If ever one man was a contrast to another, Boniface was to Celestine. His will was indomitable, his craft

unfathomable, his ambition beyond the dreams of
even his most ambitious predecessors. He was
determined to push the domination of the spiritual
power to its extremest point, and for a while it
seemed as if he would succeed; but all over Europe
men were beginning to think. The universities were
heaving in the throes of discussions on civil and religious liberty, and a body of great lawyers was coming to the front, who could oppose, in the fashion of
the day, imperial precedent to papal pretension with
equal learning and with splendid ability. The Pope's
most powerful foe was the King of France, like himself strong-willed, crafty, ambitious, resolved to put
his foot on the neck of priestly domination. His
was not a noble, unselfish nature, but he was an able
man, and, like many another of as coarse a grain, he
was to be the instrument, under God, of checking the
career of papal supremacy, which was at that time a
menace to the liberty of every subject of every European kingdom.

It is not within the limits of this book to enter
into all the details of the quarrel over supremacy
between the Pope and the kingdom of France, the
insulting documents which hurtled through the air
between Rome and Paris, the unfounded charges
against Boniface's private character, the forged mes-
sages on either side, and the ever-garbled statements.
A reading of the document put forth in 1302 by the
Pope, styled "Unam Sanctam," and which is of un-
disputed authority, shows to what height papal claims
could climb, and the good grounds on which the
French king, clergy, and people rested their opposi-

tion. In this "constitution," as it is called, Boniface
lays down in the strongest terms the superiority of
the spiritual to the temporal authority. With that
false exegesis so common then, so utterly repudiated
now by the most superficial scholars, he cites St.
Peter in the garden saying to our Lord, "Behold,
here are two swords." This, he says, shows clearly
that the temporal as well as the spiritual sword was
in St. Peter's hands, and our Lord confirms that
opinion by saying not, "It is too much," but, "It is
enough." The spiritual sword is to be exercised by
the church, the temporal sword by laymen under the
direction of the church. The temporal must always
be subject to the spiritual, as being a lower power.
God Himself, in Jeremiah i. 10, by the words, "See,
I have this day set thee over the nations and over
the kingdoms, to root out, and to pull down, and to
destroy, and to throw down, to build, and to plant,"
clearly shows the authority He meant the Pope to
have. Kings are accountable to the Pope, but he is
accountable to no one except God. It is no wonder
that this document drove the whole French nation
into absolute fury, the flame of which Philip diligently fanned. Then followed more insulting and
defying words, and at last the Pope not only excommunicated the king, but forbade any election to any
church office until the king repented, suspended the
universities from teaching, and gave notice that he
was about to publish a bull deposing Philip and re-
leasing his subjects from all allegiance.

Boniface had one great ally, which Philip could
not match: he had plenty of money for bribing and

the gaining of support, and he obtained this money
at the jubilee which marked the opening year of this
century. This jubilee merits a few words. During
the year 1299 one of those curious and unaccounta-
ble waves of feeling swept over the European world.
A general conviction was evident that great indulgences and spiritual privileges were to be obtained at
Rome at the beginning of the new century, and from
all over Europe a crowd of pilgrims about Christmas-
tide thronged every church and every street in Rome.
The Pope took advantage of this movement, and,
actuated perhaps by sagacity, perhaps by religious
enthusiasm, mounted the pulpit in the Basilica of St.
Peter on February 22, A.D. 1300, and ordered the
immediate promulgation of a bull which granted extraordinary indulgences to all who within that year
should with penitence and devotion visit the tombs
of St. Peter and St. Paul. This was to be called the
jubilee, and it was to be celebrated every hundredth
year.

The effect of this bull was tremendous. All Europe was fired with religious frenzy, and throughout
Germany, Italy, and even England the roads were
crowded with pilgrims. As many as two hundred
thousand strangers were in Rome at one time, and
so admirable was the management that every one
easily found good lodgings and good food at reasonable prices. The offerings were enormous. Priests
stood raking away from the altars the gold and silver
coins thrown down before them, and all this money
was for the Pope alone. He had the sole distribu-
tion of it, and who can doubt that he used much of

YORK COLLEGE LIBRARY

it to advance his interests in his quarrel with France and England? The world and the church have greatly changed since the first jubilee, but these pilgrimages still continue. The time has been successively shortened to fifty years, thirty-three years, and twenty-five years. It stands at that figure now, and the last ordinary jubilee was held in the year 1875. The next will be due in the year 1900.

CHAPTER II.

HE insult to Philip conveyed by the papal bulls was too deep for that proud king to brook, and just when the Pope seemed most triumphant the knell of his doom had struck.

He had left Rome on account of the excessive heat and gone to his native place, Anagni, where he got ready the document degrading Philip from his throne, and he intended to publish it in the cathedral of Anagni on the 8th of September, 1303. Of course creatures of Philip in the papal court kept him informed of all the Pope's movements, and on September 7th an armed force, commanded by William de Nogaret and Sciarra Colonna, and in the pay of France, burst into the papal palace with cries of, "Death to Boniface!" "Long live the King of France!" The Pope robed himself in the papal vestments of ceremony, put the crown of Constantine on his head, and, taking his seat on the papal throne, awaited their coming. They paused a moment at the sight of the brave old man, but the rude Colonna dragged him from his throne, and with buffets and jeers the ribald soldiery paraded the venerable pontiff through the streets of the town mounted on a horse with his face to the tail.   After this cruel insult they threw him into prison, but on the second day his townspeople rescued him, and, escorted by papal troops, he got back to Rome.

He was at that time eighty-one years old, and all this suffering told deeply on his enfeebled frame, so it was not surprising that on the 11th of October he was found dead in his room.   Of course his death was attributed to poison.   In those days and for centuries after, the sudden death of any prominent person was always supposed to come from poison, but there is not the slightest proof of it in this case. He certainly had undergone enough to kill him.   All Christendom shuddered when it heard of this outrage on the Vicar of Christ, and Dante, while he has branded Boniface with his bitterest words and consigned him to a very low place in the other world, well expresses the general feeling in those lines in the " Purgatorio " (xx., 89) :

> " I see the flower-de-luce Anagni enter,
>   And Christ, in his own Vicar, captive made;
>   I see him yet another time derided;
>   I see renewed the vinegar and gall,
>   And between living thieves I see him slain."

The Sacred College consisted at that time of twenty cardinals; but two of them were of the Colonna family and had been expressly excommunicated by the late Pope, therefore they could not vote.   The other eighteen assembled immediately, and eleven days after Boniface's death unanimously raised Nico-

las, Bishop of Ostia, to the papal throne. He took
the name of Benedict, and was the eleventh Pope of
that name. The choice seemed a very wise one.
Benedict had been a loyal and steadfast friend of
Boniface, and was a man of calm, wise character,
very anxious to do all he could to make peace. This
was shown by his immediate despatch of officers to
France to remove the excommunication from king,
clergy, and people. He restored to the French
cathedral chapters their right of election and to the
universities their privileges, and granted the tithe of
all the French benefices to Philip for two years. He
did more; he pardoned the Colonnas and restored
the two Colonna cardinals to their dignity. In fact,
he pardoned nearly every one except William de
Nogaret, and a few others who had been personally
engaged in the outrage at Anagni. Surely he would
have been wanting in the first principles of manhood
if he had pardoned those ruffians.

If Philip of France had been in any way reasonable, all the disasters which darkened down upon the
church during this just opening century might have
been avoided; but Philip, as far as the dead Boniface
was concerned, had the ferocity of a tiger, and nothing would appease him but the calling of a council
which should brand the dead pontiff with heresy,
simony, impurity, and all imaginable crimes. Benedict was too true, too brave, too honest, to consent
to any such thing. How could he lend himself to
such a degradation of the Papacy as would be presented by the spectacle of a general council sitting in
judgment on a Pope already dead? He had tried

conciliation; it had produced no effect, and he now resolved to change his tactics. He left Rome, not only on account of the heat, but because he had no liberty of action there, for the city was filled with jarring factions, and a liberal supply of French gold was a powerful weapon in the hands of his enemies. He retired to Perugia, and there, on the 7th of June, 1304, he issued a bull denouncing William de Nogaret and fourteen others, excommunicating them all and citing them to appear before him on the feast of St. Peter and St. Paul, June 29th. On the 27th of June the Pope, after a short illness, died of dysentery, brought on by overindulgence in ripe figs, of which he was very fond. Of course poison, as usual, was suspected, but there is not a shred of evidence to justify the suspicion.

The cardinals hurried together, and now there commenced in Perugia a conclave noted for its squabbles, its factions, and its delays. It is said that nearly a year had passed when the people of Perugia, wearied out by the unending strife, threatened to deprive the august body of all provisions, and even to loot their palaces. There were two factions in the conclave, the French and the Italian, and neither could elect without some help from the other. The French faction was headed by Napoleon Orsini and the Cardinal of Prato, as wily and astute a man as ever lived, and (though the other cardinals were not aware of it) the confidential agent of King Philip. The leaders of the Italian faction were Matthew Orsini and Francis Gaetani, nephew of Pope Boniface. Both factions felt that something must be done; very shame forced them to a decision.

The French faction, through the Cardinal of Prato, proposed that the Italian party should nominate three candidates, not cardinals (for at that time the election was not restricted to the members of the Sacred College); these candidates must be prelates living beyond the Alps, and Prato pledged his side to agree on one of the three. He was playing a deep game, but its success proved his keen sagacity. The three were nominated, and the choice of the Sacred College fell upon one of them, Bertrand de Got, Archbishop of Bordeaux. Momentous choice it was, and full of momentous consequences.

If ever a side considered itself a winner it was the Italian party in the Perugia conclave when they had secured the election of Bertrand de Got. He was, though a Frenchman, a subject of the King of England, who then ruled over Bordeaux and much else of France. He had been involved in a well-known quarrel with King Philip's brother, and was therefore not thought to be *persona grata* to the king. He had been a firm friend of Boniface in the French quarrel, and he owed his high ecclesiastical position entirely to the favor of Boniface. If any man seemed likely to stand by the memory of the accused Pope he did, but the Cardinal of Prato knew his man better than his colleagues. It had been arranged in the conclave, probably by Prato to gain time, that forty days should elapse between the nomination and the election of a new Pope. As soon as Bertrand had been nominated Cardinal Prato hurried off a secret messenger to King Philip, urging him to see the Archbishop of Bordeaux, flatter him, promise him his full support, and make his own terms with him. The king lost no time in doing so.

It has often been stated that the two met in secret in the forest of St. Jean d'Angely, but from documents lately discovered a personal interview seems improbable. The negotiations were doubtless carried on by go-betweens. We know all about them, however, for the king did not conceal from his intimate friends the conditions he had made with Bertrand in exchange for the promise of his favor and support. These conditions were six in number: 1. The excommunication of the king was to be withdrawn (this Benedict had offered) and he was to be pronounced without blame. 2. All his agents in the struggle with the Pope were to be absolved. 3. He was to have for five years a tenth of all clerical incomes. 4. The memory of Boniface was to be condemned. 5. The Colonna cardinals were to be cleared of all ecclesiastical disability. The sixth condition was kept secret, and unending have been the conjectures as to its import. No one knows for certain, but the general opinion is that it was the condemnation of the Templars.

Philip sent word immediately to the Cardinal of Prato that everything was all arranged, and the cardinal forthwith notified his brethren that his side was ready to proceed to the election without delay. Bertrand, in whom both parties saw their man, was unanimously elected, and took the name of Clement V.

Of course, as he was not present, much of the ceremonial had to be omitted. The Italians in the conclave were soon awakened from their dream of trust in the new Pope by receiving a summons from him to come to Lyons for his coronation. They had not imagined that any other place than Rome could be the papal residence, but many a long year would pass before the realization of any such hope, for now was to commence the "Babylonish captivity," as Roman Catholic historians designate the residence of the popes in Avignon, calling it that because it lasted, like the captivity of the Jews, just seventy years. Protestant historians often apply the word "Babylon" to papal Rome, which proves it to be a convenient word of cursing, the use of which depends on your point of view.

The coronation of the Pope was not a very happy affair, for a wall crowded with spectators fell just as Clement, mounted on horseback, was passing in procession. The Duke of Brittany, who was leading the papal horse, was killed, the Pope knocked off his steed, his tiara sent rolling in the mire, and the king's brother very badly hurt. As soon as possible after his coronation Clement began to carry out his agreement. He absolved the king and declared him free from all blame. He gave him the tenths. He restored the Colonna cardinals and created ten new cardinals, all French, and then he paused, for he could not, servile tool though he might be, bring himself to pronounce pardon on all those who had so abused Pope Boniface, nor could he condemn Boniface as a heretic and a villain, for, if he did, it would seem to invalidate his own election by cardinals whom Boniface had created. No wonder he shirked these questions, but he was in the hands of a deadly hater. Philip was determined not to let go until Boniface had been pronounced by the Pope a heretic, and his body dug up and burned. Clement did at last absolve Nogaret and his companions on condition of their performing certain penances, and he managed to stave off the affair of Boniface to a general council which he announced he would soon call at Vienne. He hoped the king would die, or something turn up that would let him out of the net in which he struggled. His hopes were realized; something did turn up. It was the famous affair of the Templars, which was now absorbing Philip, the Pope, and every one else.

CHAPTER III.

THE FALL OF THE TEMPLARS.

HE military order of the Temple was the noblest, the most famous, the bravest in the world. For nearly two hundred years had the Templars been the bulwark of the Christian power in Palestine, and now that all hope of any further Christian rule was over, and their last battle fought, the remnant came back to join their brethren in France, where the order was the most numerous and its installation the most splendid. The Grand Master was James de Molay, and with a long and magnificent train of knights and serving-men, twelve horses loaded with gold ducats, and sumpter-mules by scores bearing silver and tapestries and precious Eastern treasures, he landed from Cyprus and travelled through France to Paris, where, in the Temple, so well known in modern times as the prison of Louis XVI., was the chief seat and treasure-house of the order. King Philip marked the splendid home-coming and resolved on the destruction of the whole body.

A great deal of mystery has been thrown around his action by historians, but the motives which actuated him are evident enough. In the first place, Philip was one of the most avaricious men known in history, and was always in pecuniary difficulty. He knew that the Templar body was the richest corporation in the world and would prove a splendid booty. He owed them immense sums, and no man loves his creditors. But there was a far deeper reason than this. Philip was an able and far-seeing king, and he was confronted with the spectacle of a body of eight thousand knights and a vast host of servitors and clergy camped right in the centre of his kingdom, armed better than any of his soldiers, more thoroughly trained, and under the absolute command of one man, who might at any time take a notion to make himself king, and in that case had power to summon to his aid not only the French knights, but eight thousand more scattered over Europe. Such a course, especially if the religious difficulties were kept up, would be sure of papal support, for the order of the Temple had always been devoted papalists.

Philip doubtless reasoned that he would be able to offer very little resistance to such a force, and so, for reasons of state, the king determined to down this gigantic spectre which threatened his very life. He knew that he would not be without sympathy, for the Templars were cordially hated. The French clergy hated them because they had so many privileges; for example, whenever an interdict spread its ghastly pall over a land, and the parish churches were all shut, and only with maimed rite were children secretly baptized and the dead buried, by papal decree the churches of the Templars were exempted.

There the lights blazed, the censer swung, the mass was chanted, and all the rites of the church were openly performed. The nobles hated them for their haughtiness and exclusiveness and because they had come by inheritance into possession of so many of their family estates, and the people hated them because they were proud and rich, luxurious and overbearing.

Rumors of grave scandals existing in their order had been floating about Europe for many years, but the Templars had always disdained to notice such reports. Their power and their wealth made them feel thoroughly secure, but it proved a false security. The king laid all his plans with the secrecy of the grave. On October 12, 1307, the Grand Master, De Molay, was one of the pall-bearers at the funeral of the king's sister, and was treated by the king with distinguished courtesy. He woke at dawn of day to find the armed soldiers of the king by his bedside, and before the night of the 13th had come everywhere in France the highest and the noblest of the knights were dragged to prison, over nine hundred in Paris alone. The news flew like lightning over Christendom, and men asked everywhere in amazement, "What are the charges and who made them?"

The originators of the charges seem to have been two apostate Templars, Squin of Béziers and a Florentine named Naffo, both men of bad reputation and who made each other's acquaintance in prison. From such wretched creatures Philip listened to the following accusations: 1. That the candidates for Templar knighthood were compelled to deny Christ and spit on the cross. 2. That they worshipped an idol. 3. That they were allowed to practise sodomy and committed other indecencies. 4. That parts of the mass were omitted in Templar churches. 5. That the Grand Master and other chief officers, though laymen, gave absolution. 6. That they often had betrayed the Christian cause in Palestine. The truth or falsity of these charges has been one of the " vexed questions " over which whole volumes have been written, and even now, with the keen light of nineteenth-century researches thrown upon it, it is difficult to come to a perfectly fair conclusion.

Of course, if the charges had never been sustained the case would have begun and ended with the first informers, but the difficulty lies in the number of admissions made by many of the knights in their examinations before courts and councils. Yet when we look into these admissions we find that they were wrung from tortured men, worn out by harsh treatment in loathsome prisons, men used to luxury and unable to bear physical torture, while brave as lions on the battle-field. Courage and endurance of physical pain are two entirely different things, and there are but few natures which can long withstand horrible torture. Most men will confess almost anything to have the torture stopped. Against the admissions must be offset the conduct of hundreds of knights who, under the severest torture and amid the flames of the stake, would not acknowledge one atom of the crimes charged. Indeed, of those who confessed, the vast majority retracted everything the moment the pressure was removed. For example, it was said that the Grand Master, De Molay, confessed that every accusation was true to a commission of cardinals sent by the Pope to Chinon, and yet when this confession was read over to him in Paris he started with horror and declared that it was all a forgery and a lie, that he had never said such words. The aged and high-born chief lifted his arms and fervently recited the Apostles' Creed to show his perfect orthodoxy.

Some of the charges can be explained. The denial of Christ and the spitting on or near the cross were probably meant as a trial of faith. The candidate was asked to do this, and if he complied he was shown the lesson of constancy and faith, and adjured never to yield to such a temptation. No idol (the idol's name was said to be Baphomet) was ever found, though all the commanderies were searched thoroughly and suddenly before the inmates had time to secrete anything. As to impurity, there was doubtless much of it. It was likely to exist more or less in communities of high-living, drinking soldiers, but there was not the slightest proof that it was a common or acknowledged thing. The omission of part of the canon of the mass rests on the vaguest and most unreliable testimony. The absolution by the Grand Master seems merely to have been the remission of certain penalties for violation of discipline, which was perfectly within his power as a layman; and the secret treaties with the Saracens can be explained by those courtesies of war which had grown up from the long intercourse of Turkish and Christian warriors in Palestine.

Every secret society rising to prominence has always been the subject of much gossip and slander. The Masonic body in America, in the early part of this century, came very near being as ruined as the Templar order, from the rumors and accusations against it, which its members in vain denied.

Whether the Templars were guilty or not did not much influence Philip. He was determined to have their blood and their money, and the Pope was too much in his power and too servilely his henchman not to aid him in every way. On May 12, 1308, fifty-four Templar knights were burned alive in Paris, every one of them protesting until the smoke suffocated him that the order of the Temple was entirely innocent of the charges brought against it. Hundreds of others were burned all over France, but there is no true evidence that one recanted at the stake, and it seems scarcely credible that all these high-born men, noted for their honor, were liars and deceivers.

The Pope had put off for some time the Council of Vienne, but he and Philip came to a secret understanding about Boniface and the Templars, and he was no longer afraid to call it. He summoned it, therefore, for October 16, 1311, and it was attended by nearly two hundred bishops and abbots. Philip had secretly agreed that, if the Pope would allow him to carry out his designs on the Templars and sweep them from the face of the earth, he would abate his demands about Boniface's memory, and would say nothing more about any heresy or his wish to have the body dug up and burned. So on April 4, 1311, a bull was issued which annulled Boniface's acts against the king and kingdom of France and ordered them to be torn out of the papal registers, but nothing was said about heresy or evil living on the part of the Pope. Philip was pronounced as innocent as a lamb of all personal hatred of Boniface, and to have been merely actuated by great zeal for the church.

So this great matter of Boniface, which had convulsed the Christian world for so many years, was settled, and in the Council of Vienne but little was said about it; both sides dropped it. Clement labored hard to get the order of the Temple condemned, when nine Templars suddenly appeared before the council, prepared to defend the order and demanding to be heard; and the whole assembly, except three French prelates who had been concerned in the burning of some Templars, declared that they ought to be heard. The Pope adjourned the council, and for many months argued and strove with the bishops; but they would not consent to condemn the Templars unheard, although the King of France bullied the council at its very doors. At last the Pope, in a secret consistory of the bishops on whom he could depend, announced that he was going to dissolve the Templar order, not as a condemnation for crime, but as a question of expediency, in order to put an end to all the trouble. This was agreed to, and on April 3, 1312, the act of dissolution was read in a general session of the council, the king and his family being present.

The Pope did not dare openly to give the vast wealth of the order to Philip, but reserved to himself

YORK COLLEGE LIBRARY

and to the church the disposition of the knights and of their possessions; the king, however, laid hands on a great deal of their treasure. In France most of their lands and castles were given to the Knights of St. John, who, however, did not profit much by their legacy, for Philip put in so many claims for rent and caretaking and repairs that he eventually got a great part away from them. In the other countries of Europe trials of Templars were here and there held, but they suffered no severe punishment. Of course everywhere, on the receipt of the decree of the council, the order was dissolved, and generally their possessions were given to the Knights of St. John, save in Spain, where they were given to the crown to use in the crusades against the Moors. Many of the Templars became Hospitallers, many went back to civil life, and in a few years this magnificent order had completely vanished away.

It is one of the strangest episodes in history, a ruin so complete, so quietly accomplished, and about which there was so little regret. It only shows how completely their race was run and their errand accomplished. It is not worth while to bring up a modern theory, which has been advanced by some German writers (Wilcke, Von Hammer), that they had within themselves a secret section, where was taught a sort of Oriental mysticism, tinctured with Gnosticism, into which members after long probation were initiated, and that this gave rise to the heretical charges against them; for the theory rests only on vague grounds and far-fetched conclusions. It is not history. St. Antonino of Florence puts in one sentence reason enough for their ruin: "The whole affair was woven together by avarice, that these religious Templars might be despoiled of their goods."

But one more scene need be shown from their romantic history. For six years and a half the Grand Master, De Molay, and three other chief officers of the Temple had been immured in a Paris prison, and on March 11, 1314, they were brought out for execution. The Archbishop of Albi mounted a pulpit and began to read their confessions, but the Grand Master, undaunted by his dreadful sufferings and fate, interrupted him, and, according to Milman, used the following words: "Before heaven and earth, on the verge of death, when the least falsehood bears like an intolerable weight upon the soul, I protest that we have richly deserved death, not on account of any heresy or sin of which ourselves or our order has been guilty, but because we have yielded, to save our lives, to the seductive words of the Pope and the king, and so by our confessions brought shame and ruin on our blameless, holy, and orthodox brotherhood." This made a profound sensation in the great crowd present, and the moment the king heard of it he ordered the wood to be got ready for their burning, and the stakes were set up just where the statue of Henri Quatre now stands in Paris. There De Molay and one of his officers—for the other two recanted—were burned alive, the cruel king sitting by and feasting his eyes on the horrible spectacle. There went about the rumor for many years that De Molay in his dying moments had summoned Clement and Philip to meet him within forty days before the throne of the Most High, but there is no good authority for any such statement. Neither Clement nor Philip died until the year after, but their base and unrighteous conduct is not forgotten, and there is a secret order now extant and flourishing which never meets without repeating in the most solemn way, " Remember Clement V. ; remember Philip the Fair."

CHAPTER IV.

AVIGNON.

T was not until 1309 that Clement, after dwelling for a while in various cities in southern France, settled himself at Avignon, in Provence. Although in France, it was not then French territory; it belonged to the countship of Provence, and therefore at that time to the kingdom of Naples, for the kings of Naples were counts of Provence. The popes bought it from Joanna of Naples when she was a minor, in 1348, and promised to pay her eighty thousand crowns of gold for it; but she always said they cheated her out of that, and she got nothing. She was a lady, however, who had as little regard for truth as she had for some other virtues. Avignon remained papal territory through all the centuries down to 1791, when it was definitely united to France. It is still surrounded by the lofty walls built by Clement VI. in the middle of the fourteenth century and still in perfect repair, though they enclose much empty space, for the population has greatly dwindled since the popes reigned there.

In the midst of the modern town, which is well

worth a visit, rises the vast and gloomy palace of the popes, its ugliness a good type of that ugly period of church history. Clement V. commenced it, but it was enlarged and completed by Benedict XII. It has served for many years as a barrack, and its vast halls, where many a conclave sat, are cut up into many stories and filled with the iron cots of the soldiery and all their arms and trappings. All this is, however, to be changed. The French government has constituted it an historical monument, and it will soon be restored as nearly as possible to its ancient splendor. Petrarch was entertained here, and here Rienzi was long a prisoner, and here are still the ruins of the chamber of torture, and still are the frescoes visible in what was the private chapel of the popes. Seven popes reigned there, all Frenchmen: 1305, Clement V.; 1316, John XXII.; 1334, Benedict XII.; 1342, Clement VI.; 1352, Innocent VI.; 1362, Urban V.; 1370, Gregory XI., who quitted Avignon for Rome. But there came afterwards the antipopes who resided at Avignon forty years: 1378, Clement VII.; 1394, Benedict XIII.; 1424, Clement VIII. It is a pleasant town with lovely views, and the papal tombs in the old cathedral are interesting, though there is an old proverb which does not speak very well for its climate: "Avenio ventosa; sine vento, venenosa; cum vento, fastidiosa." ("Avignon the windy; without wind, malarious; with wind, nauseating.")

Clement did not long enjoy the quiet he anticipated after the long-drawn-out and trying cases of Boniface and the Templars were settled. His health became so precarious in 1314 that he resolved to try the air of his native place, but he got no farther than Roquemaure, on the Rhone, where he died April 20, 1314, and his body was removed to Carpentras for burial. While it is true that he had sold himself to the French king, it is also true that he skilfully evaded complying with all that pushing monarch's claims. He really managed the affair of Boniface with great cleverness, and escaped, when escape did not seem possible, censuring in terms the memory of that much-abused pontiff.

He also got the better of Philip in a much more important matter, for which Europe owes him a debt of gratitude. Philip at one time seemed to be in a fair way of getting the sway over most of Europe. French princes ruled in Naples and Hungary, and in England Edward II. was married to Philip's daughter and completely under his thumb, and he exhausted every power of intrigue to have his near relative, Charles of Valois, chosen Emperor of Germany. This would have made French influence paramount not only in Germany, but in Italy. Clement realized the danger of this, and, as he was quite as good an intriguer as the king, quietly, yet very astutely, he separated himself from Philip's candidate and threw in his lot with Henry of Luxemburg, who was elected, and crowned by papal authority. One must read Dante's " De Monarchia " to understand the feelings of the imperialists, or Ghibellines, as those were called who, seeing the failure of the papal scheme for universal monarchy, imagined it could be realized by a secular prince, the Emperor of Germany. To them, and to Dante especially, Henry of Luxemburg was the ideal of this universal king.

As for morals, Clement did not even have the slight merit of hiding his immorality. He led a life of almost open profligacy, and suitors for papal favor well knew that the person first to be gained over, if they would win their cause, was the Pope's mistress, the well-known sister of the Count of Foix.

Clement was very severely blamed then, and has been ever since, for not going directly to Rome on his election, but there is very much to be said on his side of the question. Rome was anything but a pleasant residence at that time, and the life of a Pope, exposed to the sudden riots and violent outbreaks of the Roman populace when their will was crossed in the slightest way, could not have been a very enviable one. Few men, with a safe retreat from which they could freely exercise their pontifical authority, would have considered it their bounden duty to transfer themselves to a place where their slightest act was immediately arraigned before the bar of a rough populace, and where the streets of their capital echoed unceasingly to the clang of arms, as the contending barons, who had turned the whole city into a collection of frowning fortresses, met in conflict.

It was not alone the influence of the French monarchy and the endearing charms of their native land that kept the Avignon popes so long away from Rome ; it was a wholesome and well-founded dislike to imperilling their lives and their liberty. Documents now in course of publication by the Vatican show how extensive were their connections with the whole world during that period, and that they were by no means idle in missionary and other enterprises. Of

course the removal of the papal court and the vast
crowd of strangers in attendance upon it worked
most disastrously on the fortunes of the Eternal City.
Rome soon became a scene of isolation and of an-
archy. The churches were so neglected that even in
St. Peter and in St. John Lateran cattle grazed up to
the very foot of the altar. Many of the churches
were roofless, and as ruined as the remnants of classic
days. A legate sold the marble blocks of the Colos-
seum to be burned for lime, and the records of the
cathedral of Orvieto show more marble imported
from Rome than from Carrara.

The only public work which can be positively
traced to the Avignon exile are those grand marble
steps which lead up to the church of Ara Cœli. As
travellers of those days looked from the baths of Dio-
cletian, their eyes ranged over a wide space of un-
cultivated fields, solitary churches, scattered rows of
houses, masses of ancient and modern ruins, with
nothing to distinguish it from the open country but
the circuit of the old walls of Aurelian. Two ruined
cities, the classic and the mediæval, made up the one
ruined Rome.

CHAPTER V.

JOHN XXII.

HE cardinals who had assembled at Carpentras for Clement's funeral resolved to hold the conclave for the election of the new Pope in the same place, and it shows how completely and how swiftly the residence in France had changed the complexion of that body, when we find that of the twenty-three composing the Sacred College only six were Italians. Dante wrote a letter to the conclave, which is still extant, urging the return of the papal court to Rome. He uses very plain language: "You, the chiefs of the church militant, have neglected to guide the chariot of the bride of the Crucified One along the path so clearly marked out to her. One only remedy now remains. You who have been the authors of the confusion must go forth manfully with one heart and one mind into the fray in defence of the bride of Christ, whose seat is in Rome. You must work to the disgrace of the covetous Gascons, seeking to rob the Latins of their name." From other high sources also earnest appeals were made to the cardinals to elect a Pope pledged to go back to Rome.

Although the great majority were Frenchmen, they were divided among themselves. Gascons could not agree with Limousins, and while they were hesitating and bickering a mob headed by two of Clement's nephews burst in upon them with shouts of "Death to the Gascons!" and amid the blaze of the building where they were gathered, the frightened cardinals fled away from Carpentras. Two years passed away before they could be induced to meet again, Louis, Philip's successor, persuading them to come to Lyons, promising that they should not be shut up in the electing-room, as the rule was; but the king suddenly died, and Philip V., his successor, did not consider his brother's promise binding. He immediately walled up and guarded the convent where the conclave was meeting, so the cardinals were forced by hard necessity to elect, and they chose the Cardinal of Porto, who took the name of John XXII.

He was of humble origin, simple in his habits and decent in his morals. He had a very violent and easily aroused temper, was well read, a good preacher, skilled in affairs and very active in prosecuting them. There are now reposing in the papal archives sixty thousand documents written in the time of John XXII. and connected with him. It is said that he secured the votes of the Italian cardinals by pledging himself never to mount a horse except to return to Rome, and that he evaded the spirit of his vow by going from Lyons to Avignon in a boat and never leaving it to mount anything. This was quite in the taste of the times.

The new Pope did not have to contend with an

adversary of as strong a character as Philip the Fair, for the French kings of his time were not cast in so vigorous a mould; but he had to meet two adversaries of very different character and very determined. One was " the Spirituals," under which head may be placed all those who were horrified and shocked at the worldliness and sinfulness of the church as exemplified in its highest prelates, and the other was the rapidly growing party which held that the empire and the Papacy were entirely separate and each ought to confine itself to its own department.

Dante is to us the best-known champion of that theory. He held that the empire (the Roman, of course) existed before the church, which received from Christ no authority over the empire, and has none. " Yet let Cæsar be reverent to Peter as a first-born son to a father." Egidio Colonna and John of Paris both asserted that the temporal and spiritual powers were alike independent, each with its own sphere of action. Christ did not exercise jurisdiction in temporal matters, therefore Christ's successors should not.

John very soon found himself in a violent quarrel with the extreme party in the Franciscan order. That party held that no Pope and no priest had any right to hold property, that our Lord and His apostles had the use but not the ownership of whatever was necessary for life, and so the Pope should only have the use of what was needed for the life of the church, but no power of disposing of it or of hoarding treasure or using it for luxury. They used the curious argument that St. Francis had owned nothing, therefore if the Saviour did, it would prove Him less perfect than St. Francis, which would be blasphemous. This doctrine is, of course, right in the face of all social polity, and it is no wonder that John XXII. could not stomach it, and that he issued bull after bull, and employed fire and sword, as well as bell, book, and candle, to put down so pestilent an error. The Franciscans were, however, mutinous and obstinate, and did not hesitate to accuse the Pope of heresy. They set him forth as the head of a carnal church, full of luxury and worldliness, and they opposed to him their own spiritual church, simple, poor, God-fearing. All the tongues of all the wandering Franciscan friars, the idols of the people, wagged incessantly, preaching everywhere that the Pope and the Roman court were the mystical Antichrist and the great Babylonish harlot mentioned in the Bible. Such very plain speaking in the Church of Rome had never been heard before.

While John was in the midst of this difficulty, another loomed up—the succession to the German empire. Two claimants, Frederic of Austria and Louis of Bavaria, laid their cases before the Pope, and each begged his confirmation. He at last took sides for Frederic, and then of course the Spiritual Franciscans took sides for Louis. John arrogantly asserted his right to decide who should be emperor, and commanded Louis to give up or be excommunicated. Louis had not the slightest intention of submitting, and was soon excommunicated and put under the ban. Such high-handed action in a Pope aroused great and wide-spread resistance. Everywhere great lawyers and casuists arrayed themselves on the emperor's side, and now commenced the publication of some of the most remarkable documents that ever have appeared on the principles of the liberty of the subject and the independence of the civil government in regard to the church. Some were from the clerical, some from the lay element.

Among the former let us cite two, the General of the Franciscans, Cesena, and William of Occam, called the "Invincible Doctor." Cesena (Tractate against the errors of the Pope) appeals from the Pope to the universal church and a general council which in faith and morals is superior to the Pope, since a Pope can err in faith and morals, for many Roman pontiffs have fallen from the faith, but the universal church cannot err, and a council representing the universal church is likewise free from error. William of Occam (Tractate on the decisions of the Pope) says: "It is not necessary that there should be one primate over the church, for the head of the church is Christ, and by its union with Him the church has unity." Occam lays down the doctrine of the supreme authority of Scripture in plain terms. The Pope may err, a general council may err, the fathers are not entirely exempt from error; only Holy Scripture and the beliefs of the universal church are of absolute validity.

On the lay side, the most remarkable book of all, and one well worth reading now, was the "Defensor Pacis," written principally by Marsiglio, an Italian of Padua, professor in the University of Paris, forming one of that brilliant group of which William of Occam was a member. It is astonishing to find in the beginning of the fourteenth century, and amid all the tyranny and despotism, both clerical and lay, everywhere prevailing, a man laying down the very principles on which the American government is founded. He says: " The legislator, or the first efficient source of law, is the people, or the community of citizens, expressing their will by a majority in a general assembly."

This book made a great sensation and had a wonderful influence, and the brilliant arguments which were made in the reforming councils owed their might to the study the speakers had made of this keen and unsurpassed analysis of power. " The church," he says, " is the community of all who believe in Christ. So far as a priest has property it must be subject to the general laws of property. Christ exercised no coercive jurisdiction and did not confer any on the apostles; on the contrary, He warned them by precept and by example to keep away from it. Priests have no power to compel men to obey God's law, but as doctors advise for the body, so can they advise for the soul. Civil punishment attaches to heresy only so far as it interferes with civil law. St. Peter had no authority over the other apostles, and the legend that he was the first Bishop of Rome rests on no Scripture authority and has no historical evidence. No decretals of popes are necessary to support Catholic faith; that rests on Scripture alone; and when doubts arise about the meaning of Scripture they can only be settled in a general council of the faithful in which both clergy and laity have seats. The authority of the Roman bishop is necessary to give a head to the church and a president to its councils, but he has no power of coercion beyond what a council bestows. His primacy springs from convenience and respect." There is really no book which had greater weight in the development of European politics and in preparation for the Reformation than this treatise of the Paduan lawyer.

All efforts to reconcile the Pope and the Emperor Louis proved ineffectual, and the Pope's bitter hatred aroused deeper and deeper opposition to him among the Spiritual Franciscans, and indeed among all holy-minded and peace-loving people. The Franciscans eagerly watched John's every word, and the Pope, being a good talker and preacher and priding himself on his knowledge of theology, uttered a great many. With great joy they discovered that he had fallen into heresy. He asserted in a sermon that the saints would not enjoy the beatific vision of our blessed Lord until the end of the world; that even St. Peter and the Blessed Virgin would not have that privilege. Now, of course, this is a matter of pure speculation. Nobody can possibly know anything about it, and the Scriptures do not favor any particular view; but that did not make any difference. Europe rang with the cry and counter-cry of heresy, and the King of France referred the matter to the theological faculty of Paris, which fiercely debated this purely imaginary question. The Pope spent much money and many arguments in trying to get a decision in his favor, but the university would not hear to it, and the French king declared: " If the saints do not behold the Godhead, of what value is their intercession?" which is a *non sequitur.* The storm raged so fiercely that John had to succumb, and he declared that he had only intended to state an opinion, not to decide in favor of it. It was not, however, until he lay down to die that he abjured his pet doctrine and professed the ordinary opinion that souls not in purgatory are in heaven and see God face to face as far as separate souls can so do.

The quarrel between the Pope and Louis cannot be followed in all its details, but January, 1328, witnessed the crowning of Louis in Rome at St. Peter's by two bishops, already excommunicated. As soon as the Pope heard of it he excommunicated everybody connected with it, and Louis retorted by summoning an assembly at Rome which declared John a heretic and a traitor and deposed him from the papal throne. This same assembly a few days after elected by acclamation Peter, a humble monk, once married, but now separated from his wife, to be Pope. This assumption by the Roman people of the right to name the emperor and the Pope was most extraordinary. What possible right could they have had in the matter? Louis, however, invested this shadow Pope with the papal mantle, and he took the name of Nicolas V., and forthwith named seven cardinals, commenced to sell offices and preferments in regular papal style, and to put money in his purse. His power was, however, short-lived. The Romans soon grew tired of Louis, and he fled away from Rome, taking the antipope with him. In less than two years he was back in Germany and Nicolas left behind at Pisa, where the noble with whom he had

taken refuge gave him up to the real Pope on consideration that his life should be spared. He went to
Avignon, put a rope around his neck, and threw himself at the feet of John, who raised him up, took off
the rope, and assigned him an apartment in the papal
palace, where he lived in seclusion until his death.

The feeling against the Pope grew more and more
intense, the Franciscans always fanning the flame.
It was not only the fruit of his hard nature, but his
avarice, his terrible greed, and his utter worldliness.
No Pope before him had ever so plunged into politics ;
no Pope, avaricious as many had been, had ever
reached out such cruel, grasping hands as he had.
He was a very ardent promoter of that hideous
abuse called " annates," which reserved to the Pope
the first year's income of all ecclesiastical dignities ;
and it was the attempt to press that tax in England
that led, in 1351, to the passage of those famous
statutes of " provisors " and " premunire," the former
directed against papal presentations to benefices, and
the latter forbidding the faulting of judgments rendered in the royal courts and any resort to foreign
tribunals. Long after, they served Henry VIII. many
a good turn in his war against papal supremacy.

And now the time had come for John to die and
leave all his treasures and his worldly politics. He
was over ninety. He had been an able pontiff, and
held his own well against the sovereigns of Europe,
but he was not a very notable example to the flock.
He was the second cobbler's son who rose to the
papal throne, a fact which speaks well for the church
in those days, when a feudal aristocracy had its iron

heel on everything. So narrow was he in his ideas of the Papacy that he could scarcely be brought to confer the cardinalate on any one outside his native diocese of Cahors. Loud was the outcry after his death when the enormous treasure he had accumulated came to light. There were eighteen millions of gold florins, and seven millions in plate and jewels. No wonder Villani, the historian, says, " He had forgotten those words of Scripture, ' Lay not up for yourselves treasures upon earth.' " Yet cruel, avaricious, simoniacal, and worldly as he was, he never one day neglected to hear mass and perform the outward duties of religion, so possible is it to disconnect entirely outward form from inward holiness.

CHAPTER VI.

BENEDICT XII.

HEN John died, A.D. 1334, he left a college of cardinals twenty-four in number, mostly French, and it is curious to see at their head a name which centuries later was everywhere heard in the world of Napoleon and the Restoration, Cardinal de Talleyrand-Périgord. The conclave met in Avignon, and was shut up according to the usual form in the papal palace. They all agreed to offer the vacant tiara to the Cardinal de Comminges, but they wanted a pledge from him first that he would not remove from Avignon. He absolutely refused to be bound by any such pledge, and it was necessary to choose some one else. They juggled and traded with their votes, and by an accident happened to choose, December 30, 1334, the one they least expected and perhaps least wanted, James Fournier, Bishop of Mirepoix and Cardinal of St. Prisca, who took the name of Benedict XII. As soon as his election was announced to him he said, " Brethren, you have chosen an ass." It would have been much nearer the truth if he had said, " You have chosen a fox,"

for there was nothing of the ass in his character, but a great deal of shrewdness and excellent sense.

Nothing worth noticing stands against his moral character, though Petrarch declares he was over-fond of eating and drinking. He certainly labored earnestly to purge the Augean stable of Avignon. The city was crowded with idle priests, greedy for crumbs which might fall from the Pope's table of preferment. He drove them away to their convents and their rectories. He did away with that pretty custom of his predecessors of promoting six or eight persons whenever a vacancy occurred, and thus pocketing six or eight fees. He ordered that no canonries in cathedrals should be bestowed on boys under fourteen years of age, and that they ever should have been bestowed on men under thirty is a bitter comment on the worldliness which ruled the church. His remark to the French king, Philip VI., speaks well for him. When that king insisted on his keeping up a bitter quarrel with Louis of Bavaria, he replied, " If I had two souls, I would willingly sacrifice one to do your Majesty service; but as I have only one, I cannot go beyond what I think is right."

He differed from the popes before him in refusing to advance his family, and said that a Pope should be like Melchizedek, without father, without mother, without genealogy. He tried bravely to reform the monastic institutions, but his attempt only aroused a fierce animosity, and it was a monk who wrote the famous couplet about him:

> " Nero he was, to laymen death, a viper to a monk;
> He never told the truth and constantly was drunk."

But such couplets, especially in those times, must be received with a great deal of allowance. He was a peace-loving man, and it was a bitter grief to him that he could not act as he wished, and make up the quarrel with the emperor. Louis fretted deeply under his excommunication, although the civil authority in Germany ordered it everywhere to be utterly disregarded. The imperial electors, with the exception of Bohemia, stood bravely by him, and at a meeting at Rhense in 1338 they resolved that the empire was held directly under God, and that an emperor chosen by all or only a majority of the electors needed no confirmation from the Pope. But all this did not calm the soul of the frightened Louis. The papal interdict hung over him like a poised sword, and in 1341 he made abject attempts at reconciliation. In 1342, however, he did a thing which placed his pardon further off than ever, and at which all Europe stood aghast.

Margaret, Duchess of Tyrol, called generally Margaret Maultasch, or " Pocket-mouthed Meg " (though Hefele says the name came from the castle where she was born), had been married to a very young Bohemian prince. It was an ill match, and Louis wanted her and her vast heritage for his son. No bishop could be found to grant a divorce and dispensation, for Margaret and the emperor's son were related within the prohibited degrees. Louis was foolish enough to decree the divorce himself, and grant a dispensation for her marriage to his son. He had an evil adviser in this, Marsiglio, who wrote the " Defensor Pacis." His argument was the one which now prevails extensively, that if a marriage or a divorce be against the law of God, neither church nor state can make it lawful; but if the impediment be one properly removable by human law, the civil power, and not the ecclesiastical, ought to remove it. Civil power does that everywhere now, but then it was considered almost blasphemy thus to intrude into the province of the church, and certainly as matters stood between Louis and the church nothing could have been more foolhardy than this arbitrary exercise of power, especially as it was not to uphold a general principle, but for a selfish advantage. This counsel of Marsiglio was a great blow to the rapidly spreading church-reform party, and its effects were seen when the great schism came into existence.

The quarrel between church and state, as personified in Benedict and Louis, was blazing as fiercely as ever when the death of Benedict occurred, April 25, 1342. It is said that when dying he was asked to empower some one to absolve him, but he replied, " I will not give my glory to another, but submit myself to the mercy of God." The monkish chroniclers, who, as has been said, disliked him for his attempt to reform the monastic orders, finish their account of him by saying, " Nobody cried much for him."

CHAPTER VII.

CLEMENT VI.

GAIN the conclave gathered at Avignon. It was not a long one, and the choice fell, as was to be expected, on a Frenchman, the Archbishop of Rouen and Cardinal of St. Nereo, who took the name of Clement VI., and immediately named ten cardinals, all Frenchmen but one. He was in every sense a Frenchman, gallant, gay, generous, brilliant, and in every way the reverse of his predecessor. His morals were of an easy kind, and no one in the world loved ease and splendor and good living more than he. He forgave and forgot with truly royal nobleness. He scattered bishoprics and abbacies and rich preferments with a lavish hand, and put forth a brief that any poor priest who should present himself at the palace in Avignon within two months would find it greatly to his advantage. It is said that one hundred thousand availed themselves of this invitation, and each man went away with something in his cassock pocket. He intended not only to help others to have a good time, but to have one himself, and the court of the ruler of Western Christendom soon became the talk of the world for hard drinking and free living. The great Avignon palace spread out its boundaries, and painters and decorators thronged its vast halls.

Petrarch, not much of a moralist himself, for he left two natural children, has bequeathed to us some bitter words about the vice and worldliness of the papal city. Much that he said cannot be decently transcribed. He calls Avignon the sink of Christendom. "Whatever you have read of the gates of hell," he says, "will apply to this place." His utterances, however, must be taken with some salt, for he was enraged at the steady refusal of the Pope and cardinals to go back to Rome. That vice, not only of the popes, but of all unscrupulous men in power, nepotism, never reached a greater height than under Clement. He heaped rich revenues on even his remotest cousins, even on every applicant from his own town. One of his nephews he made a cardinal at eighteen.

Merciful and easy-going as Clement was, there was one man towards whom his heart was as hard as the nether millstone, and that was the German emperor, Louis. It was indeed very hard for any one to get on with Louis, for his life was a continual see-saw between the church and the state. One day he was governed by the one and the next day submissive to the other. He began by threatening not to acknowledge Clement for Pope, and then when the Pope excommunicated him over again he licked the very dust under the papal slipper, begged the Pope to dictate the terms of his submission, was ready to take back anything and everything, and in set terms, which we can read, to submit his affairs, his state, his wishes, and his objections (*velle et nolle*, retaining nothing within the power of his own judgment) absolutely and freely to "our lord the Pope." All this was promised for the emperor by his ambassadors. This would seem humiliation enough for the head of the empire, the first sovereign in the world, before the haughty worldling in the chair of St. Peter; but the Pope insisted on more. He laid down, as necessary terms to a reconciliation, that Louis should beg him to grant the privilege of administering the empire, and should promise to make no law without special permission of the Holy See.

No wonder that when Louis appeared before the diet in Frankfort, September, 1344, there was a loud and bitter outcry and murmurs that an emperor who had fallen so low should be driven from the throne. Under such a storm of obloquy, Louis hesitated to ratify the papal demands, and Clement then launched another bull, which is as pretty a model of fancy cursing as exists in the whole papal repertory, already very rich in such documents. Here are a few elegant extracts: "Let him be accursed coming in and going out. The Lord smite him with folly and blindness and frenzy of mind. Let the heavens send their lightnings upon him. Let the whole earth fight against him. Let the ground open and swallow him up alive. Let all the merits of the saints above confound him and make open display of vengeance upon him in this life, and let him with his own eyes see his children destroyed in the hands of enemies." A distinguished Roman Catholic writer of modern times (Baader) has added this comment: "Thou ravest, O Peter. Thy great pride hath made thee mad."

And now commenced in the conclave and throughout Germany a violent war of words, which seemed the precursor of a terrible civil war. The Pope took up Charles of Bohemia, who put himself under the papal slipper, but Germany would have none of him, and when he was away at the battle of Cressy, where he had accompanied his father, the blind King John, his chances sank lower than ever. Louis, turncoat that he was, had many followers, and each side was about to appeal to arms when Louis was killed by a fall in the hunting-field, and the cause of so much and such long-continued strife was removed. It was not, however, until Charles submitted to a new election in Frankfort and received his crown expressly from the electors, and not from the Pope, that Germany would acknowledge him as the lawful emperor.

As we review the long controversy, it would seem as if the Pope got the best of it; and it is true that there was as yet no organized resistance to the Pope which was enduring, but popular opinion was being educated, and never again would the Papacy be blindly accepted as a divine and untrammelled institution. Henceforth it would be sharply criticised, and instead of being the supreme power in Europe, it would take its place among the other powers, as one state among other states. Creighton makes a very just remark when he says that the conflict with Louis of Bavaria ends the mediæval period of the history of the Papacy.

Clement had not long been Pope when the Romans

sent an embassy to beg him to return to Rome and to shorten the period of the jubilee. Boniface had fixed it at once in a century, but the Christian world in general thought that too long, and they entreated Clement to shorten it to fifty years. This request he graciously granted, while he evaded the other very urgent one to return to Rome. The bull which he issued about the jubilee is most curious, for in it he sets forth the papal power over the holy angels in these remarkable words: " If any one dies on the way to the celebration, we command the angels of paradise immediately to free his soul from purgatory and introduce it into the glories of paradise." Among the ambassadors from Rome were two famous men, whose names still live in history: Petrarch, who had just been crowned with laurel in the Capitol at Rome, Easter, 1341, and Rienzi, whose eloquence pleased the Pope so much that he bestowed on him the place of papal notary, the salary of which afforded him a suitable living. His character and astonishing career well merit a detailed account. They throw much light on the condition of Rome and the popular movement in the Italian cities. This seems the proper place to sketch his life, and also those other two remarkable events in the pontificate of Clement, the Black Death and the story of the Flagellants.

CHAPTER VIII.

RIENZI.

ICOLAS GABRINI, whom we call Rienzi from a diminutive of his name Lorenzo, just as we call him Cola di Rienzi from the diminutive of his name Nicolo, was born at Rome in 1313 or 1314. The palace they show you now in Rome was never at all connected with him. His father was a small innkeeper, and his mother took in washing to help pay the family expenses. This, at least, was the general opinion, though Rienzi, in a letter to the Emperor Charles IV., states that he was the natural son of the Emperor Henry VII., who, hiding from some enemies, took refuge in his father's inn and there had a liaison with his mother. Rienzi, however, was often untruthful, and always very imaginative. He was a handsome man of rather feminine complexion, unfathomable eyes, and one of the most charming voices man ever possessed. It was to its silver tones he owed much of his success. He was well educated by a relative who was a priest, and was especially well versed in the classic Roman writers and in the Bible, which he always most extensively quoted.

When he became a man, Rome really had no government, for both popes and Cæsars had abandoned her. There were sometimes senators and sometimes legates, but they were generally puppets in the hands of the great barons, Colonnas, Orsinis, Savellis, Frangipanis, etc., who had partitioned out the city among themselves. The population had actually dwindled down to thirty thousand souls. Rienzi at twenty-eight was well known in Rome. He was a notary to the Roman tribunals, and so kind and attentive was he that he was called the consul of the orphans. His brother was killed accidentally by a Roman baron, and that served to set him against the nobles, so that henceforth he spent his time in inflaming the passions of the populace by describing to them, in burning words or by using the allegorical pictures so common at that time, the virtues of the ancient Romans and the power and splendor of ancient Rome. He was sent as a deputy to Clement VI. to induce him to come back to Rome and to request a new jubilee. His mellifluous tongue pleased the Pope, and he was sent back home, some say as papal notary, others as apostolic vicar, Cardinal Aymeric being joined with him as papal legate and a Colonna and an Orsini named senators. He came back from Avignon full of enthusiasm and loyalty to the Pope, but he soon saw that there was no change for the better. The legate was after money only, and the nobles went on fighting and pillaging. Then he commenced again to gather the people together, and by word and by picture brace them up to assume the authority which he taught them had belonged to them in the old time.

Finally he convoked the people in a mass-meeting

at the Capitol on the 20th of May, 1347. He invited them in the name of the Holy Spirit, and on the Spirit's festival, Whitsunday. The constant reference to the Holy Spirit in all Rienzi's acts shows that he was imbued with the teachings of the Spiritual Franciscans, for the constant indwelling of the Holy Spirit was one of their principal tenets. On the day appointed he stood in full armor on the steps of the Capitol, having heard since midnight thirty masses of the Holy Spirit, and read to an immense concourse a summary of reforms which was certainly well calculated to enlist the sympathy and the aid of all who listened.

These reforms were to produce the " Good Estate " (*Il buon stato*). Every homicide was to be condemned to death without the slightest delay; the old classic ruins were to be repaired; a civic guard of one hundred and fifty men was to be established in each quarter; every noble was to give up his fortified castle to the people; the tax on salt and the harbor and river duties to go to the municipality instead of the Pope, and to be used for city improvements; the keeping of the roads to be the duty of the barons; public granaries to be built; pensions for soldiers and for their widows and orphans to be arranged.

He chose for himself the title of " Tribune," and with great wisdom he requested that the Pope's vicar, the Bishop of Orvieto, might be joined with him as an equal head of the government. This scheme took like wild-fire. The senators were expelled and the new officers installed in the Capitol with such rapidity that Rienzi might well say the Holy Spirit had aided him. Stephen, the head of the Colonnas, laughed all this to scorn, and replied to a message from Rienzi that he expected to come over soon and throw him out of one of the windows of the Capitol. The populace flew to arms and drove out old Colonna without any ceremony, and soon he and all the other barons were forced to appear and swear fealty to the Roman people. Two medals are extant at Rome which were struck at this time; on one side is " Roma Caput Mundi," and on the other " Nicolas, Tribunus, Augustus." Everywhere now in the city formerly so fractious, peace and harmony prevailed. The nobles were overawed; the husbandman could till his fields in security; the roads were safe, the taxes light—too light, indeed, and this was a fatal weakness. Embassies came not only from the Italian republics, but from foreign sovereigns, and all over Christian Europe flew the news that a new, republican, Christian Rome was rising like the sun (Rienzi's crest) over the world. The Pope was favorable, the Kaiser was silent.

This moment was the brightest in Rienzi's career. If he had exercised common prudence it seems as if he really might have brought about what it took so many centuries of blood and suffering to effect—the union of Italy. It was in his mind, and he attempted to realize it. There went forth from him to all the princes and cities of Italy messengers with silver wands, convoking them to a congress the object of which was to be the union and pacification of the peninsula. All but one promised to come, and that one yielded to the presence of an armed force.

This success seemed to have turned Rienzi's head,

for then commenced those extravagant and theatric performances which showed that he had lost his balance. The splendid processions, the gorgeous dresses, the institution of the knighthood of the Holy Ghost, the bathing in Constantine's font, may all be ascribed to the tribune's conviction that pomp and show were necessary to impress an ignorant populace; but nothing could have been more imprudent than his proclamation that, by the grace of the Holy Ghost, the choice of an emperor and the domination of the empire belonged by right to the city of Rome and to Italy, and that all electors, counts, princes, etc., who pretended to power in the empire were summoned to appear before him, or be proceeded against as rebels. This totally ignored the authority of the Pope in his own city, and really seems too insane to have been tolerated by even an excited people. Their attention, however, was absorbed in a banquet free to all, where Rienzi sat, with a golden crown on his head and the Pope's vicar by his side, at a table reserved always for the Pope.

A few days after a messenger from the Pope attempted to recall him to his senses and warn him that his sovereign and pontiff would not allow such extravagances. His only answer was another theatrical and allegorical display, costly and extravagant beyond measure, and the putting forth of new laws interdicting to every foreign prince the entrance into Italy. He now had a crown made for himself like the one the ancient Cæsars wore, and even compared himself to Jesus Christ, which shows the inherent weakness and vanity of the man. Then came another piece of almost criminal madness on his part. He invited the great nobles to a supper, and suddenly at a signal from him his soldiery entered the room and haled them all to prison, where priests were in readiness to prepare them for death. Then Rienzi mounted a tribune, ostentatiously forgave them, loaded them with distinctions, and tribune and nobles took the sacrament together.

This was mere folly and child's play, and infuriated the nobles greatly, who sent a strong embassy to the Pope to beg him to put down this masquerader, for such he had become. The Pope despatched Cardinal de Deux to Rome with full powers, spiritual and temporal, to proceed against the tribune. Rienzi was confident, however, that the people would support him, and on his call twenty thousand flocked to his banner and completely routed the army of the nobles. He returned to Rome in imperial armor, the imperial crown on his head and the sceptre in his hand, and, calling the legate to him, asked him what he wanted. The astonished cardinal had hardly time to reply before he was ordered out of the city, and then came another wild decree, ordering the Pope and all other Romans back to Rome. Another manifesto summoned deputies from all Italy to meet at Rome on the next Whitsunday to elect an emperor who was to be an Italian.

Rienzi sets forth in this paper ideas which in our day have been realized—the separation of the temporal and the spiritual authority, the unification of Italy under an Italian king, and the division of the land into constitutional provinces; but the follies, extravagances, and treacheries of Rienzi had made the Italian world so distrustful of him that the message fell flat. The legate now excommunicated Rienzi, and, awed by that, the Roman people turned against him. He then took the unmanly step of annulling all his previous decrees and promising to obey the Pope. But this had no effect on the excited populace, and " Death to the tribune!" was the cry that fell upon the frightened ears of Rienzi. The bell of the Capitol called the people to arms, and the tribune tried to soothe them with the magic of his eloquence, but all in vain. The gates of the city were thrown open to the nobles, and Rienzi and his wife took refuge in St. Angelo; but he feared that sooner or later some one would give him up to the legate, and in January, 1348, he fled away.

It was not the excommunication alone that caused his fall, but his own erratic, puerile, mystical course. He could not be relied upon, and men came to know it. It would not be possible here to follow the wanderings of Rienzi over the face of Europe. He took refuge for a while with the Spiritual Franciscans in a lonely convent in the Apennines. He went back in disguise to Rome during the jubilee year and tried to stir up a revolution against the legate, but the Romans had too keen an eye to the profits they were reaping from the crowd of strangers to do anything to disturb matters.

Then we find him at Prague at the feet of Charles IV., who listened calmly to his chimerical harangues, in one of which he said that the Pope, the emperor, and Rienzi would give to the world the image of the

Holy Trinity. The correspondence between Rienzi and the emperor has been published by Papencordt, and shows that the sovereign had no mean opinion of the tribune's talents. The epilepsy to which Rienzi had for many years been subject now became more violent in its attacks, and the Archbishop of Prague took care of him in the kindest manner. He persuaded him to go to Avignon and submit himself entirely to the Pope (1351). He did go there, and was thrown immediately into prison. The prison-cell is to this day shown in the papal palace.

Then he was tried for heresy and condemned to die; but the people of Avignon could not bear to see so brilliant a scholar and distinguished a man brought to the block, and they surrounded the papal palace with such riotous manifestations that the Pope yielded, spared the tribune's life, and ordered his prison discipline to be greatly ameliorated. Books were given him, especially the Bible and Livy, the two he most highly prized, and his food was sent him from the papal kitchen. It was then he commenced to fall into those habits of intemperance which achieved his full ruin.

As if his checkered life had not been dramatic enough, another exciting act had to be played out before its close. The state of Rome was worse than before Rienzi left it. Fightings and ruins everywhere prevailed, and the new Pope, Innocent VI., was resolved to take some strong measures. He determined to send Cardinal Albornoz, a warlike prelate who had served successfully in Spain against the Moors, and knowing how popular Rienzi had

once been with the Roman people and how persuasive he was, he sent him with the cardinal. So the
two set out (1353), but Rienzi was too observant not
to find out very soon that he was to be only the cat's-
paw of the cardinal, and he resolved to act on his
own responsibility. The cardinal would gladly have
put him out of the way if he had dared, but the
tribune seemed too powerful. He gave Rienzi the
title of " Senator," and Rome welcomed back her
senator and tribune with shouts of joy. Gorgeously
attired, and mounted on a snow-white horse, he rode
to the Capitol and addressed the people, and for a
time it seemed as if all his old power and influence
had returned; but his intemperate habits had marred
his eloquent voice and clouded his intellect. He
showed himself cruel, heartless, and crafty, and condemned to death any who made the least resistance.

The legate soon saw that Rienzi would hang himself
if rope enough was given, and he waited quietly at
Montefiascone. He did not have long to wait. On
the 8th of October, 1354, a furious mob attacked the
Capitol and demanded the senator's head. He tried
to calm them, but in vain; and, fleeing to a remote
corner of the palace, he disguised himself as a common porter, and, taking up a load, was passing out,
when a man called out, " Stop Rienzi! " and soon his
blood stained the marble lion where he had ordered
so many to be executed. For three days his poor
body was exposed to every outrage, and was then
buried by the Jews. His second ruin has been attributed to the unpopular tax on salt which he established, but the Romans had been taxed for salt before.

His ruin was the direct outcome of his tyranny and cruelty, and, more than all, his unjust execution of Pandolfo di Guido, a man universally beloved. And so fell Rienzi, his character a singular mixture of imagination, credulity, courage, noble aspirations, sensual excesses, and at last the evil qualities which flow from such excesses—heartlessness, injustice, and utter selfishness.

CHAPTER IX.

THE BLACK DEATH—THE FLAGELLANTS—THE JEWS.

HE world has been afflicted with many pestilences, which carried off vast numbers of people. We have suffered from them in modern times, and have to be constantly on our guard against them now. The faintest rumor of a pestilence in Arabia or in China arouses immediate attention at every European seaport, and measures are taken to prevent the bringing in of the infection. But in the whole dreadful history of pestilence there is nothing that will for a moment compare with the ravages of the Black Death in the pontificate of Clement VI., and which was at its height from 1347 to 1350. The distinguished German physician Hecker has given us the most systematic account of this horrible visitation, and it is in his treatise that those who would thoroughly investigate it will find the most reliable material. It is with justice supposed that twenty-five millions of souls perished in it, and in England alone the population was reduced by a half, perhaps by two thirds. Seeboken, who has gone into minute estimates, shows from English records that this is no mere guesswork, but based on awful facts.

It had its origin in China, where, in 1334, the Chinese records say, five million persons died of it. From China it came by the caravans through central Asia to Tunis. Ships carried it thence to Constantinople, then the capital of commerce, and it was easy for ships to spread it from that point through Asia, Europe, and Africa. Everywhere it found all things swept and garnished for it, for sanitation was unknown, the habits of the populace filthy, the laws of contagion scarcely outlined even, except by a few of the learned. Ignorance and superstition were its chosen handmaids. Hecker considers that an assemblage of cosmical disturbances and physical changes happening at the time of the Black Death accounts for it, such as numerous earthquakes, deluges, famines; but his conclusions seem very unscientific, and modern investigation would consider the filth in which it was engendered and the filth it everywhere met as amply sufficient cause for its terrific ravages.

One curious fact is mentioned by all contemporary writers and is borne out by modern experience, and that is of a thick, evil-smelling mist, which, advancing from the East, spread over Italy, infecting the air of the sea as well as the land, so that many vessels were found drifting about the ocean without a living man on board; all had suddenly perished. A similar mist spread over Chicago at the last visitation of cholera, and for the two days it prevailed the mortality rose from fifteen a day to over one hundred, subsiding when the air cleared. Boccaccio, in the " Decamerone," gives us the most vivid picture extant of the destruction wrought in Florence by this fell malady, for it numbered sixty thousand victims in that fair city. He says it commenced with tumors in the groin and the armpits about the size of an egg. Then came tumors all over the body, with black-and-blue spots on the arms and thighs. No medicine brought relief, and nearly all attacked died within the first three days, and without fever. Animals were also affected by the contagion. Boccaccio saw two hogs rooting among the rags of a beggar who had died of the Black Death, and suddenly they fell over and died. Other writers mention fever and spitting of blood as accompanying it. In Avignon it raged with fury, counting sixty thousand victims in that one town, and the Pope consecrated the river Rhone so that bodies might be thrown in, as it was hard to find persons to bury the dead. Clement showed the greatest kindness and wisdom in his instructions and regulations, and in the fierce hate against the Jews, not only there, but in all parts of Europe (an ignorant populace and a bigoted clergy accusing them of being the authors of the plague), he protected them, and whenever he had power forbade their arrest and torture. Even the cold of Iceland and Greenland did not protect those countries; vast proportions of their people were carried off. England suffered cruelly. In London alone one hundred thousand perished, and about two millions in the whole realm.

This led to very important economic results. The price of land was greatly lowered, so many estates being thrown into the market by death, and the price of labor was greatly heightened, there being so few to till the land. The laborers of England combined in what may be called the first " strike " in order to get their pay increased, and it was this movement which led within the next half-century to the cessation of serfage in England. The moral effects of this frightful calamity were, on the whole, deplorable. Some, indeed, it brought to penitence and a better life, but it engendered great selfishness, and with many great recklessness of conduct. The ladies and gentlemen in the " Decamerone " are an example. There they sit amid the flowers, feasting and idling and telling loose stories, while their fellow-citizens are dying like sheep. Even the parish priests fled from their cures, or shut themselves up and refused to console or to bury their people.

The orders of begging friars were alone indefatigable in the sacred work of alleviating and soothing the suffering, and their devotion won them universal love, so that men vied with one another in heaping upon them gifts and legacies. When this angel of terror had passed over, Europe awoke as from a stupor; everywhere empty houses, desolate families, and bitter mourning. There were vast crowds of widows and orphans, and many years passed before the sad recollections of those awful years could be effaced from the memories of men.

Usually in great calamities fanatics and cranks are engendered or come to the surface, and in the midst of the ravages of the Black Death there appeared a strange religious phenomenon, which had been seen before and which can be seen to this day, the Flagel-

lants, as they were called; a body of people of both
sexes and all ages, who as a mark of penance went
about in public flogging themselves. This mode of penance did not originate at this time. As far back as the
eleventh century many believers in Asia and in southern Europe afflicted themselves in this way. It has
never ceased in convents and in individual cases, and
even at this day and in this century of light, public
processions of men lashing themselves until the blood
flows from their wounds, and walking over beds of
the prickly-pear, may be seen in some of the interior
towns of Mexico. The outbreak of this singular
mania in connection with the Black Death began in
Hungary in 1349, and soon spread over Germany,
where they were also called the "cross-bearers."
Their avowed object was to do penance for their own
sins and to atone for the sins of other people, and
they joined to their flagellations prayers for the stay-
ing of the plague. The participants were at first confined to persons of the lower class, many sincerely
penitent, and many attracted by the life of idleness.
The infatuation, however, soon seized the nobles and
clergy, and very often honorable women and nuns
were found among the number.

They marched through the cities in well-organized
processions, the lower part of the face masked, draped
in black, with red crosses on the front and back of
the tunic and on the black cap. Each one carried a
scourge of three knotted cords, tipped with iron.
Splendid banners and blazing torches were borne in
their midst, and with the ringing of bells and the
singing of exciting hymns they marched to the

designated place of scourging. There they stripped the upper part of their bodies and put off their shoes. Then they lay down in a large circle, in different positions, according to their sin, and the master then castigated them, some more, some less. Then they arose and flogged themselves, singing aloud psalms, of which some are still extant.

It can easily be imagined what an effect this had upon an ignorant and credulous people. The parish priests were entirely deserted for these new-comers, and they came in such numbers that they could take possession of any church they fancied and hold their meetings there. They sometimes pretended to be able to work miracles, as in Strasburg, where they tried in vain to bring to life a dead child. They gave out that their pilgrimage would continue for thirty-four years. At this not only the church became alarmed, but society everywhere turned against them, for they rapidly degenerated, and thieving and violence followed their footsteps. Pope Clement, who in the whole matter of the pestilence and the Flagellants acted with great wisdom, issued, in conjunction with the emperor, strict orders that the public processions should stop, and everywhere the sovereigns used against them the severest measures. Gradually they dwindled away, though of course the crowds had greatly increased the plague, and the gloomy exercises had tended to deepen still further the wretchedness and despondency of the people.

During the prevalence of the Black Death the Jews suffered horribly, for everywhere, and without the slightest reason, they were accused of having poisoned the wells and the air. They often under torture confessed to having done so, but confession elicited under torture is worthless, for almost any required answer may be obtained under the rack. It is scarcely possible to comprehend the panic everywhere in Europe about poisoned wells. Nobody would use anything but river and rain water, and everywhere men bound themselves by oath to destroy all Jews. Even some of the higher clergy countenanced this dreadful resolve. In Mayence alone twelve thousand Jews are said to have been put to a cruel death. These utterly unjust attacks aroused the Jews to great fanaticism, and at Esslingen the whole Jewish community collected in the synagogue and deliberately set it on fire, all willingly perishing rather than submit to baptism.

Pope Clement protected them in Avignon, and issued two bulls, in which he declared the Jews innocent of any attempt to spread the plague; but his words were as idle dreams against the fury of the fanaticism. The King of Poland, Casimir (1333–70), also protected them, and opened his dominions to thousands of Jewish fugitives. It was in this way that Poland came to number so many Jews among its people—Jews of a very fanatic and retrograde type. This dreadful visitation of the plague seemed to steel the hearts of men. They became cruel and merciless, not only to Jews, but to their own sick, and everywhere the influence and authority of every law, human and divine, vanished away.

CHAPTER X.

HE jubilee of 1350 brought out an astonishing display of fervent devotion and
unreasoning faith. Doubtless the terrible pestilence we have just described had
done much in inclining the hearts of the
people towards a better life, and, according to the ideas
of those times, no better way could be found for
gaining the grace and pardon of God than by a pilgrimage to the capital of Christianity and the tomb
of its chief apostle. Reliable historians estimate the
number of visitors between Christmas and Easter at
about a million, and between Ascension and Whit-
suntide at half a million.

Even granting the loose estimate of numbers so
common then, the crowd was prodigious, and the
streets leading to the principal churches were so
crowded that only by a slow movement could any
progress be made, and many were crushed to death.
No one suffered from any want of accommodations,
though, as was to be expected, the prices ran high.
Enormous sums, of course, were paid into the papal
treasury, but Clement did not survive long to enjoy

his wealth, for on the 6th of December, 1352, he died from a tumor. His last important act redeems his character, in our estimation, from that of a mere pleasure-loving worldling, and shows that he could rise to the level of his lofty place.

The begging friars had shown such devotion and self-sacrifice during the Black Death that nearly everything men wished to leave to the church was left to them. This made the secular clergy very jealous, and they thronged to Avignon demanding the suppression of the friars. Clement rose in his place and defended them with generous eloquence. " Suppose," he said, " the friars were to stop preaching. What would you preach? Humility? *You*, proudest of all conditions of men? Poverty? You who are so greedy that all the benefices on earth are not enough for you? Chastity? I am silent. God alone knows how your bodies are pampered. The friars well deserve any benefits they have reaped from legacies. It is a fit reward of their courage and their zeal, and you are opposing them not from principle, but out of sheer envy."

Just before Clement died he made a law which made the condition of the cardinals shut in to elect a Pope much more comfortable. Each one now was to have a little chamber curtained off from the great hall, so that he could have some privacy. He was to be allowed two attendants, and after the third day a more generous allowance of food was provided than had been the former custom. Under these conditions the college met. Their first idea was to elect the General of the Carthusians, not a cardinal; but they recollected that he, a foe to luxury, would oblige them to give up the splendor and luxury in which they lived, so they turned their attention in another direction. Before proceeding to the election, they passed a law which, if they had been able to carry it out, would have made all future popes the mere tools of the college of cardinals. There were never to be more than twenty cardinals, and no new ones could be made until the present number sank to sixteen. No cardinal could be created or deprived without the consent of the whole body, and half the revenues of the papal see were to be turned over to them. They all took an oath to observe the law, but many qualified the oath by the words, " Unless it should prove contrary to papal law."

They then proceeded to the vote, and on the 18th of December, 1352, Stephen Aubert, Bishop of Ostia, was chosen, who took the name of Innocent VI. The first thing he did was to repudiate his oath, declaring that it was contrary to the power of St. Peter, which no cardinals could limit. Nobody opposed this, for every man felt that he would have done exactly the same thing if he had been chosen.

Innocent was a great improvement on any of the former Avignon popes. His morals seem to have been good, and he was a man of force and learning. He knew how to rule and he ruled wisely. He favored his family, as was natural, but only when they were competent for office. He cleansed the papal court of the immense crowd of idle bishops and parish priests who left their cures to be ravaged by the devil while they revelled in the luxury of Avignon.

He forced the cardinals to live in greater simplicity, and exerted himself to put down one of the most tremendous vices of that time, pluralities, one man often holding seven or eight benefices in different parts of Europe. Although virtually in France, he was perfectly independent of the French king, and his strong arm was felt in church and state throughout the Western world. Two great things were accomplished during his wise pontificate of ten years, the recovery of the papal possessions in Italy, and the settlement of that unending cause of dispute, the election of the emperor.

After the fall of Rienzi for the second time, as has been related, the papal legate, Cardinal Albornoz, turned his attention to the pacification of Italy. He was stern and cruel, but, oddly as it sounds in speaking of a cardinal, perfectly competent to command an army and to conquer. Steadily he attacked one recalcitrant province after another, and within three or four years recovered Bologna and the whole Romagna for the Pope. The papal authority was firmly established in the city of Rome, and it became once more possible for a Pope to think of going back there again, especially as the distracted state of France made it impossible to rely much on that secular arm, and brigands had already appeared at the very gates of Avignon.

It must always be remembered that the popes did not settle themselves at Avignon for pleasure merely. It was a measure forced upon them by the conduct of the Romans. If it had not been Avignon it would have been some other place, and, as things were,

Avignon was as good a choice as could have been made. To have remained in Rome would have been an intolerable captivity for any Pope. Even of Clement V. it cannot be said that he was an enemy of Italy. If the Italians had possessed any national policy his course would have helped them, for his absence would have left them free to follow their natural destiny, while his presence forced Italy to be everything to everybody, a sort of neutral ground, and, like all forced neutrals, weak. Just as soon as it was safe to go to Rome the popes made an honest attempt to go there. Their living at Avignon never lessened one whit their immense influence in Europe. The Papacy did not seem at all bound up in Rome, nor is it now, when it does not even possess Avignon or a foot of land anywhere. It is evidently not tied to any temporal power, great as the cry may be. This influence without any territory is so immense that not a court in Europe dares for a moment to ignore it or to insult it.

Indeed, it must be said in fairness that the long residence of the popes in Avignon had surrounded the dignity of the Papacy with a lustre it had not for a long time enjoyed. It was cut loose from the bondage of a degraded and ruined little town like Rome. Above all, it showed the world that the city of Rome was but of small importance compared with the church of God. A French writer, Gayet, has made an estimate that between 1100 A.D. and 1304 the popes had been exiled from Rome one hundred and twenty-two years, forty years in excess of the time they had spent in that city. Viewed in that light, " Babylonish captivity " seems a misnomer. It was a period of unwonted freedom, and the Pope (Gregory XI.) who terminated it would most probably, if he had lived, have gone back to Avignon. The consequences of his not doing it helped to make the great schism, though that was imminent from other causes. The Italians had determined to have a Pope.

The Emperor Charles IV., who had succeeded the unlucky Louis of Bavaria, observed to the letter the contract he had made with the Pope. He went to Rome in a quiet way with a small train, was quietly crowned there by the papal legate, and came quietly away. The " golden bull " which Charles published attached the electoral dignity to certain fiefs, seven in all—Bohemia, Saxony, Brandenburg, the Palatine, Mayence, Treves, and Cologne. Nothing was said about the Pope's power to confirm the election, and Innocent wisely let that question alone. In fact, both he and Charles acted in this matter with great wisdom and forbearance, and we hear henceforth not so much of emperors of Rome as of emperors of Germany. On the 12th of September, 1362, Innocent died and was buried at Villeneuve, just over the French border, where now, in the chapel of the hospital, can be seen his splendid tomb.

CHAPTER XI.

WENTY cardinals made up the conclave which met on October 28, 1362, to elect a successor to Innocent. So full of plots and jealousies and fears of one another were they that they gave up all idea of electing one of their own number, and chose William de Grimoard, Abbot of St. Victor in Marseilles, not even a bishop, who took the name of Urban V. He was in Italy at the time, and the cardinals were so afraid that the Italians would keep him there if they knew he had been elected Pope that they did not tell him, but sent for him to come immediately to Avignon. They would never have chosen him if they had been aware that he had said publicly at Florence that he would be willing to die if he could only see the chair of St. Peter restored to Rome.

As far as purity of character and a religious and holy life are concerned, he stands first of all the French popes, and he labored hard and successfully to reform his court and put down simony. He steadily refused to advance his family, and spent the vast sums which came into his possession, not on vice and luxury, but on repairing the Roman churches, building a noble college at Montpellier, and supporting a thousand students in the different European universities. He played rather a sharp trick on the Abbot of St. Paul without the Walls, in Rome. The abbot offered him a large sum of money to make him a cardinal. He took the money, used it to repair the church, and left the abbot just where he was before. Of course there was no redress, nor ought there to have been.

In April, 1367, Urban resolved to go to Rome. The country seemed in a quiet state, and a residence there seemed possible. Great was the weeping and wailing among the cardinals, who loved the fleshpots of Avignon too well to leave them without a struggle ; but as Urban had never been a cardinal, he could not enter very deeply into their feelings. They threatened they would not go, but as the Pope immediately commenced creating cardinals who would go, they concluded that discretion was the better part of valor, and at last, with many groanings, all but five set out for Rome. The Pope had received many letters on the subject of his return to Rome, among the lengthiest and most tiresome of which was one from Petrarch. He tries to entice the cardinals by asserting that the Roman wines are quite as good as those of Provence. He compares desolate and bleeding Rome with fat and fair Avignon rolling in vice and luxury, and he ends by asking Urban " whether, at the day of judgment, he would rather rise among the famous sinners of Avignon than with Peter and Paul, Stephen and Lawrence," as if it could possibly make any difference to a soul in what company it rose from the dead!

The Pope set sail from Marseilles, and a brilliant fleet of galleys formed his escort. After a short junketing at Genoa, he landed at Corneto and kept Whitsunday. Then he went on to Viterbo, where he met Cardinal Albornoz, his able legate—but merely met him, for the cardinal died suddenly a few days after his arrival. There was a riot at Viterbo while the Pope was there, and the cardinals were rather glad of it, for they hoped it would disgust the Pope with living in Italy, and that he would then and there turn back. The Pope, however, stood firm and went on to Rome, where he was received with fervent outbursts of loyalty, and for the first time since the pontificate of Boniface VIII. a Pope stood at the altar of St. Peter's. Things looked forlorn enough,— dilapidation and decay on all sides, and the population dwindled down to that of a fourth- or fifth-rate town,—but Urban abated not one iota of papal supremacy. The emperors of the East and West visited Rome and held his bridle-rein, much to the exaltation of the clergy and the disgust of the laymen who dreaded the despotism of the spiritual power.

There was no suitable house for Urban in Rome, and he fixed his residence at Montefiascone, but ever with him were the murmuring, groaning cardinals begging him to leave the ruins and the barbarism and the surly people and go back to dear Avignon. Urban saw that he was not equal to the task of facing the ever-seditious Romans. He weakened and gave way, and, after a short three years, set sail again for his beloved France and the great palace at Avignon, which had been growing in size and beauty during his absence. He returned, however, only to die; for three months after his return, on December 19, 1370, he was gathered to the long line of his predecessors and sleeps under his marble tomb at Avignon.

Only a few days elapsed between the death of Urban and the choice of his successor. He was Peter Roger, who took the name of Gregory XI., and had been a cardinal since he was eighteen years old, created by his uncle, Clement VI. Of course such a creation was outrageous and in violation of all church law, but in this case it did not have the evil effect that might have been anticipated, for the young cardinal applied himself diligently to his studies and his religious duties. He was a man of elegant manners, charming address, and blameless morals. His greatest fault was the one into which most popes fell, the elevation of his family. Two women meddled a great deal with his affairs, both of whom have since been canonized by the Church of Rome, St. Bridget of Sweden and St. Catherine of Siena. Both had the same object in view, the inducing the Pope to return to Rome, and it is not giving too much credit to St. Catherine to say that her entreaties finally persuaded him. This remarkable woman, whose influence on her times was so great, merits our attention. In these days of hypnotic experiences, and when so much light has been thrown upon hysteria, much that appeared miraculous to her contemporaries appears very commonplace to us. She was a hysterical, cataleptic subject, but by no means a weak-minded one, for her letters, which are published, show great vigor of intellect and much eloquence and force. They have been quoted with admiration by the most celebrated Italian critics, and, in fact, rank with Petrarch and Boccaccio as Italian classics of that period.

At Siena in the library are seventy-nine works on the subject of St. Catherine, but they all have for their basis a life of her which was written by her confessor, Raimondo, and they must be read with many grains of salt. It is a melancholy exhibit of what made a saint in those days, and to us moderns seems like the account of a lunatic rather than of a holy and very distinguished woman. At six years of age she habitually flogged herself for her sins. At seven she would watch a monk pass and then run to kiss the spot where his foot had rested. At twelve she refused to wash her face and comb her hair, except at rare intervals, saying she would make no such sacrifice to vanity. She then gave up all animal food, but continued taking wine until she was fifteen. Finally (according to her biographer) she gave up eating altogether and lived without food for many years. Our Lord Christ was in the constant habit of appearing in her cell and teaching her religion. She was at last married to Him, and said that she saw always on her finger the betrothal ring He placed there. Once our Saviour took out her heart and put His own in its place.

But the most noted thing about her were the stigmata, or the marks of the nails in her hands and feet, in imitation of those of the Lord on the cross. St. Francis had hitherto been supposed to have a monopoly of these, but when St. Catherine obtained them the Dominicans got even with the Franciscans. She had a trance, as she very often had, after receiving the sacrament, and when she came out of the trance she said, " I now have in my body the marks of the crucifixion of our Lord Jesus, but I have prayed Him that they may be internal only and not visible." This must not be thought imposture. The history of hypnotism and its kindred subjects gives many well-authenticated cases of such beliefs, even resulting in outward and visible appearances. There is no doubt that such signs as the stigmata could be brought about by hypnotic influence. Cases are on record, and there is such a thing as self-hypnotism. St. Catherine was able to throw herself into a state where the appearance of her Lord seemed to her to be real, and she was as convinced as any person could be that in reality He had come into her presence and talked with her.

But there is another aspect, and a very important one, in which Catherine of Siena ought to be viewed. She was not only a subject of hysterical visions, she did not only give rise to wild and absurd devotions, but she was a distinguished politician and exerted immense influence in the distracting years which preceded the return of Gregory XI. to Rome. There are things of more moment to be attributed to her courage and sound sense than incredible and even blasphemous accounts of interviews with the Saviour of mankind. Catherine was for years well known in her native city as a consoler of the poor, as a minister to the sick, as a maker of peace between divided families and quarrelling communes, but it is not easy to fix the precise time of her taking part in public affairs. However, in 1372 we find her in correspondence with most important personages, and her letters to the Nuncio in Tuscany, urging him to intercede with the Pope to put down nepotism, to stop the luxury of the bishops, and to create only good and virtuous cardinals, can be read and admired.

Florence rebelled against the edicts of the Pope, and so fanned the flame of revolution that before the end of 1375 the whole papal domain, with the exception of Bologna, was in revolt. The Pope sent an army against Florence, but also employed an engine of war which was then quite as powerful—a bull of excommunication. This brought the Florentines to their senses. They determined to send a mediator to the Pope, and they chose for their mediator Catherine of Siena, who had been in the midst of the tumult and had managed by her counsels to keep Lucca and Pisa out of the disturbance. This strange ambassador, a saintly woman, arrived in Avignon June, 1376, and was received by the Pope with the greatest kindness. He placed the whole question of the peace in her hands, but the embassy from Florence which came after her had an impression that they could make better terms by dealing directly with the Pope, and they declined to make use of her as intermediary.

She was, however, to bring about a thing much more important to the Christian world than the mere getting a peace for Florence. Gregory XI., of whose pure and gentle character we have already spoken, had secretly made a vow that he would return to Rome, and he openly avowed his desire to do so, but

everything was against him.   He was a French noble
of one of the most powerful Limousin families, surrounded by French nobles and French cardinals all
strongly interested in keeping him where he was.
His health was very delicate and he feared (with
justice) that the air of Rome would completely destroy the little constitution he had.   He loved peace
and quiet, and shrank from encountering the rude and
barbarous Romans.   To such a character, yearning
to lean upon some strong arm, the advent of a strong
nature like Catherine's was a great boon.   She at
once won his perfect confidence and set herself to
work to bring him to determine that, no matter what
the obstacles might be, he would restore the Papacy
to its own city, Rome.

It is not meant to convey the idea that there were
not many reasons to induce him to do this, the chief
ones being the impossibility of any longer governing
Rome from a distance, and the possibility of the
Romans setting up an antipope from among the Italian bishops.   It was Catherine, however, who induced
him to give these reasons their proper weight, and who
braced his weak will to the point of determination.
She spoke in public many times in Avignon, as she
had done in Florence and elsewhere, but the opposition was very powerful.   She even begged the Pope
to steal away secretly; but at length her victory was
won, and on September 13, 1376, amid a sullen court,
his aged father at his feet imploring him not to go,
Gregory XI. left Avignon, never to return.

As he journeyed through France he met everywhere tears and gloom.   Marseilles, where he was to

embark, was filled with crowds of mourning people, and soon after the embarkation there came on a terrible storm. The little fleet was sixteen days going from Marseilles to Genoa, where Catherine with her companions had preceded on foot the papal cortège. Then came the news that Rome and Florence were in commotion and would oppose him to the last; so a consistory was held at Genoa, and it was resolved to proceed no farther with the journey. All seemed lost, but Catherine secretly visited the Pope and by her words of courage induced him to go on. Ten days were spent at Genoa, then another delay at Leghorn of eleven days, and then, when again the galleys had put to sea, a fearful storm drove them all back nearly shipwrecked.

One of the aged cardinals died at Pisa from the effects of seasickness, but at last Corneto was reached on December 1st, two months after leaving Marseilles. There was a long delay there, and it was not until January 17, 1377, that the Pope landed near the great Basilica of St. Paul, and the " Babylonish captivity " was over, though its fatal consequences had only just begun. The fickle Romans received him with such wild joy that it must, for a time at least, have surmounted the mournful feelings with which he had bidden adieu to his native France.

To finish here with the history of St. Catherine, it will suffice to say that her public life did not end here. The Pope sent her as ambassador to Florence in 1378, and the effect of her three orations in the Palazzo Vecchio was to bring back that city to its obedience. A treaty was signed in July, and Catherine retired to the tranquillity of Siena, where she composed the " Dialogue," a work in mystical theology over which we need not linger. When the great schism broke out she wrote to the Italian cardinals begging them to stand by the Pope, and she was even summoned to Rome by Urban to be his counsellor. She did all she could to restrain his stern and impracticable temperament, but in vain, and while it is going beyond credibility to agree with her priest biographer that her prayers to God stopped the popular tumults, she undoubtedly influenced the Romans in favor of peace. Her long fasts and vigils had completely exhausted her, and just before Quinquagesima, 1380, she passed away, her last thoughts and her last words being about the schism which had broken her great heart. Hers was a singular life, a mixture of hysterical religious exaltation and of extreme and enlightened common sense. Among the many strange biographies of that eventful time there is none stranger than that of this weak, untaught woman of a little Tuscan city, the counsellor of popes and correspondent of kings.

CHAPTER XII.

DEATH OF GREGORY XI.—ELECTION OF URBAN VI.

OPE GREGORY did not feel at all at home in his capital city. Everywhere around him he saw ruins, crumbling walls, and tottering churches. The many wars and riots had bred a rude and ungentle manner in the people, even towards their sovereign. He could not speak Italian and so could not understand the popular language, and it is thought that he would soon have gone back to Avignon if the climate, as he feared, had not seized on his weak constitution and carried him off at the early age of forty-seven, March 27, 1378. There is a story, not very well authenticated, that on his death-bed he urged those around him not to listen to overzealous men or women who had, or thought they had, revelations from God. He left a will in which is this noble sentiment: "If either in the consistory or in public, by any slip of the tongue arising from reckless joy, or from self-complacency at being in company with magnates, or from any other disturbance of mind, we have spoken anything against the Catholic faith, we revoke it expressly and consider it as not spoken."

It was not often in those days that a Pope was

seen as gentle, as humble, as truly devout as Gregory
XI. He died with a heart filled with the greatest
anxiety. The Romans had now for a long while
been accustomed to much freedom of action. They
had conquered the patrician families and put down
their influence. They called themselves the heirs of
the old Roman republic, and Gregory had found, to
his sorrow, that they would illy tolerate the royal
authority which as Pope King he was called upon to
assert. He only wished to exercise his legal rights,
but murmurs long and loud called him an oppressor,
and he was so convinced that his death would be the
signal for much trouble that only eight days before
his demise, in a consistory, he released the cardinals
from any obedience to the laws then existing for
their governance. They were to be allowed to hold
their election when and where they pleased, without
even waiting for the ninth day's funeral ceremonies
for the dead, without any formal conclave, a majority
of votes to be sufficient. The guardian of the Castle
of St. Angelo received the strictest orders not to give
up the castle to the new Pope until the consent of
the six cardinals who had remained at Avignon had
been received.

It is not difficult to account for these precautions.
Gregory knew how deeply the Romans were concerned in the election, and how determined they were
to have an Italian Pope, and he wished to empower
the cardinals to hold the election before the Romans
could take any action. He felt sure that in this way
he could secure the election of a French Pope, for of
the sixteen cardinals then in Rome eleven were

Frenchmen, much more than a mere majority, and Gregory considered the others as not of much account.

No sooner was the breath out of the Pope's body than the Roman officials appeared before the cardinals and pictured to them in the most moving manner the pitiable state of their city, which had been for hundreds of years the head of the world and was now deprived of all her glory. Rome was the seat of St. Peter and his successors, and it was a bitter wrong for the bride to be so long separated from the bridegroom. It was the direct providence of God that had brought the last Pope back to Rome, they said, and it was the same providence that had taken him away when he thought of going back to Avignon, and they begged the cardinals to give them some information before going into the conclave about their intentions, for if they did not they could not answer for the peace of the city. The cardinals fought off the giving of any direct reply. They would do anything, they said, for the good of the Catholic Church, and try to choose the right man, but also, on their part, they threatened the Romans that unless they kept quiet they would again quit Rome for good and all.

Two things the cardinals asked : that the great crowd of peasants which had collected in Rome should be sent home, and that the great square of St. Peter's, with the bridges and gates which led to it, should be kept free so that the populace might not get near the Vatican. The officials were anxious to carry out the wishes of the Sacred College, but the city was in the highest state of commotion. Groups everywhere were discussing the situation, and a car-

dinal could not appear on the street or be at peace
in his house without excited citizens informing him
that a Pope must be chosen to suit the Romans. The
cardinals did not much relish this talk, but they were
not much frightened by it; if they had been they
would have availed themselves of some of the permissions of Gregory; but they did not, and did not
even think it necessary to hold the election in the
Castle of St. Angelo, where they would have been
safe from any interruption. They sent their own
valuables there, and all the papal jewels and ornaments, for fear of the thieving Romans, but they did
not go there themselves.

Rome was full of wire-pullers of the episcopal
order, and not the least conspicuous was Bartholomew
Prignani, Archbishop of Bari, the coming Pope; but
the gossip that he pulled wires for his own election
originated entirely with his enemies and is not worth
much notice. He was a Neapolitan by birth, from
the lower classes, and owed his advancement entirely
to his own energy and industry. The late Pope had
intrusted him with the temporary vice-chancellorship
in the absence of the Cardinal of Pampeluna. He
was a man of earnest and irreproachable character and
of spotless morals, dull by nature, without any clear
perception of his own interests or of those of his
fellows. He certainly had no genius for intrigue, in
spite of what his enemies have said, for his subsequent
conduct showed how little judgment he had even in
advancing his own interests.

There is no doubt that he was a very prominent
man in Rome at that time, and openly and every-

where avowed his intention of doing everything in
his power to keep the Papacy at Rome.   Gayet finds
a reason for thinking that he aspired to the Papacy
in the fact that he bought a house in Rome just before the death of Gregory in order to qualify himself
as a Roman citizen; but when you consider that he
held a high place in the Roman curia, there was nothing strange in his buying a house.   His election was
due neither to terror nor to his own efforts.   The
many new documents which have been unearthed of
late years by Souchon and Gayet, and the results of
which are summed up in a monograph on the election
by Dr. Jahr, place it on very different grounds.

The Sacred College at Gregory's death consisted
of twenty-three members; six, with Gregory's permission, had remained in Avignon, one was Nuncio
at Florence, so that there were sixteen in Rome to
go on with the election.   These sixteen were by no
means agreed, and it was these disagreements and
not the terror caused by the tumult of the Romans
that favored the cause of the Archbishop of Bari.
This can be shown by letters and recorded conversa-
tions, though in the letter which the cardinals sent
over the world they affirm that they chose Bari solely
from fear of the Roman people.   There were three
groups: 1. The Limousin cardinals, that is, those
from Limoges and the region round about; these
were six in number.   2. The other French cardinals,
three in number.   3. The four Italian cardinals.
Then there were Cardinals Glandeve and St. Eustache,
who were on the fence, and Cardinal St. Angelo, who
kept his inclinations strictly to himself.   All except

the Limousins were determined that no Limoges cardinal should be elected. The last three popes had been from Limoges, and that party were bent on electing this one, but they soon saw that they could not hope to do it, and they then began to support the name of the Archbishop of Bari.

There is no question that before the conclave met or there was any fear of a Roman mob his name had been freely mentioned as the most likely candidate in case an Italian had to be chosen. The cardinals knew before they went into the conclave that they could not agree to elect a Frenchman, and no more eligible Italian presented himself than Bari. He was a subject of the Countess of Provence, the ruler of Naples, and therefore in a quasi way a Frenchman, and perhaps could be got to return to Avignon, and there was every reason to think he would suit the Romans. One of the greatest proofs that his name had been favorably canvassed is that when proposed in the conclave so very little was said against him.

This, then, was the state of things among the cardinals when, on the evening of April 7, 1378, they went into the conclave at the Vatican. The Piazza of St. Peter was full of armed men, for the guards had been unable to keep the crowd from approaching the palace. Naturally enough, the Romans did not wish to lose the spectacle. They had been deprived of it for nearly a century, and they did not forget that many a time in the years past the voices of the people of Rome had greatly influenced the choice of a Pope. Some writers say that the storm in the heavens above was as violent that day as the storm of human passion below. Louder and louder rang out the cry, "We must have a Roman or at least an Italian;" but the loudest cries were, "A Roman, only a Roman!" The palace was full of angry, noisy men, and it was only after considerable time and much trouble that the officials were able to close and lock the doors, and the customary bricking up of the door into the conclave had to be foregone. It must be always remembered that the statement of great tumult and noise comes from the Pope's enemies.

Cardinal di Luna says there was indeed a great deal of excitement, but that he was not frightened; and the suggestion that the cardinals were old men and therefore easily terrified will not hold water, for the cardinals for the most part were in middle life, and men were not easily alarmed in that rough age. The rooms under the conclave hall could not be cleared; they were filled with citizens, who broke into the papal wine-cellar, drank the wines, and added the noise of drunken riot to all the other excitement. It was late and the cardinals were trying to enjoy a little rest when there appeared at the door the heads of the city wards, who begged an interview with the cardinals. They unwillingly assented, and the delegation, begging pardon for such late interviewing, besought the cardinals to give them some assurance that an Italian and if possible a Roman would be chosen. The cardinals refused, and Florence reprimanded them in very heated words for their presumption. Sleeping was tried again, but there was too much noise, and the conclave met between four and five in the morning for the mass of the Holy

Ghost, and then went to the chapel for the voting, the cries and shouts outside rising higher and higher, all uniting in one yell, " Give us a Roman!" Some one got the keys of the bell-tower of St. Peter's, and there was a tremendous bell-ringing, though there is much controversy as to whether the bell-ringing was before or after the election.

The voting began about 8 A.M. The Cardinal of Florence was just about to vote, he coming first, when the guardians of the conclave appeared at the window and begged the cardinals to hurry, as the mob could not much longer be restrained. The Cardinal of Florence stood hesitating, when Agrifolio and Orsini rushed to the window and gave an assurance that a Roman would be chosen. The Cardinal of Florence then proposed a Roman, the Cardinal of St. Peter's, saying, " I would have proposed a Frenchman if you had not given this assurance." The turn of the Cardinal of Limoges came next. He nominated the Archbishop of Bari, and then all the rest voted for him except Orsini, who, being a Roman, was most anxious to be Pope.

There was some talk about going to another and a safer place so that they might vote over again for Bari, but nothing came of it. They were afraid to tell the people (the riot was so great) that a Roman had not been chosen, and they sent three of their number to say to them that if they would wait patiently for a day a Roman or an Italian would certainly be elected. Very unwillingly the mob retired from about the palace, and after sending for Bari and some other prelates the cardinals sat down to luncheon, not being too frightened to eat. Indeed, the Bishop of Marseilles entertained at a festive meal the prelates who had been summoned.

The coming of the summoned prelates, however, excited anew the multitude, for they were perfectly certain the choice had fallen on one of them, and they began clamoring to know the name. After luncheon the cardinals went back to the chapel to counsel as to what course it was best to take. " Let us stick to what we have done," was the conclusion. Again the votes were cast for Bari, and this time all present voted and it was unanimous. Cardinal Orsini went to the window and called out, " Go to St. Peter's," meaning to convey the intention of the cardinals to publish their choice there. His words were entirely misapprehended. The mob understood him to say, " Cardinal of St. Peter's," and according to custom they rushed off to plunder his house, that being always the people's privilege. A crowd burst into the conclave chamber, and surrounding the aged Cardinal of St. Peter's, kissed his feet and struggled to embrace him, he crying out all the time that the Archbishop of Bari and not he had been elected. At last he fainted and his attendants got him into another room, while the mob rushed raging through the palace to find Bari and force him to decline or be killed, for they were determined to have a Roman. The cardinals took advantage of this dispersion to flee away, many leaving in their haste their mantles and hats. Some went to their homes, some to St. Angelo, and some to the adjacent country.

The Bishop of Lodi hid the newly elected Pope in

an out-of-the-way room and so the night passed. It certainly could not have been a very happy night for Bari. He knew that he had been chosen Pope, but with such a furious people against him and all the cardinals in hiding, how small an honor it must have seemed! He acted, however, with moderation and prudence. He sent early for the city authorities, who were eager to recognize him as Pope, but he declined to be so recognized until he was enthroned and crowned. The authorities now went to work to bring back the cardinals, but it was three in the afternoon before the fears of twelve could be overcome and they got to the palace, the crowd having now dispersed. These went to the chapel, again proclaimed Bari, and Agrifolio brought him out of his hiding-place. Florence then formally notified him of his election, he accepted, took the name of Urban VI., and mounted the pontifical throne.

On Saturday, April 10th, he was escorted by the cardinals to St. Peter's, where he celebrated mass. On the same day the cardinals who had fled into the country came back and adored him, and the coronation was set for Easter, April 18th, when Orsini placed the papal crown upon his head. The cardinals notified, in the meantime, their brethren in Avignon, using these conclusive words : " Since weighty matters are often misinterpreted through false reports, we notify you that freely and uncontrolled we chose the Archbishop of Bari to succeed Gregory." Urban, for his part, wrote to all the sovereigns of Europe. He entered undisturbed on his duties as Pope, assisted in every way by the cardinals, and he bestowed on them and others bishoprics and preferments without a sign of dissatisfaction. Two letters are extant, one from his bitter enemy, Cardinal Robert of Geneva, the coming antipope, which declare that the archbishop was freely chosen and make no mention of any "force majeure" on the part of the people.

The story of Urban's election has been made thus minute in order to show how perfectly legal that election was. Even granting that the cardinals were terrified,—and their actions prove that that supposition was much exaggerated,—when they were freed from the cause of fear they persisted in their choice and everywhere acknowledged as their Pope and sovereign Urban VI. Their renunciation of him and the schism they caused sprang from their disappointment at his persistence in remaining at Rome and from the defects of character which soon manifested themselves in him. The plea that they had chosen him because forced to do so was only an excuse. He was not a pleasant Pope, but it was their solemn duty to have borne with him and stood by him, and bitter woes came upon the church by their taking another course.

Early in May some of the cardinals betook themselves to Anagni, the summer resort of the popes, and by the 24th of June all were there except the four Italians who remained with Urban. Messengers were constantly passing between the Pope and the college, and outwardly there was perfect concord, but the hatred of the cardinals for their chosen one grew daily deeper. The Pope was so rude in his speeches to them, so haughty in his demeanor, especially when it is remembered that they were for the most part nobles and he low-born, that they could not endure it. He showed an utter absence of tact, for almost his very first act was publicly to rebuke in his chapel the bishops who were present for being absent from their sees. One was not afraid to answer, "I am here on necessary business." He charged the nuncios in the consistory with taking bribes, and the Cardinal of St. Marcello said, "As you are Pope, I cannot reply, but if you were still the little Archbishop of Bari [*archiepiscopellus*] I would tell you that you lied." He declared in season and out of season that he would not leave Rome and that he would make so many Italian cardinals that the Frenchmen would have no chance. This was not calculated to increase their loyalty. Common speeches of his to the cardinals were, "Shut up!" "Stop your talk!" It caused quite a flutter when he called the high-born Orsini a fool.

Dietrich von Niem, who was the secretary of briefs to Urban as to several other popes, says of him: "There was in this man a hard and restless nature, no humanity, no conciliation of dispositions. He was contumacious, threatening, rough, more willing to be shunned and to be feared than to be loved." Catherine of Siena, although on his side and working for him, did not hesitate to remonstrate with him strongly. In her nineteenth letter she says: "Mitigate a little, for the love of Christ, these sudden impulses. You have a great heart, but these sudden passions are the plague of your soul." He changed so perfectly after his accession that the cardinals were not much out of the way in thinking him mad, for he often acted like it.

As has been said, the cardinals were at Anagni, and they asked the Pope to come there. He declined and summoned them to Tivoli, where he and the four Italian cardinals were. They declined to come, for they were secretly plotting to dethrone him. They wrote letters to the most eminent jurists, trying to get opinions that the election of Urban was illegal and forced on them. They received, however, but cold comfort, as the general opinion was that no flaw could be found in it. On the 9th of August the thirteen cardinals who were at Anagni put forth a paper in which they called Urban all the ugly names in the rich repertory of the ecclesiastical dictionary,— "Antichrist, devil, apostate, tyrant, deceiver, elected by force," etc.,—and called upon him immediately to give up the throne.

It was a base and cowardly act, not dictated at all by a love for the church, but because they were afraid of having to give up the life of power and luxury and ease which had so long been theirs. They knew perfectly well that the election of Urban was as valid as that of any Pope had ever been, and they also knew that the kingdom of France would support them in whatever extremity they put themselves, for France wanted to keep a Pope of her own choosing. Thomas d'Acerno gives six reasons for their action: 1. The Pope's limitation of their luxury, especially of their expensive dinners. 2. The strict prohibition of simony, which was their common vice. 3. The Pope's threat to make cardinals, which every Pope has always done. 4. His determination to stay at Rome, which was his proper place and the seat of the

Papacy from the first. 5. His insulting language, which was not agreeable, certainly, but was not the slightest excuse for denying his authority. 6. His refusal to go to Anagni and summoning them to him; certainly he would have been a very cowardly sovereign if he had done otherwise. No excuse at this point can be made for the cardinals; nothing guided them but self-interest. It is no excuse to say that they had no idea of the fatal consequences, for they could not help knowing that the election of another Pope would throw the whole church into the most terrible disorder. In the providence of God, their action ultimately brought about the lowering of the extravagant demands of the Papacy and loosed the bonds in which it had so long held the European powers, but that is no excuse for them.

After their manifesto of the 9th of August, the recalcitrant cardinals took measures to protect themselves. There was a large force of Breton soldiers in Italy under the banner of the Count of Geneva, also a cardinal. These they called to their support. The Romans tried to stop the coming of these troops to Anagni, but failed, although three hundred dead were left upon the field. The cardinals removed from Anagni to Fondi, which was in Neapolitan and not papal territory, and, by promising each one secretly that he should be the new Pope, induced three of the Italian cardinals to join them. Urban now had only one cardinal left with him, the old Cardinal of St. Peter's; but he soon died, leaving a will in which he strongly asserted the legality of Urban's election. Then the Pope, without one particle of tact or prudence, made twenty-nine new cardinals at once, a thing totally unprecedented and unnecessary; and as if he did not need all the friends he could muster, he embroiled himself with Joanna, Queen of Naples, who had been anxious to do all she could to help him. The Archbishop of Arles stole away from the Castle of St. Angelo with all the papal jewels and insignia and joined the cardinals at Fondi. There, on the 20th of September, 1378, the cardinals went through the mad and guilty ceremony of choosing a new Pope in place of Urban, whom they deposed with bell, book, and candle.

Their choice fell not on a man of piety, learning, and good repute, but on a soldier, a captain of freelances, the Count of Geneva, a cardinal indeed, but a mockery of every quality that should grace a cardinal. He was connected by birth with many of the royal houses of Europe, but his life had been passed on battle-fields and not in churches, and the blood of more than one massacre was on his armor. He took the name of Clement VII., and bitter were the gibes and jests on one so fierce by nature calling himself " Clement." And so began the great schism which for more than forty years tore Christendom to pieces and dragged the banner of the Prince of Peace in the vilest mud ; everywhere hateful words, lies, perjury, trickery, simony, and the grossest and most unblushing immorality on the part of those set highest in the church. The laws of the church were everywhere set at naught, and one hideous game of grab occupied popes, kings, priests, and potentates from Norway to Italy.

It is one of the greatest proofs of the divine origin
of the church and of the eternal vitality of Christianity that it lived through this horrible period, and that
in the hours of the deepest degradation God was not
without far more than the seven thousand who had
not bowed the knee to Baal.   Not only among the
Spiritual Franciscans and other mystics, not only in
convents and monasteries, but everywhere in humble
parishes and in quiet city homes were thousands of
devout people who looked with horror on the witches'
dance of sin and lawlessness going on around them
and considered it the curse of God upon the church
for its sinfulness.   Daily and hourly many devout
prayers went up to the throne of heaven that this
life-crushing burden might be removed from His
long-suffering people.

It would be amusing if it were not so sad to note
how political affinities and race animosities dictated
which Pope a country should acknowledge without
any regard to the justice of his claims or the holiness
of his character.   France declared for Clement, and
of course England then took sides with Urban.   Italy
stuck to her own son.   Germany, sick of French
popes, was all for Urban.   If England was for Urban,
why of course Scotland was for Clement.   Spain was
engineered into the Clementine ranks, but since
France was that way why Flanders must be the
other way and shout for Urban.   Even now it is
hard to tell which Pope deserved obedience, and
Roman Catholic writers do not always agree about
the line.   The councils which met about the schism
carefully shirked that question, and even such a his-

torian as Gieseler prints Clement VII. and Benedict XIII. in the genuine series, and if Alexander VI. was a right numbering then certainly Alexander V. must be counted in. It is a pretty question for casuists, and to casuists let us commit it.

CHAPTER XIII.

URBAN VI. AND CLEMENT VII.

HERE stood, then, the two rival popes, and as a matter of course the first thing they did was to call each other names. Each was Antichrist, and each was the arch-apostate, and all the spiritual weapons in their arsenals were at once wheeled into line. Urban excommunicated four of the French cardinals and a whole crowd of noblemen, and Clement did the same for a select company of the Urbanists. Clement went to Naples, and the queen and many of the nobles greeted him warmly; but the great bulk of the people were for Urban, and a riot soon broke out. Clement fled before it, soon embarked for France, and hastened to Avignon, which was all swept and garnished and tenanted by seven other spirits more determined than even he was to perpetuate the schism.

The great difficulty that stared Urban in the face was the want of money. The great river of wealth which usually flowed into the papal coffers was much choked by the confusion in men's minds as to which Pope ought to receive it, and it was very hard to reap anything from soil which had been so harried and exhausted as his own dominions. To make up for all this he entered on a course of the most unblushing rapacity and simony. He ransacked the Roman churches for their plate and ornaments, and traded with dealers for the property of parishes and monasteries, and even instituted a commission to sell property without the consent of bishop, rector, or superior.

At last he got together enough to pay an army, and was able to drive out the robbing Bretons and get possession of the Castle of St. Angelo. He then turned his attention to Joanna, Queen of Naples, called her in bulls all the names he could conjure up, and declared that she was deprived of her kingdom, which he gave to her nephew, Charles of Durazzo. Catherine of Siena had a finger in this pie, as we see from several of her letters. Clement in Avignon was on Joanna's side, since Urban was on the other; and since the latter had given the kingdom to Charles, Clement and Joanna gave it to Louis of Anjou, for whom Clement created a principality in the Italian territory —an easy thing to do on paper, for Clement was in Avignon and could not control a foot of Italian soil. Battles and sieges took place; Joanna, who had had four husbands, and who, according to what historian you follow, was either a Messalina or a Lucretia, disappeared from the earth, and Charles reigned in her place, for Louis died of the plague in Italy.

Urban came to Naples to confer with the new king, and there acted with that utter absence of self-control and common wisdom which seems to have marked his whole pontificate. He was cursed with a nephew, named Butilio, who was constantly getting him into trouble by his acts of violence. He carried off a nun, for which sacrilege the courts condemned him to die; but the Pope said it was only a youthful escapade not worth noticing, and he annulled the sentence. The affair was patched up, and the Pope and cardinals (and most unwilling cardinals they were, never knowing from one day to the other how his Holiness was going to act) left Naples for Nocera. There Urban tried hard to make some new cardinals, but he could not get anybody to accept the dignity; it had been made too cheap.

Charles tried to have a conference with him, but the haughty Pope sent word, " Kings have been accustomed to come to popes, not popes to go to kings." The angry king replied, " I will come, but at the head of an army." He was as good as his word. Nocera was soon invested, and every day the old and furious Pope marched around the battlements with bell, book, and candle, excommunicating all his enemies beneath the walls. The cardinals, more and more frightened at the Pope's actions, now began to consult eminent lawyers as to what course they had better take, for some of them considered the pontiff totally insane. Urban got wind of this, and he seized on six cardinals whose names had been given him, put them in a loathsome prison, then brought them to trial and tortured them to make them confess.

What a spectacle! the Vicar of Christ gloating over the sufferings of his chief counsellors! For while they were shrieking with pain he was walking up and down in a garden near by reading his breviary, and his miserable nephew stood laughing by the side of the sufferers. All this and much more about Urban and his successors is told us by Dietrich von Niem, whose Latin memoir of the schism is most interesting and most vigorous.   Urban at last was able to escape from Nocera, and, dragging the six wretched cardinals with him, he managed to reach Trani, and there found Genoese galleys which conveyed him and his suite to Genoa.   The canny Genoese sent in a heavy bill for these galleys, and the Pope had to make over to them a seaport in payment.   On the land journey one of the prisoners, the Bishop of Aquila, could not keep up, and the Pope coolly ordered him to be murdered and his body left by the roadside.

While at Genoa the other accused cardinals were secretly made way with, excepting one, an Englishman, the Bishop of London, who escaped death by the intercession of his sovereign, Richard II., but he was kept in prison until after Urban's death.   Urban could not be peaceful anywhere.   He soon quarrelled with the Genoese, moved to Lucca, and then to Perugia.   There his evil-genius nephew, Butilio, again came to the front and by his acts of violence and lust made the place too hot to hold his uncle, and in August, 1388, Urban returned to Rome.   He now evolved a new scheme for raising money and proclaimed a jubilee.   Clement VI. had fixed the period between the jubilees at fifty years, but Urban reduced it to thirty-three years, the time of our Saviour's earthly life, and fixed on the next year as the proper one.

He was very busy getting ready for it, when he was thrown by his mule, and the shock was so great that after a lingering illness he died October 15, 1389.

No one regretted him, and when one reviews his acts and marks his fearful temper, his silly obstinacy, and his want of judgment on the most ordinary occasions, one is inclined to believe that those of his time who thought him mad were not far out of the way. The epigram of Tacitus on the Emperor Galba will well apply to him : " Omnium consensu, capax imperii nisi imperasset " (" All men thought him capable of ruling, until he ruled ").

CHAPTER XIV.

CLEMENT VII.—BONIFACE IX.

EANWHILE the Avignon Pope was comparatively quiet. The fierce Count of Geneva had much changed since he had been made Pope. He was much more affable and tractable than his adversary, who had been a monk from his youth and of the strictest manner of life all his days. Clement, like Urban, wanted always money, money. He had the rich kingdom of France to bleed, and he bled it to the last drop. The French clergy shrieked and complained, and some lamented loudly and bitterly that they had ever taken him as Pope; but Clement had thirty-six cardinals to provide for, and even one cardinal absorbed considerable cash. The Sacred College kept men employed all over the kingdom to notify them when a rich parish or a cathedral stall or an abbacy became vacant, and then with the quickness of lightning a papal bull put them in possession of it. The papal officers sold "reversions," that is, the title to a benefice, which was good as soon as the present holder should die or vacate. The effect was most disastrous on religion. The parishes were neglected, the abbeys could no longer help the poor, and the great University of Paris was depleted of students.

This university did its utmost to put an end to the

schism. It contained among its teaching staff many enlightened and conscientious men, and they appealed solemnly to Clement to call a general council and submit to it the question. He seemed to give heed to what they said, but there were too many French prelates and French politicians interested in keeping up a French Pope to allow him, even supposing him to have been sincere, to carry out such a purpose. When Urban died he and his cardinals fondly hoped that the schism would finish and that the world would acknowledge him as Pope; but the Italian cardinals had no thought of such a thing, nor can we see any reason why they should have thought so. They could not with any consistency acknowledge Clement as having been legally chosen, so they met immediately and elected Peter Tomacelli, Cardinal of St. Anastasia, who took the name of Boniface IX.

Some say he was only thirty years old; his secretary, Dietrich von Niem, says he was forty-four. Thirty seems very young for a cardinal, but Clement VII. beatified one named Peter, Bishop of Metz, who was only eighteen. Such a saint was this youth reputed that the king and the University of Paris sent Peter d'Ailly to Avignon to plead for his canonization. In his plea he stated that the youthful prelate had raised seventy-five persons from the dead. " Credat Judæus," etc.

Boniface was a man of glittering generalities, superficial, fluent, not accused of immorality, but generally and constantly accused of the worst simony under which the church had ever suffered. Clement, bad as he was, was not worthy in this respect to tie the

YORK COLLEGE LIBRARY

latchet of Boniface's shoes. In one fell swoop he reserved to himself one year's income of all bishoprics and abbacies. If you wanted to buy a bishopric (and nothing was more common), you had to pay down the money in advance for it, and there were regular offices in Rome where you could get the money advanced and give a lien on the income of your see, after the Pope had pocketed the first year. He invented a new mode of squeezing clients. He sold reversions, as others had done, and then sold them again to some one else; so that when the abbot of a fat place died three or four would come forward with the proper papers showing that they had bought and paid for it, and the one who had a form marked " preference above all other preferences " got it.

For a hundred gold florins, if you were a mendicant friar, you could get yourself transferred to an order which was not mendicant. People wondered, and justly, how mendicant friars vowed to poverty could have a hundred gold florins, but they did have them and paid them over. The Pope's mother and his three brothers were greedier than he was; they made hay while the sun shone, and laid tribute on every one who had business with the Papacy. So many wretched and unfit persons were put in responsible places that there came to be a saying in the church, " The Bonifacian plantations, which the heavenly Father planted not."

It was very hard for Boniface to get money, for the rich mines of France and Spain were worked by the antipope. England did indeed acknowledge him, but the English were very sensitive about so much money going out of the kingdom, and under Edward III. the famous statutes called " provisors " had been passed in A.D. 1350. They forbade any man to receive any provision or preferment from the court of Rome; that the king should present when proper, but that elections to bishoprics be free. In 1353 a statute of " premunire " provided that " any one who should carry to a foreign tribunal matter which was cognizable in the king's court, or who should try to impeach in any foreign court a judgment which had been pronounced by the king's court, should be cited to answer before the king, and if he did not appear should be outlawed, forfeit his property, and be committed to prison." This was the strongest antipapal act passed before Henry VIII.'s time, and it shows how long before the Reformation the English people were preparing for it. Pope Boniface stormed over such laws, but in vain. Then he tried humbling himself, and in April, 1371, sent a piteous letter to the Archbishop of Canterbury and the English clergy begging for money. They were very obdurate, and there is a statement extant showing that all he realized from this moving appeal was about fifteen hundred dollars.

Mournful as this picture is, it is not without its bright side. The very horror of it all, the venality, the utter disregard of the commonest honesty, the gross sensuality, the greed of the highest prelates, brought many earnest souls closer to God and drove them to their knees in prayer for the afflicted church. There were many devotedly religious people, and every hamlet had its simple and pious souls who lived in an atmosphere very different from the tainted one of papal and royal courts. There are sermons, devotional treatises, etc., of that time which breathe the truest spirit of piety. One natural consequence of the papal greed was that everywhere in Europe was to be found an ever-increasing number of learned and sensible men who believed no longer in the prevailing doctrine of the superiority of the Pope to all law. It had been held and taught that a Pope's every word, his every decree and manifest, no matter how contrary to civil law or to the revealed law of God, was not to be questioned; but the actions of the popes themselves were fast letting light in upon that darkness.

The jubilee which Urban VI. had arranged, but did not live to see, took place in 1390, and that the real religious spirit still had some vigor is shown by the large number of persons who in spite of all the disturbances and difficulties appeared at Rome. This jubilee brought in a great deal of money to Boniface, and he sent agents all over Europe to hawk indulgences for those who wanted to come to Rome, but were hindered from doing so. This increased his store, and some of the money he laid out in repairs on some of the almost ruined Roman churches. The jubilee was such an easy way of coining money that Boniface had the ingenuity and the coolness to declare that the last one was irregular and ought not to have been held at thirty-three years' interval, that fifty years was the proper time, so that one was due in 1400, and he issued a bull providing for it.

He was not living at Rome then, for the Romans,

when they had a Pope, never could treat him well
for any length of time.   They were miserable without him and made him miserable when he was with
them, so since 1393 Boniface had been living in
Perugia and other places.   As the jubilee drew near,
the Romans felt that in some way or other he must
be got back, for a jubilee without a Pope would be
as "Hamlet" with Hamlet left out; so they humbled
themselves, and Boniface took advantage of their
necessities.   They agreed that the "bannerets," as
they were called, the popular rulers of the city, should
be done away forever and that the Pope should be the
real and not the titular sovereign of Rome.   This
jubilee was a wonderful success.   The French, who
had not been able to attend the last, flocked to this
one, and indulgences were granted, of course for pay,
to those who would promise to visit certain designated
churches in their own neighborhood in lieu of going
to Rome.   So much money came in from this source
that the Pope was able to clear out the choked harbor
of Ostia, put in repair the Castle of St. Angelo (and
in doing this he was obliged to hang thirty-one of
the Colonnas who attacked him), improve the Vatican, and obtain a foothold and an authority in Rome
which his predecessors had not enjoyed for well-nigh
two centuries.

To return to the schism, Boniface as soon as he had
been made Pope sent letters to all the sovereigns,
expressing his great regret over the division in the
church and his earnest desire to put an end to it; but
as he alluded to Pope Clement under the title, "son
of Belial," these letters were not productive of much

harmony. The University of Paris, however, did not cease its constant efforts to close up the ghastly breach, and memorialized the king, the unhappy Charles the Mad, begging him to take up the business. They proposed that one of three plans should be agreed upon : arbitration, resignation of both popes, trial of the case before a general council. It is said that ten thousand individual opinions in the case were collected by the university. A copy of this memorial was sent to Clement. He foamed with rage over it, and, calling his cardinals together, laid it before them. What was his amazement to hear them say that they agreed with it, and thought he ought to strive to carry it out! He answered not a word, shut himself up in his room, and three days after died in a fit of apoplexy doubtless caused by his agitation, September 16, 1394.

The moment he was dead the university memorialized the king, who happened to be sane at that time, begging him to prevent the cardinals at Avignon from electing a new Pope, and he lost no time in writing them to that effect. His letter found them already assembled in conclave, and having an inkling as to its contents, they resolved not to open it until the election had been held. So on they went in the woful course of division, although never had a better opportunity offered for taking the first steps to heal it. They elected the very one of their number who by cunning and double-dealing would be the most apt to prevent the closing of the strife, Peter di Luna, a Spaniard, who took the title of Benedict XIII.

CHAPTER XV.

BENEDICT XIII.—INNOCENT VII.

BENEDICT XIII. had been one of the most active in starting the schism by the election of Clement at Fondi, though no one more than he had in words bewailed that step. He had declared that he would make any sacrifice to put an end to it, but all that was mere talk, for neither he nor his cardinals had the slightest idea of giving up. The cardinals all took an oath at the election that if it would help the matter they would, if elected, resign, but not one of them meant one word of it. There was too much to be got out of it for such as they to give up. They were perfectly ready to heal the schism if their Pope could be the Pope, otherwise not. The University of Paris still persisted in its laudable efforts and advised Benedict to take earnest steps towards a reunion, but he gave only polite words in reply. The whole kingdom of France was, however, becoming aroused on the subject, and, whether it took many years or few, men were resolved that there should be no peace until this frightful chasm was filled. On February 2, 1395, a national council met in Paris. The king was again insane and could not attend, but there was a large number of bishops, monks, and distinguished university people. The judgment of the university that the Pope should resign was adopted by a vote of eighty-seven to twenty-two.

A deputation of the noblest names in France was selected to carry this message to Avignon and present it to the Pope, and prayers were ordered to be offered in all the churches of France for the success of the embassy. The ambassadors had hard work to obtain an interview with the Pope, but the cardinals, finding the pressure very great, after much talking of a very heated nature, agreed to support the embassy and secure their admission to the pontifical presence. Benedict tried to stave the matter off by submitting the project of a meeting between himself and Boniface, but the ambassadors replied that such a scheme was perfectly impracticable and impossible to realize. The Pope, of course, knew that as well as anybody, but he tried to bully them into assenting to it. " I am your sovereign," he said,—" not only yours, but of all who are living." This sort of talk greatly disgusted the embassy, and refusing even to dine with the Pope, they went back to Paris. The general opinion was that if the two popes should meet they would divide Christendom between them, and there would be two popes forever.

The university now decided to send trusty persons to the different kings in Europe and endeavor to induce them to join in an effort to put down the schism, but nothing came of it. Benedict now attempted to interfere with the university, but the faculty greatly resented this and appealed from any act of his to a "future, true, and only Pope." Benedict declared that any such language was unlawful. They immediately repeated it and declared their belief that schismatical popes were subject to general councils, and that after death their acts were referable to the judgment of their true successors, which is something widely different from the modern papal doctrine. In 1398, after a meeting of the French king and the German emperor to talk over the schism and their failure to get both popes to resign, there was again a council in France.

This was not simply an ecclesiastical affair, for many of the lay dignitaries were present. Long and earnestly they debated whether the kingdom of France should continue to acknowledge Benedict. After twelve days' discussion, by a vote of two hundred and forty-seven out of three hundred, they decided no longer to do so, and the king communicated the decision to the whole realm. No one was to obey Benedict, or pray for him, or, what was much worse, pay any money to him. When this was made known at Avignon all the cardinals but two forsook Benedict and fled over the Rhone to Villeneuve, which was a French town and not in the papal dominion. Benedict sent after them the usual number of curses, but they returned not. As the Pope was so recalcitrant, the French king sent an army under Marshal Boucicault to Avignon to besiege the papal palace. They did not attempt to storm it, and for a wonder the Pope did not come out and curse them. This siege was kept up seven months, and the papal household was very short of provisions, although a great stock had been laid in.

The turncoat cardinals kept urging the king to seize Benedict, and things became so warm that the Pope was forced to yield and agree to be kept under the guard of the cardinals and the chief citizens of Avignon. They pledged the king that the Pope should not be allowed to leave his palace, and he remained there a prisoner from April, 1399, until March, 1403, obstinately refusing to abdicate. Strict as the watch was which was kept, Benedict managed one day to slip past his guards in disguise, hide in a friendly house in Avignon until the next day, when swift rowers carried him down the Rhone to the strong castle of Renaud, in Provence, and therefore subject to Louis, King of Sicily and Count of Provence, the Pope's sworn friend and loyal subject.

Benedict had chosen the nick of time. France was torn to pieces by the rival factions of Orleans and Burgundy, and whoever was the enemy of one side was the friend of the other. Burgundy was against Benedict; therefore Orleans, the king's brother, was for him, and Orleans controlled the mad king. Again there was a great assembly at Paris, and the king, at the moment sane, came in with his brother, Orleans, and declared that, since none of the other sovereign powers would withdraw from Benedict, he would not, and that again he acknowledged him as Pope. Swift as the wind the cardinals turned again and took their places at Benedict's side, and he was once more the Pope of much of Europe, especially of England, France, and Spain. To obtain this favor from Charles the Pope had faithfully promised to do what he could to extinguish the schism, and he did forthwith send an embassy to Rome to confer with Boniface. The Romans gave a safe-conduct, and the ambassadors arrived safely in Rome, but Boniface would only receive them as Pope.

With the usual good sense of Frenchmen, they agreed not to press that question, and at the first interview they laid before him a scheme for meeting in some place and discussing the whole subject of the schism. "Very well," said he; "but remember, I am the only Pope; your master is an antipope." "That may be," said the angry deputies, "but at all events he is not a simoniac." The thrust went home, and the Pope, who had for some time been in wretched health, now took to his bed and in a day or two departed to his eternal rest. Dietrich von Niem says that when dying he exclaimed, "If I had money I would be well." But Dietrich is not always free from gossip.

It must be said for Boniface that he ruled his little kingdom with far more ability and justice than his predecessors had done. He had to fight many a hard battle with rebellious burghers, not only of Rome, but of Perugia, of Assisi, and everywhere in Italy, where Guelph and Ghibelline were springing at each other's throats. When his greatest foe, Visconti, Duke of Milan, who was rapidly conquering all Italy, came against him and his cause seemed desperate, a providential plague carried the duke off, and the pontiff gave devout thanks. These contests cost the Pope much money, and this probably was the great cause of the Pope's marvellous rapacity and unscrupulous simony. Improbable as it seems, it rests on excellent testimony that he "absolutely cancelled all his own grants, indulgences, and dispensations, and those of his predecessors, so that they all might be regranted over again for five years and new fees collected."

On the death of Boniface, Benedict fondly hoped that his claims would be recognized and that the Italian party would elect no other Pope, but his hopes were soon rudely shattered. The Italians had every reason to go on with an election, for they thought with justice that their line was the only true one; so without any delay, on October 17, 1404, they chose Cosimo Megliorotto, Cardinal of the Holy Cross, who took the name of Innocent VII., a gentle, pure-hearted, excellent old man, not distinguished for anything in particular, but anxious to have peace and to lead a quiet life, which was perfectly impossible for a Pope of those times, especially for one who was so ill-fated as to have to live in Rome. The stern rule of Boniface had kept the quarrelsome burghers well under, but the new Pope was too weak and yielding to cope with them. Colonnas and Savellis swooped down from their mountain fastnesses to swell the tide of insurrection, and Orsinis, as usual, took up arms for the pontiff. As had happened often before, the streets ran blood, the palaces were looted, the cause of religion disgraced.

Ladislas, the King of Naples, was in Rome at the time with strong hankerings after some of the papal territory. Innocent tried to purchase his mediation by ceding to him for a limited time the possession of the Maremma, and the king tried to mediate; but since the Pope had to surrender twenty thousand florins of income, the royal mediation did not do him much good. The city was divided into two hostile camps, and the Tiber was the dividing line, the Pope on one side at St. Angelo, and the people on the other at the Capitol. In August, 1405, less than a year after his coronation, Innocent was forced to flee away to Viterbo, and there his nephew, a hot-headed young man, got into a quarrel with some of the citizens, killed eleven of them, and threw their bodies out of the window, while the Pope, helpless and horrified, sat weeping in his apartments. Then there was a fierce combat; the palaces of the cardinals flamed in the air, the Abbot of St. Peter's was murdered before the Pope's eyes, the Colonnas were masters of the situation, and all was tumult and confusion.

The King of Naples had an army all ready near Rome, and he thought it a good time to push it forward and get a slice of what was going; but the Romans, even if they had driven out their rightful lord, the Pope, had not the least desire to have the King of Naples for their master; so, after a bloody conflict, Ladislas was obliged to retreat, and in March, 1406, the Pope came back again and used the well-worn papal weapons of excommunication against the king. Ladislas gave way before this and surrendered the Castle of St. Angelo.

This was accomplished in November, 1406, and before the month was out the poor, weary Pope was done with all the trials of this world and at rest among the long line of his predecessors. The Roman cardinals,

fifteen in number, really hesitated about going on with a
new election, but if Rome was to be kept for the popes
it was necessary to have a head there immediately.
They had no alternative but to proceed, their very
lives depended on it, and so they went into conclave.
How they all protested and swore that the election
they were going to hold was a pure matter of form,
and that whoever was elected was to be simply an
instrument for resigning whenever his rival should
hold out any hopes of doing likewise! The iron-clad
oath which they took, that whoever was elected
should always stand ready to resign, is extant in the
useful chronicles of Dietrich von Niem, who still keeps
up through all these reigns his budget of news.

No one swore more loudly or protested more earnestly than the Cardinal of St. Mark, Angelo Corario,
a native of Venice and nearly eighty years of age.
He certainly seemed a safe man to elect, and elected
he was and took the name of Gregory XII. At
his enthronement he said " his only fear was that he
would not live to accomplish the holy work of unification." Fine words, these, but Von Niem, who was
in a position to know, implies that he did not mean
them. Oaths were easily made and broken then.
However that may be, Gregory immediately took
steps in the right direction and sent a letter to Benedict which was earnest and well conceived. He addressed it to " Peter di Luna, whom some nations
during this wretched schism call Benedict XIII."
Peter di Luna replied in the same strain and addressed
his letter to " Angelo Corario, whom some nations in
this wretched schism call Gregory XII." Both were

quits then as far as titles went, and both letters expressed the most fervent desires for peace and reunion. Benedict's words were very strong: "Haste, delay not; consider our age, the shortness of life; embrace at once the way of salvation and peace, that we may appear with our united flock before the great Shepherd."

Soon the city of Novara, in our day the seat of a flourishing commerce, was chosen as the place where the popes were to meet, each put off the papal insignia, and then the two colleges of cardinals were to unite and choose a successor. Everything looked fair and promising, when Gregory began to hedge. He could not well help it, for, although a man of excellent character, he was old, easily frightened, and entirely under the dominion of some greedy nephews who meant to make all they could out of his Papacy and to keep it up as long as possible. Ladislas, the King of Naples, was of the same way of thinking. He was afraid that, in case of reunion, there would be a French Pope chosen and that then he would have to give way to a French king. He therefore did all he could to keep the Pope from going to the appointed rendezvous and worried him by constant assaults against Rome.

However, that very slow-moving body, the papal court, was at last got in motion, and on August 9, 1407, Pope Gregory set out for Viterbo; but it took him until September to get as far as Siena, the meeting at Savona having been arranged to take place at some time between Michaelmas and All-saints. Then Gregory began to make excuses, and a long roll they were. You can judge him either a hypocrite or a terrorized old man; testimony is about even for either side. He said he had no galleys equal to those of Benedict, that the district through which he had to travel was not safe, that he was out of funds—in fine, he had twenty-two formal objections to going to Savona, and all the while his clergy and his monks were preaching at him with all their lungs. He was a coward, they said, and a traitor, and Benedict was on the lookout to murder him and all his cardinals.

Gregory got as far as Lucca, and Benedict, on the other hand, advanced to Porto Venere and then to Spezzia. They were now only fifteen leagues apart, and the whole of Christendom looked with shame on these two old men parrying and eluding, and each so afraid to give up his power. Very pungent things were said about them both. Leonard of Arezzo says it was as if one Pope, like a land animal, refused to approach the shore, and the other, like a water animal, would not leave the sea; and our old friend, Von Niem, says they were like two knights having a sham fight in a tilting-ground; they appeared in earnest, but it was all display. St. Antonino gives Benedict a pretty hard character; he says: " Benedict, although a learned man, was the most crafty and shifty of mortals. In his sharp tricks he was like an eel escaping from clasping hands, slippery and versatile. On the other hand, Gregory was like an innocent lamb, like a dove without venom." Then, again, in more biting words about the two: " They were like the two elders in the history of Susanna, from whom iniquity went forth."

The spring of 1408 saw the two popes, one at Spezzia, the other at Lucca, each endeavoring to outmanœuvre the other and each with his own trials. Benedict was well aware that his chief support, the kingdom of France, was getting very weary of the long-drawn-out game of shameful cunning, but he seems to have thought that the distracted state of the kingdom, the constant insanity of the king, and the factions of Burgundy and Armagnac would prevent any steps being taken against him. He heard the mutterings and threats that he would be deserted; but he was arrogant and blind enough to issue two bulls attacking the King of France and the university, which was a great power in France, threatening them with excommunication and the kingdom with interdict. These bulls, however, only infuriated the French.

The king summoned an assembly at Paris, and the preacher at the opening session charged Benedict with heresy and schism and branded him as an enemy of Christ. The assembly declared the two bulls of Benedict to be illegal and treasonable, and Charles commanded his chancellor, the famous Gerson, to do what he liked with them. He ripped them in two and gave the princes one half and the university the other, and both parties tore them to atoms. The Pope's messengers were treated with the greatest indignity, dressed in fantastic costumes, and mounted on a high scaffold for the derision of all the populace. The die was cast; the neutrality of France was proclaimed to the world, the long and fateful spell of a French Pope was broken, and the first really valuable step taken in the mending of the rent garment of the church.

The French marshal, Boucicault, was ordered to seize Benedict, but the Pope was too quick for him. His galleys lay at anchor at Porto Venere, and as soon as he got wind of what was intended he set sail and was soon at Perpignan, in the kingdom of Aragon. The master mind in the attainment of this great decision from the French church and nation was Gerson, one of the most illustrious of Frenchmen in any age. He was most active and conspicuous in this whole matter of the schism and was one of the principal figures in the councils of Pisa and Constance. Some notice of his life and works will not be out of place here.

John Gerson, or, perhaps better, John Charlier, was born at Gerson, near Rheims, December 14, 1363. He was brought up by devout parents and when fourteen was sent to the University of Paris. His great talents soon attracted attention, and at twenty he was elected procurator. In 1387, when twenty-four, he was chosen one of the ambassadors to Avignon in the matter of the Immaculate Conception, and from that time devoted his great abilities to the elevation of the tone of the clergy and the university and to the putting an end to the schism. He became when only thirty-two chancellor of the University of Paris, one of the highest honors that could befall a Frenchman. He was a most prolific writer, and no one now would have the courage to wade through all his treatises, but they are easily divided into three parts: the improvement of the university studies, the matter of the schism, and, in later years, devotional and spiritual writings. He labored diligently to supplant the foolish and idle questions over which the school-men split hairs, by the study of the Bible and the fathers.

He held the doctrine, which is most reasonable and catholic, that a general council could be summoned without the authority of the Pope, and that the authority of the church resides in the whole body of the episcopate. He held, indeed, that in a case of emergency a council could be summoned by faithful laymen. Perhaps the word "Gallican" will sum up better than any other the general trend of his views. They were entirely hostile to the arrogant papal pretensions. For a long while he was thought to have been the author, or at least the adapter from the Latin, of the famous "Imitatio Christi," but more profound research has fixed its authorship on Thomas à Kempis.

While these proceedings were going on against Benedict, Gregory was in no better plight. His own city of Rome was in the hands of the ever-busy King of Naples, who declared that he came there to protect the Pope's interests, and under that cloak he seized city after city of the Popedom.

The cardinals were constantly reminding Gregory of his promise to resign and the swelling words he had uttered on that subject. They tried to bribe him; offered him the patriarchate of Constantinople, two Venetian bishoprics, and the bishopric of Exeter (Milman says the archbishopric of York) if he would give up the contest. Suddenly he took a new tack

and broke all his promises by declaring his intention
to create four new cardinals. The Sacred College
protested loudly, vowed they would not recognize
any such cardinals, and made ready to flee away from
Lucca. The Pope forbade their going, but the Lord
of Lucca took their part, and shielded them from
papal violence; so that, with the exception of those
who were sick, they all reached Pisa in safety, where,
on the 14th of May, 1408, they published a bitter
letter against the Pope, in which they reminded him
of the words he had used at his coronation—" that
he would go on foot with his pilgrim's staff if it would
reunite the church."

Four cardinals of Benedict's following stole away
from Perpignan, and the Gregorian cardinals came
from Pisa to Leghorn to meet them, so that in Leghorn there were gathered from both obediences, as
they were called, fifteen cardinals, and soon after five
others joined them, and these twenty issued a call for
a general council to be held at Pisa in March of the
following year. The universities of Paris, Bologna,
Florence, with others, signified their full approval
and their conviction that such a measure was perfectly
legal. In the letters which the cardinals wrote to the
sovereigns and the universities they did not spare
either of the old men who were struggling to keep
the tiara. They showered upon them most liberally
the choicest terms of vituperation and compared them
to the Roman soldiers dividing the seamless robe of
Christ. " Perjurers and liars " were also among the
titles with which they greeted their former masters
and spiritual lords.

The old popes did not take very kindly to this idea of a general council, and they resolved to anticipate it by holding councils of their own. Benedict summoned one at Perpignan, and quite a number of prelates attended; but they soon got to quarrelling, and the council dwindled away to eighteen members. This little remnant advised unanimously the resignation of Benedict, or at least that he should send representatives to Pisa. The Pope flew into a furious rage, and as Perpignan was getting too hot to hold him, he retired to the Castle of Peníscola and there brooded over what he thought were his rights and wrongs. Gregory had hard work to find a place for his council. He could not have it in Rome, for that was in the power of the King of Naples, who professed, indeed, to be Gregory's friend, but he had slipped his leash so often that the Pope could not trust him. The Pope tried Florence, Bologna, Venice (his own city), Ravenna, Capua, but all turned a deaf ear; and at last in a little Venetian town in the Friuli a few bishops were got together, but it amounted to nothing, and nobody took any notice of it.

The fact was that Christendom in the West was tired out with the shiftings and delays of these two old men, and their adherents now were principally among those whose incomes depended directly on them. They were very different men. Gregory XII. had been chosen because he was so very old that the cardinals thought he would only hold together long enough for them to feather their own nests and arrange their own futures. He was a mere puppet pulled about by his relations and his cardinals and the troublesome King of Naples, but nothing can be said against his character; he simply had not strength enough to grapple with the enormous difficulties of his position. Benedict XIII. was a much stronger man, courageous and determined to uphold the honor of the Papacy. He had to take a great deal of bad language from the universities, and it rankled within him. His conduct was always scrupulously correct, and in ordinary times he would have made an excellent Pope, for he had many of the characteristics of a great church statesman, but he too was the victim of circumstances. He was attempting to fill an impossible position, and until the very last, when his temper entirely gave way and he showed foolish and useless anger, he calls for our pity and often for our admiration.

CHAPTER XVI.

THE COUNCIL OF PISA.

T was a great boon for Pisa that the council was appointed to meet within her walls. She had as a city met with hard luck. Her trade had fallen off, and, once first among the Italian centres of commerce, she was now in importance below both Genoa and Florence. It would not be long before she would fall into the jaws of Florence, already open to devour her. It seemed then like a return of the old glory to be chosen as the meeting-place of a great council. The council met in the beautiful cathedral which has filled so many travellers with admiration. It arrests even the attention of the American most sated with foreign churches, for it is so noble, so quietly beautiful, and with so little of meretricious display. Close by it is the graceful baptistery and that wonderful leaning tower of which architects yet debate whether it leans from purpose or from accident. Hard by is the exquisite Gothic cloister of John of Pisa, which surrounds the Campo Santo, on the walls of which the greatest painters of the Siena school had painted the drama of human life. All these buildings were

generally as we see them now when the council was
opened on Lady-day, March 25, 1409.

The procession formed in the monastery of St.
Michael and wound through the crooked streets to
the cathedral. The numbers in attendance made it
very imposing. According to D'Achery, there were
present twenty-two cardinals of both obediences, four
patriarchs, ten archbishops, sixty-nine bishops, while
thirteen archbishops and eighty-two bishops sent
proctors. There were present sixty priors, the generals of the Dominicans, Franciscans, Carmelites, and
Augustinians, the Grand Master of the Hospitallers,
and the Prior of the Teutonic Knights, besides one
hundred and nine representatives of collegiate and
cathedral chapters. Ambassadors were sent by
Wenzel, King of the Romans, by the kings of England, France, Sicily, Poland, and Cyprus, by the
dukes of Burgundy and Brabant, Cleves, Bavaria,
Pomerania, the Landgrave of Thuringia, the Margrave
of Brandenburg, the universities of Paris, Toulouse,
Angers, Montpellier, Vienna, Prague, Cologne, Cra-
cow, Bologna, Cambridge, and Oxford. One hundred
and twenty-three doctors of theology and two hundred doctors of law lent the weight of their learning,
and at least ten thousand strangers visited Pisa during the council.

It was a strange spectacle, that which the Council
of Pisa presented to the Christian world. It could
hardly believe in itself, for councils had for centuries been only summoned by the Pope, or presided
over by him or his deputies. This council had been
summoned by cardinals, and although it was very

largely attended, yet there are certain flaws in its action and certain anomalies in its conclusions which have prevented its having that weight with historians, especially those who are Roman Catholic, to which it would seem entitled. As has been already said, the doctrine of Gerson was its foundation: "If the Vicar of Christ be corporally or civilly dead, then the church, to provide itself with a head, has the right to assemble in general council, not only by the authority of the cardinals, but by the aid and support of every Christian prince." Peter d'Ailly also gave an opinion: "From Christ, its head, the church has the authority to come together or to summon a council to preserve its unity. Christ's words are: 'Where two or three are gathered together in My name, there am I in the midst.' He said not 'in the name of Peter,' or 'in the name of the Pope,' but 'in My name.'"

This all seems to us self-evident, but at that time it had only been heard in studies and university lecture-rooms; but this terrible schism brought out all such doctrines now and aired them before all the world. Everybody felt that if this council could get its decisions accepted the emergency would justify any irregularity in the way in which it had been called. To get it fully accepted, then, would be the rub, and it never was universally accepted; for certain rulings of the Council of Constance, which came after it, show that that council was not much guided by its predecessor, although it reached the same conclusions.

The president of the Council of Pisa was the Cardinal of Poitiers, chosen probably because he was the only cardinal who had not been created during the schism; his title was clear, no matter what other titles might be. The creed or profession of faith was read by the Archbishop of Pisa, and it ended with a declaration far too sweeping to go down in this our more tolerant day: "Every heretic and schismatic must share with the devil and his angels the burning of eternal fire, unless before the end of his life he be restored to the Catholic Church."

The advocate, Simon of Perugia, asked that the summons to the two rival popes be read, and with very ill-timed levity he spoke of them as "Benefictus" and "Errorius." Indeed, the literature of the council abounds not only in levity, but in coarseness. There are lampoons and satires extant about Gregory and his cardinals which are too filthy and indecent to be reprinted in our day. The two old pontiffs had so disgusted everybody that there was nothing too bad to say of them. As in courts of law, officers at the doors of the cathedral summoned Peter di Luna and Angelo Corario to appear and answer to the charges against them. Three days this farce was repeated, and the absent popes were then pronounced in contumacy.

At the fourth session of the council opposition showed itself. Four bishops appeared on the part of Rupert, Emperor of Germany, though Wenceslas also claimed that title, and fighting was going on about it. Rupert, through these prelates, propounded twenty-two objections to the council, most of which were dry technicalities, splitting of hairs, etc. April 24th was fixed as the time for answering them, but the deputation was evidently frightened at what it heard and saw, and, concluding that Gregory would stand no chance, quietly stole away and was heard of no more.

An answer was made at great length by the council on May 4th, but the point of the legality of the meeting was dropped for the safer ground set forth by Gerson, D'Ailly, and the universities, that the emergency justified the occasion. On the 24th of April the charges against the two popes were read from a document which consumed three hours in the reading. It had been drawn up by the cardinals, and it glided skilfully over their persistence in continuing the election of popes and bore down very hard on the obstinacy of the popes themselves. Then the taking of testimony began; but the council got very weary of that after a few days, and declared that the matters in question were facts of public notoriety.

In the eighth session, May 10th, a decree was passed stating that the cardinals created by both popes had withdrawn their allegiance from them and were now united together, that they pronounced the council duly assembled as representative of the universal church and with authority to settle the schism. On the 5th of June Peter di Luna and Angelo Corario were again summoned at the gates, and appeared not. The cathedral doors were then thrown open, and the Patriarch of Alexandria, with the patriarchs of Antioch and Jerusalem on either side of him, stood in the doorway and read the sentence of the council. It condemned both Benedict and Gregory to be deposed, pronounced invalid all their decisions and all their nominations of cardinals for a year past, and declared that if they would not aid in healing the division they should be handed over to the secular power.

Milman well says of this: " Such was the first solemn, deliberate, authoritative act by which a general council assumed a power superior to the Papacy and broke the long tradition of the indefensible, irresponsible autocracy of the Pope throughout Christendom. It assumed a dictatorial right in a representative body of the church to sit as a judicial tribunal, with cognizance of the title by which papal authority was exercised, of offences committed by prelates claiming to be popes, and to pronounce in the last instance on the validity of their acts. It went much beyond a decision in a contested election; it was the cashiering of both popes, and that not on account of irregularity or invalidity of title, but of crimes and excesses subject to ecclesiastical censure. It was a sentence of deprivation and deposition, not of uncanonical election."

Of course the cardinals could not take the last-mentioned ground, for it would have upset their own positions. If they granted that the popes had been uncanonically elected, then of course they were uncanonically created. The proclamation of the sentence was an occasion of great joy. All the bells were set ringing, and village after village took up the chime, so that, it is said, the news was known in Florence within three hours.

Now that the old popes were disposed of, it was of the first necessity to choose a new one; the church must not be left without a head, and the question,

" How to do it," was a most delicate one. The cardinals could not consent that the council in its corporate capacity should do this, for that would be to renounce their most coveted privilege, and would be likely to lead to great disputes and complications all over Christendom. This the prelates and doctors assembled soon realized, and there was but little question as to whether the choice should be left solely to the cardinals. They, however, put forth a paper in which they all bound themselves, in case one of their number should be chosen Pope, not to dissolve the council until (Mansi) " a rational and sufficient reformation of the church, both in its head and its members, shall have been accomplished."

Benedict still had a few supporters in Europe, and the King of Aragon sent ambassadors to insist that the envoys from that Pope should be heard in the council. They were allowed to state their case, but as soon as their spokesman said, " We come from Pope Benedict," there were everywhere cries, " He is a heretic and schismatic;" and as a riot was rapidly arising, the envoys left the council with an arrow in their side from Cardinal Cossa, who said, " If you come into my legation, I will burn you alive."

This action of the council was unwise, for the envoys were prepared to hand in Benedict's resignation, no matter whether Gregory resigned or not. On the 15th of June, 1409, the cardinals, at full liberty and under no conditions, entered into conclave at the archbishop's palace. The account of the number varies; Milman says twenty-six, Creighton twenty-four, Robertson twenty-two. Their deliberations were kept very secret. They undoubtedly would have preferred to choose Cossa, the ablest among them; but he did not think his time had come, and he persuaded them to elect Peter Philargi, Cardinal Archbishop of Milan, a Greek by birth, and a found-ling without a relation in the world. A Franciscan friar had taken him when a beggar boy, and had him carefully educated in that order. He had studied at both Oxford and Paris, was a well-read theologian, and a man of stainless character.

He was a compromise candidate and was as good a choice as the conclave could have made, one great recommendation to his brother cardinals being that he was over seventy and could not hope to reign very long. He took the name of Alexander V. This was on June 26th, and on July 1st he preached before the council, and had a decree read approving of all that the cardinals had done up to the opening of the council, declaring that all the cardinals of both obedi-ences were true cardinals, and that if there was any defect in their titles he as Pope pronounced it healed. There began now forthwith the insistence of many of the prominent members of the council on under-taking the reform of the church, but the cardinals dodged the question. It was set for July 20th, then for the 24th, then for the 27th, and on the 7th of August the Pope dissolved the council, deferring all reforms to the future council, which it was decreed should be summoned by the Pope in April, 1412.

So ended this important gathering, which, while it had ventilated quite thoroughly the great question as to which was the supreme authority in the church, the Pope or a general council, had really done nothing towards putting an end to the great schism which had been so long the bane of the church. The only result was that there had been two popes before, and now there were three; as a writer of the times makes the church say, " Bivira fueram; triviram fuerunt " ("I had two husbands before; now they have made me triple-husbanded "). Both the rival popes were so old, it would have been better to have waited until their decease; then the schism would have died a natural death.

CHAPTER XVII.

ALEXANDER V.

HE new Pope was, as has been said, learned and of spotless life, but he had very little firmness and was entirely under the control of the able and unscrupulous Cardinal Cossa, to whom he owed his election. He had no relations, and so it was thought he would not fall into the usual papal fault of nepotism, but he soon made it evident to all the world that the whole Franciscan order were his relations, and that he intended them to have a full share of all the good things he had to give away; and "giving away" was Alexander's fatal weakness. He said of himself, " I was rich as a bishop, poor as a cardinal, and a beggar as Pope." But it was not so much what he gave his fellow-monks that aroused the indignation of Europe, especially of France, as the bull he published in their favor. The mendicant orders had been steadily rising in the scale. They were stirring preachers, very democratic, and most self-sacrificing in times of plague and war. The common people were thoroughly devoted to them, and the friars were not slow to take advantage of it. They thrust themselves into every parish, heard confessions, administered the sacraments, married and buried, without the slightest consideration of the parish priests, who, as a matter of course, held them in holy horror.

The system of the church must rest on the parishes, and the rights of parish priests must be carefully defined in order that there may be regularity and lawful obedience. It is absolutely necessary to have this settled now, and it was just as necessary then, and we cannot help siding thoroughly with the parish priests and the diocesan bishops. The former saw themselves gradually supplanted in the affections of their flocks by a set of wandering friars, to whom, of course, a sinner would a great deal rather confess (as he would probably never see him again) than to his parish priest, who knew him and would keep an eye on him. The bishops were driven nearly to distraction by the constant disputes and questions arising between the regular clergy and the friars.

These pushing fellows were everywhere, and even the universities were being fast captured by them; able, eloquent, and often well read, they wormed themselves into the best chairs and boldly proclaimed their own views. This was not done without many a hard fight of words. William of St. Amour, in the middle of the thirteenth century, protested in the most pointed way against them. " For an able-bodied man who can work for his living to live off the poor is sacrilege, for St. Paul says, ' If a man will not work, neither let him eat.' Monks say," he continues, " that it is a counsel of perfection to live like Christ; but Christ teaches us to work, not beg. If any one wants to be perfect, he must either go to work in the world, or go into a monastery and live out of the world." St. Thomas Aquinas and St. Bonaventura defended the friars, and so the battle went on.

The popes had tried to do justice. Boniface VIII., in 1300, had decreed that no friar could preach in a parish church without the consent of the rector. It seems wonderful to us that any such decree could be necessary. By this decree the bishops were to have the power of forbidding any friar from hearing confessions in his diocese, and any friar performing any service in a parish for which he was paid was bound to hand over one fourth of the fee to the parish church. At the time of Alexander's election these two bodies, the regular clergy and the friars, were like two hostile armies, each one hoping for some great advantage; but the friars saw that their time had come. One of their own kidney had now mounted the papal throne, who, it was well known, was a thorough mendicant, heart and soul; so, hastening to Pisa, they procured from Alexander, October 12, 1409, a bull called " Regnans in Ecclesia," which completely knocked the bottom out of any right still remaining to the parochial clergy.

This bull gave the preaching friars, the Minorites, Carmelites, and Augustinians, full and uncontrolled power to hear confessions in every parish in Christendom. The Pope rubbed in the insult, for he ordered all the clergy to read this bull to the people from the steps of their own altars, and thus proclaim to the universe their downfall and the complete triumph of their adversaries. It was a bitter dose for a rector to have to say, " I am no longer master in my own house, but must share my rectorship with the first friar any man fancies." For a Pope elected to make peace, this bull was about as imprudent a move as could have been made. The hubbub it immediately aroused was tremendous, and the friars were soon quaking before the hornets' nest they had stirred up.

The University of Paris immediately sent deputies to Pisa, who were to insist on seeing the original bull, for they could not believe their ears. The deputies came and interviewed the cardinals, who one and all said, " We were not consulted about this bull; we had nothing to do with it, and we take no responsibility for it." The original bull with its leaden seal (*bulla*) was shown them, and, angry enough, they went back to Paris and reported that the bull was indeed genuine. The university immediately proceeded to expel all mendicants from its walls, and to prohibit their preaching in Paris. Dominicans and Carmelites hastened to say that they had wanted no such bull and had no use for it. The Franciscans attempted to carry it out, but a royal proclamation forbade any parish priest allowing friars to preach or hear confessions in the parish churches. Many universities adopted like measures, and one of the very first things Alexander's successor had to do was to repeal this obnoxious document and restore things to the *status quo ante.*

The great question now agitating Italy was the mastership of the States of the Church. It was absolutely vital for the new Pope to get possession of the city of Rome if he was to retain any temporal authority at all in the peninsula. Cossa, the Pope's dictator, felt and understood that thoroughly, and he prepared himself to march against Ladislas, King of Naples, who held the imperial city. The king's lieutenant, Orsini, deserted him, and the papal troops got possession first of the Vatican and its quarter, and, after many marchings and countermarchings, of the Castle of St. Angelo and the rest of the city. The people were glad enough to be free from the rule of Naples and to return to their old municipal elections. Meanwhile the Pope had lingered in Pisa, waiting for the clearing of the way to Rome, but the plague breaking out there, he retreated to Prato and then to Pistoja. He would like to have gone on to Rome after it was conquered for him, but his master, Cossa, objected, for he wished to be the first man in Rome, and he induced the Pope to undertake in the middle of winter the very hard and dangerous journey over the Apennines to Bologna, the capital of Cossa's legation, where Alexander settled himself at Cossa's expense, it is said.

He was not, however, to settle anywhere for very long, for he grew very ill towards the end of April, and felt that his end was drawing near. Dietrich von Niem, who is still chronicling papal doings, says, " Our lord the Pope, on his bed of sickness, in the presence of all the cardinals, preached us a beautiful Latin sermon from the text, ' Peace I leave with you, My peace I give unto you,' and begged all present to relax no effort to restore peace and unity to the church." All who heard him burst into weeping over his earnest words, and so on the 3d of May, 1410, he died, and lies buried in the church of St. Francis at Bologna, a true Franciscan monk in a Franciscan church.

As usual, his death was attributed to poison administered by order of Cossa, and it was one of the charges made against that person at the Council of Constance; but Hefele, who has thoroughly examined the charge, concludes that it rests on no foundation. Alexander enjoyed the Popedom too short a time to show what his real worth in that position would have been, but as Cossa dictated all his actions, it is probable he would have continued to do so if the Pope had lived longer.

CHAPTER XVIII.

JOHN XXIII.

HE cardinals had all followed the Pope to Bologna, and his death occurring May 3, 1410, on May 14th they entered the conclave, and on May 17th elected Baltasar Cossa, Cardinal of Bologna, Pope, who was enthroned on May 25th, and took the title of John XXIII., the last Pope ever known by that name, heretofore such a favorite, for no one since has cared to revive sleeping memories by taking John for his pontifical appellative.

The very first question that arises is, How was it possible for an assembly of the highest ecclesiastics in the world, knowing that the eyes of all Latin Christendom were on them, and realizing the gravity of the situation, to choose such a person as this John? He had been a pirate in his youth and had had two brothers hanged for piracy; but let that pass. No man ought to have brought up against him the sins of his youth if he repents of them and mends his ways. The universal condemnation of John rests on other grounds. We will also put on one side the accusations of unnatural lusts, though such were openly made at the Council of Constance; but all allowance made for the violence and injustice of enemies, John XXIII. seems to have been a monster of lust, cruelty, tyranny, and deceit.

Von Niem, his secretary, says that in Bologna it was openly said that in that city alone he had corrupted two hundred wives, widows, virgins, and even nuns. Aretino, another secretary, speaks of him as an able man without one trace of spirituality. How was it possible that a man so unholy, so thoroughly wicked, could have been made the successor of St. Peter and the Vicar of Christ? The election does not seem to have been compulsory, or else somebody would have said so at the Council of Constance, when certainly everything was brought up against John that could be hunted out.

The fact is that the cardinals, terrified at the state of Italy, and feeling the absolute need of a powerful man at the head of affairs, allowed themselves to be persuaded that no other person in the world could manage the difficult situation as well as Baltasar Cossa, liar and adulterer as he was. They seemed to forget his frightful vices and crimes in his energy, talent for affairs, and commanding personality. He was so far superior to any of them in ability that he dominated them completely, and in his presence and under his influence they acted as if hypnotized, and followed his lead exactly. This does not at all excuse their action, but it explains it. It is only one instance among many of superior ability, even if coupled with great wickedness, winning its way to the front.

In June, 1410, John created fourteen cardinals, among whom were two Englishmen, Langley, Bishop of Durham, and Robert Hallam, Bishop of Salisbury. He excommunicated, as was to be expected, the two old deposed popes, Gregory and Benedict, and declared the troublesome Ladislas deposed from his throne. To counteract Ladislas, the Pope threw in his lot with Louis of Anjou for the kingdom of Naples, and Louis hastened to Bologna to prostrate himself at the Pope's feet. The two joined their forces, and Louis set out for Rome. The Pope did not dare to go with him, for there were very evident signs that the cities of his former legation were only waiting for his absence to revolt; and that is what happened when, emboldened by some successes of Louis, the Pope left Bologna, March 31, 1411, with a splendid escort of French and Italian ecclesiastics and nobles. On April 14th, at Rome, the city magistrates appeared before him and did homage, and on April 28th he reviewed the very finest army that had ever gone out to war with Naples. On May 19th Louis gained a great victory over Ladislas, who barely escaped with his life. The captured banners were sent to John, who had them trailed through the mud of Rome.

But the winning of a battle is not enough; it must be followed up, and Louis did not prove equal to that. He delayed pursuit so long that the prisoners were enabled not only to arrange their ransoms, but also to buy back their arms, so that Ladislas, in fact, bought back his army and manned all the passes into Neapolitan territory. Louis in vain attempted to force them, and, becoming

disgusted with the whole business, hired a ship in
Rome and sailed away to Provence, so little thought
of that no one came to the wharf to see him off. He
was never heard of again and died in 1417. Now
again Ladislas came to the front, for nothing could
long keep down that restless and energetic king.
John excommunicated him over and over again, and
published a crusade against him all over Europe; but
the King of Naples laughed at all such things as the
impotent ravings of an old woman. The great leader
of the free-lances, Sforza, on whom the Pope had
greatly relied, deserted to Ladislas, and all the re-
venge the Pope could take was to have an effigy of
him made, which he hung by the right foot from
the bridge of St. Angelo, with a hoe in one hand and
a legend in the other, setting forth in coarse and cut-
ting language Sforza's many failings.

The Pope now turned entirely around and commenced dickering with Ladislas, although he had
loaded him with every epithet of vileness that even
a papal tongue could command. They both had
something to gain. Ladislas wanted to get rid of
the claims of Louis of Anjou, and John wanted to
deprive old Gregory XII. of the protection of Ladislas, under whose strong shield he was then living.
The compact was made. The Pope meanly abandoned
Louis, who had risked much for him, and agreed to
recognize Ladislas as King of Naples and to pay him
one hundred and twenty thousand ducats in two years;
and Ladislas just as meanly abandoned the cause of
Gregory, and notified the old man that he must leave
his dominions, for that, by " the grace of the Holy

Spirit " (!), he had been led to acknowledge John as the true Pope.

Poor old Gregory was at Gaeta, little expecting so summary a dismissal, and he did not know which way to turn; but the citizens of Gaeta, who were much attached to him, bought a couple of ships which happened to put in at Gaeta, and sent him off. After much cruising he landed at Cesena, and the lord of Rimini, Malatesta, gave him shelter there, for he was willing to do anything to exasperate John, whom he cordially hated.

It will be remembered that Alexander had promised at Pisa to call a council within three years for the purpose of reform, and John felt bound to carry out that promise; so he called a council at Rome, which met after various delays on February 10, 1413. Very few prelates arrived, for John did not want many and used threats to prevent from coming those he could not trust. In Rome was not a safe place then for timid bishops to venture. Nothing came of the council; it burned Wyclif's writings on the steps of St. Peter's, which certainly did him no harm, and the moment any reform questions were brought up the Pope's friends got the floor and talked them to death. Muratori, in the "Life of John XXIII.," relates the following incident, which in those superstitious times was considered ominous enough. At evening service, during the council, the Pope was just beginning the hymn, " Come, Holy Spirit," when an owl flew into the chapel and settled itself on a beam just opposite the Pope, winking and blinking at him. A cardinal called out, " What a curious shape for the Holy

Ghost!" and everybody laughed, while the brazen
Pope was visibly dismayed. John soon dissolved this
gathering, but he did not dare to let the question of
a council drop, and on March 3, 1413, issued a summons for a council to be held in December, notice of
time and place to be given later.

The hollow peace which Ladislas and the Pope had
patched up did not last long, and certainly the king
had not expected that it would. He soon found the
Romans growing very tired of their Pope and his
taxes, for John debased their coin, increased the
duties on wine so that no more was brought to
market, and then attempted to squeeze a second fee
out of all the officials Gregory had named. This was
the straw that broke the camel's back. The Pope
and the citizens, however, went through a solemn farce
of pledging faith to each other. John abolished the
obnoxious taxes and instituted the old Roman republican forms, and the citizens swore that they were
ready to die rather than submit to Ladislas, whose
army was at the very gates. A few days after this
mummery Ladislas broke through the city wall near
the Basilica of Santa Croce, and the city was his again.

The Pope and cardinals fled away, and the horsemen of Ladislas after them, and as they were mostly
old and luxurious men, many perished of fright and
misery. John got to Viterbo and thence to Montefiascone, but the peasants were so uneasy for fear
that Ladislas would come there and destroy their
crops that John was forced to go on to Florence,
which he reached on June 21st. The Florentines did
not want to let him in, but he found a lodgement in

the monastery of St. Antonio outside the walls, and Ladislas meanwhile overran the whole Roman territory. John knew not where to turn, except to Sigismund, the new sovereign of Germany, and he doubtless would have preferred even Ladislas if he had had the least idea how Sigismund would trick him and bring about his ruin.

The German situation must now be considered. There had been three claimants of the empire, as there had been three of the Popedom—the party of Wenceslas, that of his brother Sigismund, King of Hungary, and a third party, which had chosen Jobst, or Jocas, Marquis of Moravia. In this last party were the archbishops of Mayence and Cologne, who were also imperial electors. Jobst, being nearly ninety, soon died, and Wenceslas, the drunkard, and his brother Sigismund were reconciled, so that the latter had a fair field. The Archbishop of Mayence came over to him, with the stipulation that the emperor should acknowledge John XXIII. as Pope, and so Germany now definitely deserted Gregory and accepted John. Sigismund was now elected King of the Romans, with his succession to the empire assured.

The Emperor Sigismund was a strong personality, and no emperor since Frederic II. had taken so prominent a stand. He had had a stormy youth, for no man ever lived more addicted to sensuality, and his debts were so great that during his whole life he felt their embarrassment. His necessities had forced him into very shifty transactions, and he gave little promise of a great future; but he was now forty-three, and had resolved to lead a life more consonant with his

lofty position and the high aims which stirred within
him. One of his most earnest wishes was the healing
of the schism in the church; to that he determined
to devote his best energies, and, much as he has been
blamed by Protestant writers, he conscientiously endeavored to carry out that determination. He was
a man of magnificent presence, thoroughly versed in
all knightly accomplishments, fond of show and splendor, and thoroughly understanding how to dazzle all
beholders.

He had one great advantage: he was the only
sovereign of the first rank whose hands were entirely
free, for France and England were involved in deadly
war. The victory of Agincourt had turned the
head of Henry V., and he hoped to subdue all
France to the English crown. The French had a
lunatic for king, and civil war, carried on by the
Armagnacs and Burgundians, had desolated and
paralyzed the whole country. Sigismund really
stood alone, the most imposing figure in Europe,
brave, but opposed to war and determined to bring
about a meeting of a general council. The Pope was
well aware of this resolute purpose of Sigismund, and
that only by assenting to it and helping to carry it
out could he hope for any aid from the emperor.
He was too keen-sighted a man not to foresee all the
possible disadvantages of such a council. He was
certain his own abandoned life would come in question, and no Pope could view with any calmness the
probabilities of a long discussion over the question,
" Which is the supreme authority, Pope or council? "
with every prospect of a decision in favor of the latter.

But the Pope thought a subtle Italian a good match any time for a heavy German, and he had great faith in the prestige of the Papacy and the vast treasure he had it in his power to distribute. The greasing of palms was quite as influential then as now. He trusted that the many cardinals he had made would stand by him, and that he certainly had cunning enough to foment plenty of divisions after the council got under way. He talked the whole thing over with his secretary, Leonardo Aretino, who has left an account of the talk. "The whole point of the council," he said, "is in the place, and I will take care that it is not held in any place where the emperor is more powerful than myself. I will give my ambassadors the most ample powers, which they may openly show for the sake of appearances, but secretly I will restrict my commission to certain places."

This the Pope fully intended to carry out, and when he came into the room to give his last instructions to his chosen deputies, the two cardinals, Challant and Zabarella, he had a paper of secret instructions in his hand, in which he named the cities they would be allowed to accept; but "those whom the gods would destroy they first make mad," and the Pope suddenly said, "I have such faith in your wisdom and courage that I will not burden you with any conditions." He tore up the paper, which was for him a fatal step.

The Emperor Sigismund was living at Como, and thither the ambassadors hastened. As soon as the interview was arranged the emperor proposed Constance. He said it was well situated for both Italians

and Transalpines, being just at the foot of the Alps.
It was healthy, food could be easily procured all
around the lake, and he would be able to make everything very safe for everybody. The envoys wriggled
and struggled, but the emperor would not yield an
inch, or hear to any other place, and, much as they
feared the outcome, they at last gave way and consented in the Pope's name to a council being summoned at Constance for November 1, 1414. The
cunning emperor did not delay a moment. Before
the envoys had left the city messengers were flying
in all directions, announcing the time and place of
the council, and summoning to it the bishops and
sovereigns, with ample promises for their safe-conduct.

The Pope foamed with rage when the deputies returned and told him what had happened, but what
could he do? He had no other way of escape open
to him. He still hoped to bring about a change of
place, and arranged for a personal interview with the
emperor, hoping that " a fine Italian hand " would
count for something. The interview took place at Lodi,
and the emperor served the Pope's mass as deacon.
This promised well, but when they came to talk,
the Pope had to take a severe lecture from the emperor on his immoral life and the corruption of his
court, and he soon saw that no blandishments of his
would induce Sigismund to allow the council to be
held in some Lombard city. The Pope said, " It
will be so hard for us to cross the Alps." The emperor dryly replied, " And equally hard for us to do
so." It was no use. The Pope had to give up, and,

with a most unwilling pen, on December 9th he signed the summons for the council in Constance on the next All Saints' day. Sigismund, on his account, summoned the two deposed popes, and once more the empire and the Papacy joined to govern Christendom.

The two potentates made a pleasure excursion to Cremona, and while there the lord of Cremona took them to the top of a high tower to show them the view. Fondolo, the host, was a great scoundrel, and years after, when he came to his bloody end, he confessed before his execution that, when he had the Pope and the emperor up there on the lofty campanile, he had been strongly impelled to hurl them both over the parapet, not that he bore them any particular grudge, but because he felt sure that such a deed would make his name immortal. He added to this statement the cool remark that he was very sorry he had not done it. Little did the two high personages know the risk they had run. They parted in peace, and John went on to Bologna, worried enough by another outbreak of his old enemy, Ladislas, who on the 14th of March broke into Rome with his army, and rode straight up the aisle of St. John Lateran to look at the heads of St. Peter and St. Paul, which the frightened priests held up; much good the sight must have done him. Then he left Rome for Florence, and frightened the Florentines into a peace, and was on his way back to Rome when he was struck with his last illness. He managed to sail to Naples, where he died August 6, 1414, much to the joy of Pope John, the Romans, and, in fact, everybody else outside of Naples.

Ladislas was a strong man; he was rough and

cruel, but the soldiers of that time were generally so.
His grand idea of uniting all Italy in one great Italian
kingdom took centuries to realize. His arm was far-
reaching, and, as it was restrained by no considera-
tions of honor, men everywhere trembled before the
uncertainty as to where it would strike. The history
of his career is well-nigh forgotten now, but art has
conferred upon him immortality, for his monument is
conspicuous even in Naples, a city remarkable for its
magnificent tombs. It fills the whole east end of the
church of St. John Carbonara, and on it is the in-
scription, "Divus Ladislas," which hardly coincides
with the opinion of Antonio Petri, a writer of his time,
who, mentioning his death, says, "His soul was
blessed the contrary way," which is a very euphemis-
tic way of saying that it was sent to hell.

His death was a great relief to Pope John, and he
regretted bitterly that it had not happened before he
gave himself into the hands of Sigismund. He began
to question now whether he should go to Constance.
His family begged him not to go; they are reported
to have said, "You may go a Pope and come back a
private citizen;" but his cardinals felt that every sentiment of honor demanded that the Pope should keep
his plighted word. "It was too late now to retract,"
they said. Whatever John may have been, he was
not a coward, and he made up his mind to face the
dangers. His pride, moreover, dangled before him
the great honor of presiding over a general council,
which he thought he could do for a short time, and
then depute a cardinal to take his place, and come
back to Italy.

October 1st he set out, carrying with him money enough, he said, to buy up every enemy, for, like all dishonorable men, he thought every one else purchasable. A splendid train accompanied him, and in Tyrol he met Frederic, Count of Tyrol, who promised him protection if he needed it, and as Frederic's territory came close up to Constance, such a promise was not to be despised. As the papal train was descending the Arlberg, the Pope's carriage was upset, and his temper was so tried that he lay cursing in the snow as if his old pirate days had come back. As he halted on the mountain in sight of Constance, he exclaimed, "This is the way foxes are trapped!" His heart was full of foreboding, but he put on a brave front, and on the 28th of October he made his entry into Constance with nine cardinals and a train of nine hundred priests and laymen.

CHAPTER XIX.

THE COUNCIL OF CONSTANCE.

HE little city of Constance, on the lake of that name, containing only seven or eight thousand people, was now the cynosure of all eyes. In a moment it had leaped into notoriety, and there was not a hamlet in Europe where it was not often on men's lips. It is a sleepy little place now, where even the tourist delays but a few hours. The old walls surround it, and in the "Kaufhaus" is the hall where many of the doings of the famous council took place. The cathedral in its present form has no greater antiquity than the sixteenth century, but St. Stephen's Church dates from the fourteenth. The Rhine flows out of the lake just at the city's edge. The lake is very often called the "Bodensee," either from the Castle of Boden, or from the idea that it has no *boden*, or bottom. It is about forty-two miles long and a little over seven wide.

In June, 1414, the emperor's people arrived, and began to make preparations for his comfort, and in August came a cardinal to get all things in readiness for the Pope, and from that time until All Saints' day, the day set for opening the council, there was no livelier place to be found on earth than the little Swiss town. The comers were not all ecclesiastics, for every bishop had his train of men-at-arms, and merchants from all parts of the world flocked there, knowing that in such a gathering of the rich and mighty it would be easy to dispose of many wares. There was also a great crowd of singers, players, and amusement providers of all kinds.

There are various estimates of the number of strangers present at one time, varying between fifty and one hundred thousand, among whom were counted over a thousand prostitutes. Everything relating to the police, the sanitation, the provisioning of the city, was placed under the direction of the Count Palatine Louis, and well did he discharge his high trust. There never was any lack of food, and never any overcrowding. Stalls for thirty thousand horses and beds for thirty-six thousand men were provided, and that this should be done in a small town of eight thousand people shows most admirable management. There was, of course, with so many men much debauchery, but it was kept steadily in the background, and there was nothing that could be called a riot during the whole long duration of the council. The policemen were two thousand in number, and it is said that there were five hundred mysterious disappearances, the subjects of which were probably drowned in the lake.

The ecclesiastics in attendance were: twenty-nine cardinals, three patriarchs, thirty-three archbishops, one hundred and fifty bishops, one hundred abbots, fifty deans, three hundred doctors of theology, and eighteen hundred priests. The seculars included more than one hundred nobles and nearly three thousand knights. The immense suites of some of the visitors show the pomp and luxury of the age. John Huss, a simple priest, had eight attendants. The splendid processions, as each sovereign or great prelate entered the city, kept up a moving panorama of the greatest interest. One prelate, John of Nassau, Archbishop of Mayence, rode in incased in complete armor, helmet and lance and cuirass, and after him three hundred and fifty-two men and seven hundred horses. It was a curious exponent of a shepherd of the flock of Christ.

This great and magnificent company did not all arrive for the beginning; indeed, so slow were they in gathering that on All Saints' day, November 1st, when the council was to have opened, the Pope thought it best to postpone the opening until November 3d; then it was delayed until the 5th, and on that day, with much pomp and ceremony, the Pope declared the council open, and fixed the time of the first session for November 16th. On that day the Pope preached from the words, " Speak ye every man the truth," and as that was a thing he very seldom did, the sermon must have been purely theoretical. Nothing more was done that day, for nobody knew exactly what to do, and each hesitated to make the first move. The leader had not yet arrived, but there had crept into the city a poorly dressed and mean-looking man, whose name had been for some years now on the lips of vast numbers of people, and who was destined to furnish many a page for the church historian—John Huss, a poor Bohemian priest.

We possess very copious material relating to the Council of Constance. Von der Hardt (1700) gathered together and published at Leipsic an immense collection of documents of all kinds, and there exist two most interesting diaries of persons who were present, one written by a burgher of Constance who was one of the committee of arrangements, Ulric von Reichenthal, and the other by Cardinal Filastre who took a prominent part in the proceedings. Cardinal Peter d'Ailly and Cardinal Zabarella were also very conspicuous, and of the English, Robert Hallam, Bishop of Salisbury. Of English bishops there were present Bath, Hereford, Salisbury, Bangor, Winchester, London, Lichfield, and Norwich. The Emperor Sigismund, the most exalted personage next to the Pope in the council, did not appear until Christmas, and as nobody wished to show his hand on the great subject of the council's convening, the closure of the schism, it was necessary to find something to fill up the time.

One of the principal objects of the council was the consideration of the affairs of Bohemia and John Huss, and as Huss was present under the safe-conduct of the emperor, the Pope judged that they might well begin his case. What a feather in his cap it would be, if he could put down this tide of heresy! It would be interesting if we could know the thoughts which were occupying the Pope's mind at that time, but we can only conjecture them. He feared the council, and yet he was proud of it. Before him was ever the shadow of his possible deposition, but he hugged his money-bags to his breast and believed that money would smooth away all obstacles and purchase all votes. He was mistaken.

The Pope had seen Huss since his arrival in Constance, and is reported to have said, " If he had slain my brother I would not permit, as far as lay in my power, any harm to be done to him in Constance." Huss had come in perfect, and, we must think, exaggerated, confidence. True, he had a safe-conduct from Sigismund, and not only that, but certificates of orthodoxy from the emperor, from the Archbishop of Prague, and from the papal inquisitor for Bohemia, who had questioned him minutely; but it is evident he had not truly grasped the composition of the council. Certainly he had not much to hope for from it; in spite of his certificates of orthodoxy, the practical Italian cardinals saw immediately that his preaching and his publications were a direct attack on their whole system. England and France were both afraid of the socialism in his views, and even Gerson, liberal theologian as he was, sent the Archbishop of Prague a selection of twenty articles from Huss's writings which he said were dangerous and heretical. He found especial fault with that dogma of Huss that the real church was made up only of those foreordained to salvation, and that their judgment was to be supreme over all in authority—certainly a most dangerous idea in church or state. Gerson well says: " Political power is not founded on the title of predestination or grace, since that would be most uncertain, but is established according to laws ecclesiastical and civil." The peculiar views of Huss will be set forth in the chapter on John Wyclif, from whom he derived them; indeed, our best collection of Wyclif's writings is to be found in the Imperial Library at Vienna, to which they were transferred from the Bohemian convents and monasteries which were sequestered by the Austrian emperor, Joseph II.

The Pope had allowed Huss to visit the churches in Constance, but wished him to hear mass when there were few present, and he asked him not to celebrate. Huss, however, paid no attention to that wish, but every day said mass in his own house, and large numbers of people resorted to it. The house was also constantly filled with people listening to his talk. All this had been reported to the council by Huss's bitter enemies, Palecz and Michael de Causis, and on the 28th of November two bishops, with the burgomaster of Constance, came to Huss's house at dinner-time and informed him that the Pope and cardinals wished him to appear before them. Huss rose from the table, saying, " I did not come to Constance to argue with Pope and cardinals; I came to speak before a general council; but for peace' sake I will go with you." His horse was brought, and, surrounded by a guard of armed men, he rode to the papal lodging, where a number of cardinals were assembled. They accused him of heresy and read to him charges which had been formulated, and he said that if he could be proved a heretic he would recant.

He was charged at this time with teaching: (1) that it was necessary to receive the eucharist in both kinds; (2) that the validity of the sacraments depended on the moral character of the priest; and (3) that the church was to be governed wholly by the foreor-

dained and sanctified. The discussion went on until
night, when John of Chlam, Huss's most devoted
friend, who had accompanied him, was told that he
might go home, but that Huss would be under arrest
in the palace. Chlam rushed into the Pope's bed-
chamber and cried, " You have broken your promise.
Huss has the emperor's safe-conduct. You have no
right to arrest him." The Pope washed his hands of
the matter by saying, " I did not arrest him. It was
the cardinals. I cannot go against them." Huss
was then put in charge of the precentor of the cathedral and confined in his house, but on the 6th of
December he was transferred to a dungeon in the
Dominican convent on a little island near the shore.

This was a foul, unhealthy place, and Huss became
very ill there, but he kept himself occupied by writing religious tracts and lengthy answers to the charges
made against him. Like all such men, he professed
himself willing to be convinced, which in such cases
generally means having your adversary agree with
you. He was willing for himself to use the term
" transubstantiation," but he thought ordinary Christians ought to be expected only to believe in the true
presence of Christ's body and blood. He was willing
to allow that a wicked priest could administer the
eucharist, but it would be to his own damnation.
He declared the cup for the laity scriptural and prof-
itable, but he was not willing to declare it absolutely
necessary.

This certainly seems fair enough. Meanwhile
John of Chlam was filling the air of Constance with
loud protests against his friend's arrest and the viola-

tion of the safe-conduct.   He sent a swift messenger
to announce the fact to Sigismund, who had just
been crowned at Aix-la-Chapelle, and was on his
way to the council.   The emperor was very angry
and sent back word immediately to release Huss, and
if the council did not heed, he authorized the opening
of the prison doors by force.   The council, however,
did not heed, for the general sentiment in the Huss
matter was with the Pope and cardinals.   Then Chlam
nailed protests to the doors of all the churches in
Constance solemnly protesting against the false
promises of the Pope, but John Huss remained in
prison.

On December 7th a congregation of cardinals and
bishops was held in the Pope's palace, he being absent,
to try to hit upon a plan for conducting the business
of the council.   The Italian party wished the first step
to be the confirming of the acts of the Council of Pisa,
their motive being to give John a clear title, for if the
acts of Pisa deposing Gregory and Benedict were now
confirmed, then John's title was without a flaw.   The
French party, headed by Cardinal d'Ailly, were not
willing to agree to this.   They contended that the
Council of Constance was only a continuation of the
Council of Pisa, which was adjourned and not dissolved, and could not be dissolved until the church
was reformed, for that was the purpose for which it
was got together, and that purpose they were there
to carry out.   Some cardinal spoke out very bluntly
and said : " You talk about reforming the church ; you
had better first reform the Pope.   Make him say
mass every day and not put it off for pleasure or

business; make him wear the dress a Pope should wear and not behave with such lightness; make him act with a little dignity and not gabble so much with all sorts of people; make him attend to the business of his office," and they hinted much more.

This was not very reassuring talk to come to the Pope's ears, nor was the discussion in the general congregation a few days later any more to his taste. Cardinal d'Ailly argued that the better way would be to proceed with gentleness against the two old popes and make their resignation easy. The Pope's partisans would not hear to that. " They had been deposed at Pisa," they said, " and could not resign now." D'Ailly's words in answer were very signifi-cant. Von der Hardt gives them in full: " While with all probability the Council of Pisa is counted to represent the universal church, which is ruled by the Spirit and cannot err, yet it must not be concluded that every Christian is bound to believe it could not err, when many former councils reputed general have erred. Doctors have often taught that a general council can err not only in deed, but in law, and, what is more, in faith. The universal church alone has the privilege of not being able to err in faith; for when Christ said to Peter, ' Thy faith shall not fail,' He did not mean Peter's personal faith, but that of the universal church." This last sentence we would call nowadays a *non sequitur*. All this line of argument made John very uneasy, and he had not the wisdom to conceal his anxiety. He talked with everybody, and that never improves any situation.

The talk of the council, however, up to this date

was simply talking against time. The council without Sigismund was like soup without salt, and his appearance was the one absorbing topic. The emperor, who was nothing if not theatrical, had arranged that his entrée should be as imposing as possible. Before dawn on Christmas day, 1414, a vast multitude was assembled on the shore of the lake to see his arrival. He, with a splendid suite, had embarked in boats on the other side of the lake at Oberlingen, and the waters were lit up by the blazing torches as the flotilla swept to the shore amid the shouts of the crowd. Sigismund hurried to his lodgings to change his dress, and soon appeared at the cathedral magnificently attired to take part in the early mass which was to be said by the Pope. Around him clustered the ceremonial officers of his household, electors and counts of the empire, with the sceptre, the sword, and the orb. He put on a splendid dalmatic, and with the imperial crown upon his head took his place at the altar, according to ancient custom, to serve the Pope as deacon of the mass.

It was his place to read the gospel, which was the one still read on Christmas day in the Christian church: "There went out a decree from Cæsar Augustus that the world should be taxed." No wonder that a thrill ran through the assembly when they looked at that remarkably handsome man, the first sovereign in the world, standing by the Pope, and reading about the decree of Cæsar Augustus, his own common title. No wonder they felt that the decrees of the council would probably be guided by him. The emperor could not have arranged a scene calculated more strongly to advance his own influence and authority. After mass the Pope gave him a sword, with which he swore he would defend the church; and he probably meant what he said, but he meant to do it in his own way, and not according to John's wishes. All things, however, looked very fair, and emperor and Pope met most cordially. John knew how hard pressed the emperor was for money, and he offered him two hundred thousand florins; but Sigismund was obliged most reluctantly to decline, for he knew it was a bribe, and he was determined not to entangle himself in any such way.

Three days after the emperor's arrival (the exact date is not certain) Cardinal d'Ailly preached before the council on the text: "There shall be signs in the sun, and in the moon, and in the stars." In the style of sermonizing of that day, he made the sun represent the Pope, the moon the emperor, and the stars the cardinals, etc., in the firmament of the council. He hit the Pope very hard: "If the Pope have risen by bad means, if he have led a scandalous life, if he have ruled despotically, he is but the shadow of a sun." Then he foreshadowed in the following words the coming question: "The Holy Trinity of the divine persons is not more adorable than a trinity of popes abominable." But while D'Ailly shot arrows at the Pope, he stoutly upheld the traditions of the Papacy: "The imperial power," he said, "must not think to preside in the council, but to carry out its decrees. The Pope summons councils, and," he significantly added, "when once summoned their power is above the Pope." "St. James," he said, "when he presided over the first general council did not publish the decrees in the name of Peter, but said, ' It seemeth good to the Holy Ghost and to us.' "

Altogether a most significant sermon ; nobody slept under it, and the Pope must have heard it with a sinking heart. Nor did he feel much better when on January 4, 1415, it was decided after much debate that the envoys of Gregory and Benedict were to be received as cardinals, with cardinals' hats, for it showed that the old popes were still thought of as popes, and that the question of their deposition was not yet settled. These envoys were present to see in what way the abdications could best be arranged.

The first thing that occupied Sigismund on his arrival in Constance was the arrest and imprisonment of John Huss. He demanded that the Pope should release him. The Pope said, " I did not arrest him ; it was the council; seek redress there." Sigismund then went before the council and urged the question of his personal honor, for he had given a safe-conduct to Huss. The bishops replied that no one had any business to give safe-conducts to heretics, and that such a contract was invalid. Then the emperor threatened to leave Constance, and the fathers said, " If you do, we do also; the council will be broken up, and you will have to take the blame of it." This was a poser, and Sigismund thought he had nothing to do but to yield. He yielded, and Huss was left to the tender mercies of the council alone. Sigismund has been much blamed for this, and, viewed by the standards of our day, his conduct was most despicable and treacherous ; but when you put yourself back

amid the standards of that day and in his environment, you will find that much is to be said in his
defence.

In the first place, every man then held that the
church was the arbiter of duty; that in any case of
conscience her decree was omnipotent. We do not
hold any such view, for we hold that duty and honor
are far superior to any law of the church; but neither
Sigismund nor any one else then thought of such a
thing. He found himself advised, by the very highest
authorities in his world, to whom he had been accustomed to defer in all religious and moral matters, to
recede from his position, as being a position he had
wrongly taken, and therefore the changing it would be
doing right. Here was a heretic, and of all crimes
in the world heresy was then considered the most
awful. Kings were bound to do their very utmost to
put heresy down, and rash and wicked promises, he
was told, were never binding. Gerson reminded him
of Herod's wicked oath about John the Baptist, and
asked him whether it would not have been better if
the king had violated that. The King of Aragon (and
if the council was to succeed, he must be managed,
for he was Benedict's faithful champion) wrote him
that "it was impossible to break faith with one who
had already broken faith with God."

It was made very clear to Sigismund that unless
the council had power given it to settle the affair of
Huss and punish him as they saw fit the whole assembly would dissolve and all his pains be for nothing. Was one poor little Bohemian priest worth that
sacrifice? were a few possible riots in Bohemia worth

it? It is safe to say that even now, with all our changed views about the arbiter of honor, nine out of ten of the reigning sovereigns would from prudential reasons act exactly as Sigismund did. They would plead the greatest good to the greatest number. This does not indeed justify the emperor, but it shows the tremendous difficulties which met him on every side, the immense pressure brought to bear upon him, and that he does not deserve the unmeasured contempt and obloquy which have been heaped upon him by the great body of Protestant commentators.

CHAPTER XX.

COUNCIL OF CONSTANCE.

OW that the matter of Huss was put in the way of solution, the council breathed freer. It felt a freedom of action the lack of which had greatly oppressed it. The emperor had yielded to the spiritual power, and the council said, "Laus Deo." There were grave questions now to be settled, which for a while will keep the Huss question in the background. Huss is safe in prison and can wait; the council must occupy itself with more pressing matters. The first was the manner of voting.

While John had listened with ill-concealed fear and anger to the wordy attacks upon his conduct and his policy, and while he saw that the animus of the council was decidedly for reform, he said to himself, "When it comes to votes, I shall be all right. Votes are the things that determine causes; votes can be bought, and I will be able to secure the requisite majority to carry my points, for I have spent a great deal of money on very venal men. A large number of the Italian bishops, especially those *in partibus*, are dependent on me for their daily bread, and I have made fifty men bishops on purpose to have their votes. I am safe." So the Pope undoubtedly reasoned, but he was destined to receive a cruel blow. Others had thought of the Italian, or rather Latin, superiority in numbers.

The point was discussed then, as it was all over Europe during the Vatican Council of our time. It carried the day there, and Latin majorities settled all questions; but the Council of Constance, in the wise providence of God, avoided that rock, on which it certainly would have split and gone to pieces. When the question was asked, "Who are to vote?" the Italians said, "Why, only bishops and abbots, as of old." D'Ailly, always clear-headed and ready, said, "That was all very well when bishops fairly represented the Christian community; but now there were great institutions, like universities and orders of monks, which deserved representation, and as the unity of the church was under discussion, how could princes or their ambassadors be excluded from voting?" Cardinal Filastre, also a Frenchman, went further. He demanded that all priests present should vote, and he used the tolerably sharp words, "An ignorant king or bishop is a crowned or mitred ass." Neither of these schemes, however, prevailed.

The English members of the assembly were few in number, but their chairman, Robert Hallam, of Salisbury, was one of the ablest men in the council, and through him they proposed that the voting should be as in the universities, by nations. The nations were to be: (1) the Italians, including all the cardinals; (2) Germans, including Poles, Hungarians,

Danes, and Scandinavians; (3) French; (4) English; (5) Spanish, though as yet the last-named had not joined the council. The prelates, ambassadors, and doctors of each nation were to assemble and debate separately; then they were to communicate their conclusions to the other nations, and when an agreement was reached a general meeting of the nations would be called, the matter put in shape, and then confirmed in a general session of the council.

This scheme of the English was first assented to by the Germans, then the next day by the French, and the Italians, being thus rendered helpless, had to submit. No change could have been fraught with more important results.

Cardinal Filastre now put into the hands of the council a paper drawn up by him, in which he said that the shortest way to end the schism would be for all three popes to abdicate. If John was willing to do it, well and good; if not, the council ought to compel him to do it. The emperor approved very highly of this paper, but naturally the Pope thought it the work of a traitor, since he had made Filastre a cardinal. The paper of Filastre was answered by partisans of the Pope, and this discussion was wisely kept up by papers which were circulated among the members, it being thought prejudicial to have open debate until some agreement had been reached.

And now came into their midst a terrible paper. Its author was unknown, but it was a review of John's whole life, and stated in detail the vices and crimes of his strange career. It is a document which decency would prevent being reproduced now, and was indeed

so damnatory that the members of the council decided to suppress it as degrading to their common
Christianity. The Pope, however, heard of it and
read it, and it frightened him terribly. He completely lost his balance and consulted with the cardinals as to whether he had better not confess what
was true in it (for he acknowledged it was partly
true) and say to the council, " Yes, I have led a bad
life, but I am not a heretic, and popes can only be
deposed for heresy." The cardinals advised him to
wait and not commit himself.

On February 15th the plan of a common abdication of all three popes was agreed upon by the English, Germans, and French, and laid before the Italians, who saw no escape but assent. Deputies now
waited upon the Pope to inform him of this decision,
and to their surprise he consented and submitted a
form of abdication, which was immediately put before
the nations. It was found to be too vague; it could
not be accepted. Then he offered a second, but that
also was rejected. Then the emperor offered one,
but that the Pope would not accept. Then Gerson
drew up a fourth form, which the emperor himself
carried to the Pope, and presented with some rather
strong language.

The Pope struggled and wriggled, but the nations
held firmly together. There was no hope; he seemed
to resign himself to fate, and summoned a general
congregation. As has been already said, he was a
man of courage, and so, in a steady voice, which did
not show in the least the bitterness of his heart, he
read the following words (Von der Hardt) : " I, Pope

John XXIII., for the repose of the whole Christian people, profess, engage, promise, swear, and vow to God, the church, and this holy council, willingly and freely to give peace to the church by the way of my simple cession of the Papacy, and to do this and fulfil it effectually according to the determination of this present council, whenever, and as soon as, Peter di Luna and Angelo Corario, called, in their respective obediences, Benedict XIII. and Gregory XII., shall in like manner cede the Papacy, to which they pretend, either in person or by their lawful proctors, or even in any case of vacancy by decease or otherwise, when by my cession unity can be restored to the church of God through the expiration of the present schism."

Certainly this seemed very fair on the part of the Pope, and as broad a declaration as could have been expected from him. No wonder that the whole council broke out into shouts and wild expressions of joy. It seemed almost like a dream that at last, at last after so many, many years, the church was to have rest and peace. Te Deum was sung as never sung before, and the next day, at another public session, the Pope repeated this oath and accentuated it by kneeling down before the altar and saying, " So I promise." Then the emperor, taking off his crown, knelt down and kissed the Pope's feet. It was very spectacular, rather too much so to be thoroughly genuine. The council fathers evidently thought so, for, as they analyzed the Pope's oath, they saw that after all the abdication was conditional. They wished to make it absolute, and they asked the Pope to issue a bull in the prescribed form of abdication. Again he writhed and stormed and evaded, but the relentless emperor extorted from him something more definite and yet not quite full enough, for still there were loopholes.

The council now took another step. The old Pope Benedict had suggested that the emperor go to Nice to meet him and there arrange fully for his abdication. The council asked Pope John to empower the emperor to offer his at the same time. This John felt would be final and irrevocable, and he utterly refused to do it. He proposed to go himself and meet Benedict, but the council feared his trickiness and did not want to trust him out of their sight, for with him out of Constance they feared that all their work would have been in vain. Still everything was bland and smooth on the surface, and on March 10th John presented Sigismund with the golden rose, which, after all these centuries, is still being presented by the popes of our day to Catholic sovereigns. The emperor took it politely, but showed what he thought of it by immediately presenting it to the cathedral for the Virgin's altar.

The next day was an eventful one for the council, for both parties showed their hands, it being evident that the time for mincing matters was past. It could no longer be concealed that the emperor and the Pope were at daggers' points, and all could see that John's promises had been hypocritical and that force would have to be used to hold him to his word. A suspicion was taking form that the Pope intended to run away, and the emperor had all the gates guarded ;

but the Pope, to reassure everybody, promised that he would not dissolve the council, nor leave it until it was ended, though it is not probable that many believed him. Words ran high in the sessions, and the Bishop of Salisbury said openly that such a Pope as John was deserved to be burned at the stake.

The situation was strained enough. There were the emperor and the three nations of English, French, and Germans arrayed against the Pope and the Italians. The violent language used about the Pope seems for a moment to have softened the French towards him. They said that things had gone too far, and asked for an adjournment that angry passions might cool down. Eagerly the Italians caught at the proposal and even ventured to raise the question about changing back from the vote by nations to the individual voice. It must not be forgotten that it was quite as hard for Frenchmen to vote with Englishmen then as now, even more so; for the English were at that moment in the heart of France, endeavoring to conquer it all, and the battle of Agincourt took place that very year. It showed a laudable desire in the French to make the reform of the church superior to all patriotic feelings, that they had been willing at all to vote with the English. The quarrel ran very high, and hot words were spoken by Sigismund. The Pope began to take courage; but the French ambassadors informed the French bishops that their king sided entirely with Sigismund and had made the emperor his proctor, so with difficulty they patched up a peace.

The Pope now resolved on a desperate course,

which he concealed by lying. He had a strong ally at Constance in Frederic of Austria, who was a bitter enemy of Sigismund, and therefore, of course, a friend of John. Frederic's territory was within a short ride of Constance, and thither John determined to flee. Sigismund suspected him and, entering his presence, accused him of meditating flight, but the Pope with smooth duplicity declared that he had not the slightest intention of leaving Constance until the council was dissolved. The emperor seemed satisfied and left the presence-chamber, but scarcely was he out of the room when John let loose his tongue, and heaped such epithets as "fool, drunkard, beggar," and other choice words upon the sovereign.

Dietrich von Niem, who still continues his chronicle, tells us how astonished he and all the other attendants were to hear such language from the Pope, but John doubtless felt that he would soon be beyond Sigismund's power. The next day, March 20th, Frederic of Austria gave a great tournament and everybody went to see it, and while town and palace were so empty the Pope dressed himself in a groom's clothes, mounted a groom's horse, rode unrecognized out of the gates and away to Ermatingen. There a boat was ready, and the swift-flowing Rhine soon carried him to Schaffhausen, which was Austrian territory, and where Frederic had a castle.

Excited enough was Constance when the flight became known. Tumultuous crowds of ecclesiastics and laymen filled the streets, and the merchants began to shut their shops; but the police were well organized, and before a riot could materialize, peace and order were restored. Sigismund immediately summoned the council, and three cardinals and an archbishop were appointed to go to Schaffhausen and beg the Pope not to dissolve the council, but to assent to the scheme of appointing proctors to carry out his resignation. While the session was going on a letter was brought to the emperor from the Pope, stating that he had gone to Schaffhausen for his health and greater freedom of action, and that he intended fully to carry out his abdication, the letter ending with the enormous and transparent lie that his flight had been entirely without the knowledge of Frederic of Austria.

The council now took a tremendous step. It commissioned Gerson, the well-known theologian, to preach a sermon defining the basis of its authority, and so he did on the 23d of March. He laid down the general principle that the head of the church is Christ, the Pope being only head under Him. The union between Christ and the church is indissoluble, but not so with the union between the church and the Pope, which can be dissolved. A Pope is necessary, but not any particular Pope, for a council can remove a Pope if necessary; and it has the power, being under the direction of the Holy Spirit, to pass laws which even popes are bound to obey. A general council may be assembled without the consent or the call of the lawful Pope, as, for example, if he were under accusation and refused to call the council, or if there were more than one claimant of the Papacy.

The opinion of the University of Paris was also

read to the council, and such an opinion at that time carried great weight. This opinion concluded that the Pope could not dissolve the council, for to do so would involve him in the sin of schism; that the whole church is more than the Pope and superior to him; that the Pope holds his power through the church and as its representative, and that a council, if necessary, might depose him, just as any one would have the right to take a sword out of the hand of a lunatic. These views were approved by all the nations, even the Italian, excepting the cardinals, who, although a majority of them were Frenchmen, sat with the Italian nation as being the Pope's council. The cardinals had thought it more consistent with their dignity and their relations to the Pope not to be present at Gerson's sermon. One cannot help pitying the cardinals, for they really did not know what to do. Much as they disapproved of the Pope and heartily as they were ashamed of him, he was still their head, and as he asserted positively that he was intending to abdicate, they felt it their duty to stand by him, and, like all people trying to be on both sides of a fence, they came in for a great deal of suspicion from all parties. John summoned them to attend him at Schaffhausen, and seven of them obeyed, together with the household officers of the papal court.

The question has often been asked why John did not dissolve the council and excommunicate all who opposed him. It would not have taken Hildebrand long to launch the proper bull, but John, unlike Hildebrand, had behind him a bad life and the sense of a weak cause. He seems to have lost his grip, to have doubted his own authority, and he did nothing but scold and storm and lie, so that each effusion of his only served to sink him lower in the estimation of the council. That body was daily awakening to a fuller and higher sense of its dignity and authority.

Vexed with the shifting of the cardinals, the council authorities did not even summon them to the meeting which was held March 26th to prepare decrees for the general session, and the cardinals who had remained at Constance determined to stay away from that session, but the two most distinguished of their number did attend. One, D'Ailly, celebrated mass, and the other, Zabarella, read the decree which had been prepared, affirming that the council was not dissolved by the Pope's flight and ought not to be dissolved until they had ended the schism; that it could not be transferred to another place, and that the members must stay until the work was done. As soon as the cardinal had finished reading that decree he took out another paper and read it, being a protest on the part of D'Ailly and himself against precipitate action, stating that as long as John professed willingness to end the schism they must hold to him. They were present, they said, not for pleasure, but because they thought it their duty, and with the hope that the Pope would confirm the decrees. This, on their part, was a wise and courageous action, and saved their order, for the council was rapidly coming to that pass where it would not care whether the cardinals attended or not.

The envoys who had been sent to Schaffhausen

returned with offers from the Pope to appoint certain
cardinals as proctors with power to carry out his
resignation against his will, promising also not to
dissolve the council till the church was united. This
seemed a fair proposition, but when the envoys were
unwise enough to say that the Pope's withdrawal had
dissolved the council, it made all that the Pope had
written so suspicious that his words were considered
mere subterfuges and evasions and passed for nothing.

The tide had risen, and the council was going to
act, if necessary, without either Pope or cardinals, for
it was realizing that it represented the church. John
did not feel himself secure at Schaffhausen, for Frederic could no longer protect him, since the Swiss and
the empire were both arming against him. On March
29th the Pope galloped off to the Castle of Lauffenberg, farther up the Rhine; but not a cardinal went
with him; all returned to Constance. Angry and
anxious as they felt at the pretensions of the council
to command a Pope, they resolved to attend the general session called the fourth, which had been appointed for March 31st; and only two remained away,
D'Ailly and the Cardinal of Viviers. It was a memorable day. Cardinal Orsini presided, and the emperor, crowned and robed in the imperial mantle,
was present with a great crowd of nobles.

The decrees prepared were intrusted to Cardinal
Zabarella to read. He seems to have been ordinarily
the reader to the council, probably from his possess-
ing a clear voice. He began: "This council, lawfully
assembled in the name of the Holy Spirit and forming a general council representing the Catholic Church

militant, has its power immediately from Christ; and every one of every rank, even the Pope, is bound to obey it in matters pertaining to the faith and the extirpation of the present schism." The next words were, " and the general reformation of the church of God in its head and members," but the cardinal did not want to read those words. He, with his brethren, did not wish to acknowledge that the council had power to reform the church; they thought that cardinals' work; so he stumbled over the words, and stammered, and lowered his voice. Immediately there arose a tumult of voices calling out "Read" and " Do not read." More and more angry they grew, so that nothing else that he read was heard, and the session broke up in fierce anger against the cardinals.

In a few days, April 6th, another session was held, when the decree was read in its entirety and with a loud voice by the Archbishop of Posen. The part following the words which Zabarella had slighted declared that the Pope could not adjourn the council to any other place, or summon his court to attend him anywhere else, and that all promotions made henceforth by him were null and void.

The Pope's ally, Frederic of Austria, had now been put under the ban of the empire, and before a month was over had to kiss the dust before Sigismund and abandon all idea of protecting the Pope. John meanwhile was dodging about from one town to another, a wretched fugitive. From Lauffenberg he went to Freiberg in the Breisgau, and from thence to Breisach, and then to Neuenburg; then back to Freiberg, where a deputation from the council found him on April 27th, and extorted from him a promise to send proctors to the council in a few days.

The deputies returned to Constance, and on May 2d the council cited John to appear and answer to charges of heresy and schism and scandals of life, and this citation was nailed to the gates of Constance. April 18th was quite an important day for the council, for on it the cardinals presented a series of propositions declaring that the Roman Church had authority over a general council, meaning by the Roman Church the body of the cardinals in Rome. They contended that the Roman Church or the Pope had just as much authority from God over the universal church as a general council, and that without the assent of the Roman Church nothing could be decided by a council. The theologians whom they addressed found it was not as easy to answer the whole college of cardinals as the wicked Pope.

The cardinals certainly were valid representatives, and nobody could question their authority. The opponents of the cardinals could not deny that the Church of Rome was the head of all churches, for on that principle the whole church had for centuries been governed; but they tried with great ingenuity to make out a difference in councils. In councils about matters of faith, they said, the Church of Rome must take the lead, but in councils called to extinguish a schism caused by cardinals it was not proper for cardinals to interfere. The Sacred College, however, carried its point, and sat, as it had ever sat, in the council; nay, more, in the session of May 25th it ranked as a separate nation and voted as such.

On May 9th a troop of three hundred men, commanded by the Burgrave of Nuremberg, went to Freiberg to bring John to Constance. He pleaded for delay and empowered the three cardinals of Cambray, St. Mark's, and Florence to act as his proctors; but they were thoroughly disgusted with him, and refused to act in his behalf or to have anything to do with the matter. He was left to his fate, and on the 14th of May, 1415, he was condemned for contumacy and declared suspended from his functions. Commissions were now appointed to take evidence about John's life and administration, and black and awful was the tide of accusation which rolled in upon them. There were seventy-two charges formulated, but some were mere repetitions of others, and there is scarcely any nameable crime or sin which does not appear in this indictment. The Pope was charged with incest with his brother's wife, with rape, adultery, sodomy, poisoning, murder, simony, and utter want of religion. Sixteen of the charges were so indescribable that by common consent they were dropped, but on the strong testimony of the rest the council pronounced the sentence of deposition.

The soldiery had brought John to Rudolfzell, eight miles from Constance, and it was there that the sentence of deposition was made known to him. He made no resistance, gave up his seal, pulled off the ring of the fisherman, said that of his own free will he surrendered the Papacy, and that he never would attempt to resume it. That promise he certainly kept, perhaps because no one would help him to break it. He was brought to the Castle of Gottloben, just outside the walls of Constance, where John Huss was a prisoner; then transferred to Heidelberg, under the guard of the elector palatine, where he lived for nine years. Afterward he raised a large sum of money and bought his liberty from the elector. He went then to Florence, and was made Cardinal Bishop of Frascati by Martin V., but died in Florence before taking possession of his new see. John as a military man might have made a fine record, for in those times his vices in a soldier would have counted for little; but as a Pope he was an utter and horrible failure, and alienated from him even the most fanatic devotees of the Papacy.

CHAPTER XXI.

THE TRIAL OF JOHN HUSS.

OW that the momentous business of Pope John was gotten out of the way, the council turned its attention towards the extirpation of heresy, and the fathers went into that subject with a will in order to show the Christian world that however much they might have seemed to touch on the dignity of Pope and cardinals and to pursue a democratic course, there was not one spark of desire among them to allow the least tampering with the faith. They acted as persons often act who, to throw off imputations of sloth in one direction, manifest surprising activity in another. Gerson, D'Ailly, and others, liberal and moderate as their statements had been about papal domination, the terrible condition of the clergy, and urgent need of reformation, did not mean any reformation in doctrine or any change in the authority of the clergy and the finality of their decisions. If Huss had any idea that they or any one else in the council sympathized at all with him, he was doomed to bitter disappointment.

Much as we may, and very properly, blame Sigismund about the safe-conduct, it is only justice to say that if Huss were brought before a council of any of the great religious bodies to-day, while they would not condemn him to be burned,—for all that has passed away, thank God, from the life of the church, and punishment of the body is no longer used as a punishment of the soul,—yet it would be impossible for them to avoid condemning many of his doctrines. For example, his view (copied from Wyclif, as most of his views were, his treatises often being literal transcriptions of Wyclif's writings) in regard to the sinfulness of a priest destroying all the efficacy of his acts and annulling all his title to property ; what religious body could endure that? Who is to decide about the sinfulness? How easy for a grasping king to decide that six or seven rich bishops were in mortal sin, and therefore had no right to their property, and proceed to take it all away! Who could be certain whether he had been properly baptized, or whether he received a true eucharist, if the efficacy of all these things depended on the morality of the priest? It is evident that now as then any such opinion would destroy any religious organization in the world, and it was the same with the civil authority. If Huss's assertion be true, that " a king in mortal sin is no king before God," what security could there be for any ruler? At any moment demagogues might excite the people, saying, " The king is leading a sinful life and is therefore no longer the rightful king." A " sinful life " would, of course, be their conclusion as to what was sinful, and it might easily be held by many that smoking, hunting, card-playing, were infallible proofs that the king was living in mortal sin.

Even a superficial thinker must see that all such views are utterly subversive of law and order, and there is no question that the political theories of Wyclif and Huss were thoroughly pernicious and revolutionary. They could not be tolerated in our day any more than centuries ago. Huss cleared himself of any unorthodox Roman views of transubstantiation, or worship of the saints, or of any of the great doctrines of the Christian faith. Even in regard to communion in both kinds, he was not willing to assert that it was absolutely necessary to a perfect communion. He even managed to steer clear of heresy in the subtleties of nominalism and realism, but he certainly laid himself open to the gravest censure in regard to civil or ecclesiastical position depending on the moral worthiness of the holder of that position. Mournful as is the spectacle of a sincere and true-hearted man burned to death for opinions conscientiously held, it cannot be denied that the council labored hard to save him from himself and that they tried long and perseveringly to induce him to give up what they very rightly thought soul-destroying errors. This will be seen from an account of the proceedings.

On May 4, 1415, in the eighth session of the council, Wyclif's writings were publicly condemned and ordered to be burned, and his bones were ordered to be dug up from consecrated ground and burned. It is difficult to see how the friends of Huss could have had much hope after that, for, as has been said, Wyclif was Huss's model and teacher in many things; but they had plenty of courage and on May 16th presented a petition to the council asking for Huss's release from prison. To this the Patriarch of Antioch, speaking for the council, replied that they would not and could not release an untrustworthy man from prison, but that he should be heard in a public audience, which was fixed for June 5th. On that day Huss appeared, and the original manuscripts of his work " On the Church " and other treatises of his were shown him. He acknowledged their genuineness, and then commenced the reading of charges based on his written words. When asked questions, Huss would not answer yes or no, but proceeded to argue and quote the fathers. This did not at all suit the council, and the angry reproaches and abusive calls became so intolerable that it was impossible to go on, and the investigation was adjourned for two days.

On June 7th the emperor appeared to preserve order, and proclaimed that any one making a disturbance would be put out of the room. As an example of the difficulty of dealing with Huss, it may suffice to say that when Cardinal Zabarella cited the verse, " In the mouth of two or three witnesses shall every word be established," and added that there were twenty witnesses on every charge against Huss, the accused replied, " If God and my conscience witness for me that I never taught what I am accused of teaching, I am not concerned with the testimony of my enemies." To this Cardinal d'Ailly fairly and justly answered, " We cannot possibly judge you from the standpoint of your conscience, but from the tes-

timony laid before us." Huss could not be made to
see the force of this, for with him his own conscience
was everything, and he seemed totally oblivious of
the fact that other people also had consciences. We
admire his courage, but we cannot approve his rea-
soning. His friend, John of Chlam, made a very
impolitic remark at this stage of the proceedings,
which greatly angered the emperor. He said that
" there were many castles in Bohemia where Huss
could have been hidden away from the emperor, if
he had not of his own free will chosen to come to
Constance." Sigismund then and there publicly
gave Huss up. He declared that his safe-conduct
had been given so that he might have a hearing before the council; now he had had it, and his duty was
to submit. " If not," Sigismund added significantly,
" the council will know how to deal with you; as for
me, so far from defending you in your errors and in
your contumacy, I will be the first to light the fire
with my own hands." Huss made then, as before
and after, the same vague protestations that he could
not go against his conscience, and was remanded to
prison.

The next day the weary work began again. Thirty-
nine articles taken from Huss's writings were before
the judges, and D'Ailly remarked that the charges
were far more mildly drawn than the words of Huss
would justify. The discussion turned on Huss's
doctrine that the true church consisted only of the
predestined to eternal life, and therefore only virtuous
persons could hold any office in the church; a wicked
Pope or priest was not a true Pope or priest. Huss

gave specious explanations of this, which did not satisfy the council, and would not satisfy any court.

At the close of the session, Cardinal d'Ailly urged Huss to abjure his errors, and the emperor added his entreaties; indeed, appeals of the most moving nature were made to him; but he would not listen, and was sent back to prison. As soon as he had left the room, the emperor rose and said, "There is more than enough evidence. If he will not forswear his errors, let him be burned. If he does forswear them, he must be banished from Bohemia; for this evil must be rooted out from that country. When I was a boy this sect began there, and look how it has increased and multiplied." The Bohemian nobles who heard these words boiled with rage, and they were very costly words for Sigismund; for the Huss party was very strong in Bohemia, and when it was known that the emperor had publicly said that Huss ought to be burned, deep oaths were sworn that never should Sigismund be their king, and he never was their king in any peace or comfort.

Every effort was now made to induce Huss to retract. The very highest personages, among whom Sigismund was foremost, went to his cell and pleaded with him to recant. Very mild forms of abjuration were drawn up, but he would not sign; yet so tender were they of him that he was allowed to confess and receive absolution without any abjuration. His conduct seems to verge on obstinacy; but certainly no one can help admiring the firm face set against the very highest in power, and, harder still to do, the firm resistance to words of love and entreaty. The martyrdom of conscience has been a vital power in the world, though often that conscience has been misinformed and overstrained.

On the 6th of July, at the fifteenth session of the council, Huss was brought in for his final sentence. He was made to wait in the porch until mass was over, for fear that such a heretic's presence would be pollution. Then he was brought in to listen to a sermon on heresy; but he spent the time of its delivery in prayer. The charges were then read, and when he tried to interrupt, he was silenced. He did manage to say, and as he said it the emperor could not keep the blush from his cheek, that he had come to Constance of his own free will, trusting in the imperial safe-conduct. He was then degraded from the priesthood with solemn ceremony, every article of the priest's dress being put upon him and then removed. His tonsure was obliterated by clipping, and it is amusing, even at that serious moment, to read that they discussed long whether they should use razor or scissors to do it; scissors carried the day. Then a paper fool's cap painted with devils was put on his head, and a bishop said, " We commit thy body to the secular arm, and thy soul to the devil." " And I," said Huss, " commit it to my most merciful Lord Jesus Christ."

He was then led away to a meadow near the town, where the stake had been got ready for the burning. As he was on his mournful way, he was taken past a burning pile of his own books, and he remarked dryly that he did not see how they could condemn Bohemian books, since not one of them could read them. Once more Duke Louis urged him to recant, but he would not; and with prayers for his enemies, piteous appeals to his merciful Saviour, and protestations that he had not been fairly tried, he soon succumbed to the flames. His ashes and his burned clothes were thrown into the Rhine.

Creighton says with great fairness about the trial of Huss, "It is impossible that a trial for opinions should ever be considered fair by the accused. He is charged with subverting the existing system of thought; he answers that his opinions, if rightly understood, are not subversive, but amending. Into that issue his judges cannot follow him; they are appointed to execute existing laws, and until these laws are altered by the properly constituted authority the best attempts to amend them by individual protest must be reckoned as rebellion. It is useless to criticise particular points in the trial. The council was very anxious for his submission, and gave him every opportunity to make it; but it is the glory of Huss that he so deliberately asserted the rights of his individual conscience against ecclesiastical authority, and sealed his assertion with his own life-blood."

The execution of Huss set Bohemia all in a blaze, and the council tried to get over making that country the present of another martyr, in the person of Jerome of Prague, a great friend of Huss, and the one who brought him Wyclif's writings from England. Jerome did at a public session, September 23d, retract everything, and in all justice ought to have been set free; but he had Bohemian enemies who asserted that his recantation was not sincere, and February 24, 1416, the council ordered a fresh investigation. We cannot pursue that. An Italian gentleman who was present, Poggio, has left an elegantly written account of Jerome's eloquence, wit, and learning as shown in his defence, at the close of which he said that his recantation had been through fear and against his conscience, and that he now took it all back. He thought Huss a just and holy man, and he was ready to share his fate. Great efforts were made to get him again to abjure; but, as he would not, nothing remained but to burn him, that being considered, in those days, the only proper or possible thing to do with a heretic. So on May 30, 1416, he was sentenced, and led away to be burned on the very spot where Huss had suffered. Out of consideration, the executioner was about to light the fire behind him, but he called out, "Light it before my face; I am not afraid of death." His ashes also and his burned clothes were cast into the Rhine.

CHAPTER XXII.

THE AFFAIRS OF GREGORY AND BENEDICT.

HE two great causes of the Pope and the heretics were not the only ones which interested the council; there was the still existing schism, for Gregory and Benedict still had adherents. Gregory had proved easy to deal with. He seems at last to have appreciated the terrible effects of the schism, and to have been willing to do what he could to put an end to it. On the 4th of July, 1415, his constant and devoted friend, Malatesta, lord of Rimini, appeared as his proctor and formally abdicated in his name. The council winked at the summons to that particular session being in Gregory's name. He had wished that, so that his honor might be saved, and his notion that only a Pope could call a session of a council be humored. He was made Cardinal Bishop of Porto and given precedence over all the other members of the college. His cardinals were recognized and invited to take seats in the council with the other cardinals without any conditions, and all the officials he had appointed were retained. Poor old man! he did not live long to trouble anybody, but died before the adjournment of the council, at the age of ninety.

Benedict proved a much more difficult personage,

and there were to be some weary days before he at last could be disposed of, and the way opened for the election of a new Pope. The Emperor Sigismund, in whose restless brain vast projects were fermenting,—projects of being the universal peacemaker, the grand conqueror of the Turks, and other marvellous schemes,—offered to try and arrange with Benedict and his supporters, the principal ones being the kings of Scotland and Aragon. The council accepted his offer, and it was decided that Benedict should meet him and the King of Aragon at Perpignan in June. Benedict was there at the time appointed, but Sigismund, on account of the troubles arising about the flight of Pope John XXIII., could not keep his appointment before July. Before that time Benedict had departed in a huff at having been kept waiting, and it was not until September 18th that the three, Benedict, Ferdinand of Aragon, and Sigismund, were gotten together at Perpignan.

Nothing, however, could be done with Benedict; he was simply an obstinate fool, as can be seen from one of his demands, which was that he alone should name the new Pope, since he was the only cardinal who had been appointed by Gregory XI. before the schism began. Arguments and threats proved equally ineffectual; everybody grew disgusted with him, and even his great supporter, St. Vincent Ferrer, began to preach that it was all up with Benedict now, and that the Council of Constance was to be recognized. The sovereigns of Germany and Aragon were determined, however, to settle the question for which they had met, and on December 13, 1415, they agreed on certain arrangements at Narbonne, and very circuitous arrangements they were and came to nothing.

This was to be the manner of proceeding: The council was to summon all the princes and prelates who held to Benedict to come within three months to Constance and form a council; and Benedict was to summon all the other side to join them there for the same purpose. This council, which was to include Benedict's cardinals, was to depose Benedict, elect a new Pope, and proceed to reform the church. This was not such a conclusion as the council had hoped for, but it was much better than nothing, and now the fathers waited as patiently as they could for the emperor to get back to Constance and finish up the Benedict business, for nothing seemed to be able to get itself settled without him. Sigismund, however, was not ready to return immediately. He wanted to set out on his great scheme of reconciling France and England, and he reasoned well when he argued that, until they were reconciled, reform in the church did not stand much of a show.

We cannot follow the emperor in his showy journeys, which cost him a great deal of money and plunged him over ears in debt, although he pawned all the presents he received on the way. He was not at all successful in his mission to France, and only moderately so in England; and, after an absence of a year and a half, he got back to Constance January 27, 1417, very much Anglicized, with the Order of the Garter conspicuously displayed, and loud words of admiration for England. Such conduct, as a matter of course, exasperated the French and fanned the flame of discord already kindled between these two nations at the council.

Things had dragged very much in Constance since his going away, and the fathers were very tired of the long-drawn-out gathering. They had hoped to get away by Easter, 1415, then by September, 1416, and here it was January, 1417, and they were still there. A commission on reform had been appointed in July, 1415, thirty-five in number (eight from each nation, and three cardinals); but the divisions were so great that it progressed backward. On one side were the French, with the English and the Germans sometimes with and sometimes against them, and on the other side the cardinals and Italians. The great subject in dispute was the support of the Pope. The reformers wanted him to live on his own revenues, and stop the everlasting and exhausting drain on the religious foundations all over Europe; but the cardinals protested that the Pope had so little property, and Italy was so poor, that he would be penniless, and if he was so, why they would be much more so.

The tax on which the French prelates laid the most stress and which they worked the hardest to abolish was that called "annates," or the payment made to the court of Rome by any bishop, rector, or abbot on taking possession of his benefice. This had swollen so much of late years that it virtually absorbed the revenues of the first year of incumbency. The French had to pay the most of this simply because the government did not fight against it, as had always been done in Philip the Fair's time. The English would only pay for bishops, not for abbots and rectors;

and in Germany and Italy the civil authorities inter-
posed all sorts of objections, which made the tax
difficult to collect in those countries. This heavy
burden made the French struggle hard, but the other
nations, not intending to pay much of it, were not
very zealous and the cardinals fought the French
tooth and nail, so that their laudable desire failed of
approval. Nor could the nations agree on the reform
of the monastic orders, nor on simony; and all these
things worked against harmony.

The greatest obstacle to any harmony was, however, the wearisome case of Jean Petit. Petit was a
Paris lawyer, the defender of the Duke of Burgundy
when accused of murdering the king's brother, the
Duke of Orléans. This was years before the council
met, and Jean Petit died in the meantime; but there
was a violent quarrel among scholars as to his opinions.
The fact is that his opinions were monstrous, being
nothing else than legalizing murder. The French
wanted the council to condemn these opinions, which
were called the " Eight Verities "; but the majority
took the ground that they were only philosophical
notions, and were not within the province of the
council, which was concerned only with matters of
faith. This was not true, for they opposed the very
ground principles of Christianity; and the French
knew it, and the indifference of the council much
annoyed them, so that they were in no mood to
agree with anybody when Sigismund returned. The
Spaniards, having now renounced Benedict, came into
the council as a fifth nation, and this was a crumb of
comfort to the French; for the Spaniards sided with

them against the English, and, in fact, signalized their admission to the council by moving that the English be no longer counted in the council as a nation, but be incorporated with some other. This raised a fine quarrel, and it was with difficulty got under, and then only for a time.

One of the first things done on the return of Sigismund was to proceed with the affair of Benedict. He had been cited on November 28, 1416, to appear at Constance within seventy days and answer to the charges against him. The citation was renewed at Peniscola, a little castle to which Benedict had retreated, January 22, 1417. The officers sent by the council were monks, and when they came into his presence the old Pope exclaimed, " Here come the crows of the council!" " Yes," some one in the audience muttered; " and crows gather around a carcass." As the citation was read, Benedict every now and then would say, " A lie." Back went the deputation to Constance with the report that Benedict would do nothing. On April 1, 1417, the council declared him guilty of contumacy, but it was not until July 26th that sentence was passed on him, and he was pronounced a schismatic, a heretic, and a disturber of the peace, deprived of all rank, and " lopped off like a dry bough." The bells of Constance rang for joy over this sentence. It was a general holiday, and it now seemed as if the schism was really at an end. This was the last public notice of Benedict. He remained at Peniscola playing at Pope, a lonely and deserted old man, who passed away a few years after, unhonored and forgotten.

CHAPTER XXIII.

THE ARRANGEMENTS FOR THE ELECTION— MARTIN V.

SIGISMUND had returned the last of January, 1417, and early in March the French party determined to attack the English party; for politics in Constance had quite as much influence with the council as religion. The affair of Huss was championed by Sigismund quite as much to break the power of the Czechs as to put down heresy. The Jean Petit affair was purely a question of French politics, and now the old hatred between France and England was to find expression in this august body summoned to reform the church.

As soon as the election of a new Pope seemed imminent by the clearing away of the Benedictine and Gregorian factions, the question of votes became important. It will be remembered that it had been arranged that the members of the council should vote by nations and not by individuals. The "nations" were at first four, but the coming in of the Spaniards increased them to five.

The French now raised this question. Benedict

XII., they said, had recognized in Christendom four nations, Italian, German, Spanish, and French. While Spain was not present in the council England had been allowed to sit as a nation to keep up the number four; but now that the Spaniards were in, the English ought to be counted with the German nation, as Benedict XII. had arranged, and ought only to vote with it. If this were not done, the mode of voting by nations ought to be abolished. The French were not able to get in this protest without great hissing and noise, and the emperor put a quietus on it by saying that nothing could be read in the council upon which the nations had not agreed in general meeting. The English were naturally very angry, and they also put in a paper, in which they annihilated the French with statistics. The English crown, they said, ruled over eight kingdoms (unless you count the little Irish kingdoms, it would be hard to understand this); had fifty-two thousand parish churches, and France only six thousand (this must be a much exaggerated statement); one hundred and ten dioceses, while France had only sixty; and— convincing argument—had been converted by Joseph of Arimathea, while France owed her religion to a much less important personage, Dionysius the Areopagite.

This question disposed of, there came up the burning question, "Shall a Pope be elected after the reforms are decreed, or shall the election take place first and the reforms be effected afterwards?" There was much to be said on both sides of this question, and it was said by both sides with much vigor. It was argued, and from the standpoint of those times with great justice, that the church must have a head and must have one immediately, that it was perfectly incomplete without it, and that any attempt to reform it in its present mutilated state would amount to nothing. On the other hand, members of the council were reminded that the reason why the Council of Pisa had been such a failure was because they had allowed the election of a Pope to put off reform, and the very pointed argument was used that the papal office needed reforming as much as anything else, and unless that were reformed before a Pope came in, he might turn around and block any interference whatever with his office. On the side of reform stood Sigismund with the English and Germans, and on the side of the election the cardinals, the Italians and Spaniards, and the French, seemingly for no other good reason than to be opposed to the English.

It was a weary battle. Deluges of words were poured forth on all sides, sermon after sermon, protest after protest. The cardinal or the curial party, as it is better called, feeling sure of three votes out of the five, took a bold step, and on September 9, 1417, put in a paper before a general congregation, protesting against the delay in the election, and declaring that the church was taking great harm from it. This action made Sigismund very angry, and he, with a large party, rose and left the cathedral. His temper was not improved by hearing some one shout after him, " Let the heretics go." The cardinals determined to force their hand, and got up the report that the emperor intended to use troops to overawe the council; and the Castilians, with a great show of fear, prepared to leave Constance; but the city police blocked their way. This game infuriated the emperor, and he ordered the cathedral closed against the cardinals; but they came and sat on the steps of the bishop's palace, and called aloud for freedom.

The emperor saw he was going too far, and on September 11th a general congregation was held, at which the cardinals were present. There they put in another protest, which utterly ignored the English, and in which they speak of themselves as a body separate from the nations, and say that they and three nations were anxious to proceed to a vote, and they washed their hands of all consequences from delaying it. This delay they charged directly upon Sigismund and the Germans. The reason why the English were thus snubbed was because they had just lost by death their powerful head, Robert Hallam, Bishop of Salisbury, who passed away September 7th. He had kept them firmly to the side of Sigismund, but now they seemed to be headless and very wavering.

It can be imagined into what a fury their imminent defection threw the emperor, and his violent words gave rise to renewed reports that he intended to use force. The cardinals diligently fanned the flame, and went about wearing their red hats to show they were ready for martyrdom. This produced its effect: the German party dwindled away, and the sturdy emperor had to show signs of concession. Early in October he gave his consent to the election of a Pope, but wanted a guarantee that as soon as

the election was over, and before the coronation, reform should begin. The cardinals very properly said
that they had no right to pledge for the Pope. They
did, however, pass some reform measures, embodied
in the decree " Frequens," given in full by Von der
Hardt. This provided that a general council should
be held in five years, and then another in seven
years, and after that every ten years. In case of a
schism, one could be convoked at any time. No prelate could be translated against his will, nor could
the Pope take possession of the fortunes of deceased
ecclesiastics.

Now again rose the ghost which would not be
laid, " Who were to vote?" The cardinals knew very
well that they could not hope, as usual, to be the
only electors, but they intended to fight hard to reduce the opposition as low as possible. Confusion
worse confounded reigned in the council, and it
seemed as if all the years of debate and worry would
amount to nothing, when a *Deus ex machina* appeared
in the shape of Henry Beaufort, Bishop of Winchester, half-brother to the King of England, Henry IV.,
a keen politician and a man of great wisdom. He
managed to reconcile the contending parties, and it
was agreed that the council should pass a decree
guaranteeing reform work after the election of a Pope,
that the reform measures on which the nations had
agreed should immediately come before the council,
and that a commission should be appointed to arrange
the mode of election.

The commission was immediately named, October
11th, and two propositions were laid before it. One

was by the Germans, that each nation should appoint fifteen electors, and that the fifteen Italian cardinals should represent the Italian nation.   The other was by the French, and was the one adopted: the election to be made by the cardinals and six deputies from each nation, thirty in all, two thirds of the cardinals and two thirds of the deputies to agree before an election could be made.   This did not get arranged until October 30th, and decrees were then published providing that the Pope, with the council or with chosen deputies, should reform the church in its head and the Curia on eighteen points agreed to by the reform commission.   The council, struggling in the last gasps of independence, decreed also that it could not be dissolved until the Pope had granted reform.

This seems a sorry outcome after all the earnest talk about reform—eighteen points only, and the fathers not to do that even themselves, but to help the Pope do it.   The simple fact was that the Sacred College, with that astuteness which has generally marked it, had bided its time, and now, when everybody was weary to death of the long, protracted council, it with steady persistence stuck to its colors and carried its points.

And now the election was to take place.   It did not consume much time, for this legislative body, like many others of our own day, rushed through in the greatest haste the most important act, months of debate having been wasted over the pettiest things. The usual rooms for the electors, fifty-three in number, twenty-three being cardinals, were prepared in the Kaufhaus, which is still standing, and on Novem-

YORK COLLEGE LIBRARY

ber 8th everything was ready. High mass was sung in the cathedral, and the Bishop of Lodi, who seems to have been the favorite preacher of the council, gave a sharp sermon on the words, "Look even out the best" (2 Kings x. 3), in which he said he hoped they would give the church a better Pope than it had had for forty years. The electors then went into the conclave, all the Roman formalities being carefully observed. As they went in, each man took the emperor by the hand and swore to make a true and honest choice. Before noon on November 11th the election was made, and the choice was gladly announced to the eager crowd outside: "We have a Pope, Cardinal Oddo [or Otho] Colonna, and, being St. Martin's day, he has taken the name of Martin V." Sigismund flew to the Kaufhaus and kissed the papal foot. Martin mounted on horseback, and through the enormous crowd—eighty thousand, some writers say—the procession moved to the cathedral, the emperor holding the right bridle and the Elector of Brandenburg the left. The Pope was placed on the altar of the cathedral, and sat there for hours, while the people passed joyfully before him. The great schism was ended; let us now review some of its terrible effects, not to be overcome in many a year.

CHAPTER XXIV.

THE EFFECTS OF THE SCHISM.

EFORE continuing the history of the Council of Constance, it may be well, now that, by the election of Martin V., unity was restored to Western Christendom, to note briefly the condition of the church, the ruin that schism had worked in it, and the effect upon the common life of the people. It is not pretended that all the evils rampant were the direct fruits of the division; many of them had been in existence for centuries; but they were now intensified and aggravated beyond measure. That the church should have survived these horrible years, and should be now vigorous, aggressive, and the great *vis medicatrix* of the world, is, perhaps more than any other one thing, a proof of her divine origin and the impossibility of the " gates of hell " prevailing against her. Her wounds were not from strangers, but received in the house of her friends, and therefore the more grievous and piercing.

There is no lack of literature on the subject of the state of the church in the fourteenth century. Von der Hardt has made a great collection of it, which has been freely drawn upon by all historians. Among the most famous treatises are: " On the Ruin of the Church," probably by Nicolas de Clemanges; " On the Difficulty of Reform " and " The Necessity of Reforming the Church in Head and Members," by Cardinal d'Ailly, though some think by Dietrich von Niem; " Petitions for the Reform of the Church Militant," by Richard Ullerston, an Englishman; and the " Squalors of the Roman Curia," by the Bishop of Worms, in 1405.

The great causes of complaint were the corruption and sensuality of the clergy, which, as is ever the case, reacted upon the laity; the prostitution of the cure of souls to the love of money, so that everywhere benefices were bought and sold; and the tremendous exactions and abuses, simoniacal and otherwise, of the papal court. Take indulgences, for example (Froude): " Pardons, dispensations, and indulgences, permissions to do things which would be wrong without them, or remissions of penalties prescribed by the canon for offences, indulgences which were extended by popular credulity to actual pardon for sins committed, were issued whenever the Pope wanted money. Sorrowing relatives, uneasy for the fate of a soul in purgatory, could buy out their friend at a fixed rate of charges. The results were calculated beforehand. Averages could be taken from repeated experience. Sometimes a capitalist contracted on speculation for the anticipated sum, sometimes the batch was disposed of by recognized officials resident in the various countries. The price was high or low, according to the papal necessities, or according to the magnitude of the sins to which it would reach; but no one could possibly be so innocent as not to need an indulgence for something."

Complaints of these things came from all parts of Europe; the far north seemed to have been as great a sufferer as the extreme south. In many dioceses there were two bishops,—for example, in Breslau, Mayence, Liége, Basel, Lübeck, Constance,—one an Urbanist, one a Clementine. It can easily be imagined what confusion arose in the minds of laymen as to which was their true superior; for the Clementines would preach that the Urbanist masses were blasphemy, and the Urbanists would retort in the same strain. In many cases public worship was altogether stopped, for the differences between the parishioners and the poverty of the priests made it impossible to keep the churches open. The profligacy of the clergy was everywhere a matter of complaint. One writer says: " The priests frequent brothels and taverns, and spend their time in drinking, revelling, and gambling. They fight and brawl in their cups, and with their polluted lips blaspheme the name of God and the saints, and from the embraces of prostitutes hurry to the altar." Nor were many of the friars any better than the parish priests. Popular tracts in the language of the country everywhere speak of them in the coarsest terms. Chaucer (1340–1400), in his Canterbury pilgrimage, gives incidentally the general estimate of a friar in his time.

Even long after, the evil had not been rooted out; for Erasmus, speaking of some criticisms on his famous book, " Moria," or the " Praise of Folly," says: " Had I seriously wished to describe monks and theologians as they really are, ' Moria ' would seem a mild performance by the side of what I should have written. I do not condemn religious houses, but ask yourself what trace of piety is now to be found in such houses beyond forms and ceremonies. How worse than worldly almost all of them are!"

Even of nunneries Clemanges says, " It is about equal to sending a girl to prostitution to put her in a nunnery." Priests guilty of the greatest offences, if they could raise a little money, got off scot-free. In very many instances bishops sold licenses to priests to keep concubines. Indeed, this was so general in Norway and Sweden that women living in this way were socially respected, and parishes often, for the protection of their families, insisted that the rector should take a concubine and pledge himself to be faithful to her. Boccaccio, by the conversation he puts into the mouths of refined people in the " Decamerone," conversation which in our day would scarce be heard in a barrack-room, let alone a company of ladies and gentlemen, shows how low was the standard of morality among such people. The lives of some of the popes were stained with sin, and that such a person as John XXIII. could ever have been freely elected the Vicar of Christ speaks volumes for the miserable tone of Christian living which everywhere prevailed. Money may be worshipped now, and venality common enough, but the church of to-day is as white as driven snow compared with the subserviency to money which then prevailed. The popes of the schism were always impecunious, for the schism stopped the flow of wealth into the papal coffers, and all sorts of dishonest and unfair expedients were resorted to in order to raise funds. It was wittily said that, while there might be some doubt whether Peter was ever at Rome, there could be none about Simon's presence there. Popes fleeced bishops, bishops priests, and priests their flocks.

Even if a bishop was a man of pure character, and anxious to reform his diocese, he was confronted immediately with " exemptions." For example, if he had a dissolute monastery in his diocese, and wished to reform it, the monastery would get together a good sum of money, often selling the church plate to make it up, and send off to Rome to purchase an exemption from episcopal authority, becoming a " peculiar," so that the bishop had no authority within its walls. Even to this day Westminster Abbey enjoys that privilege. All sorts of favors could be purchased at the papal bureaus for money. Men would buy ten, twelve, eighteen benefices, and never go near one of them, but hire at starvation prices some wandering priest to give irregular ministrations, while they spent the rest of the income in luxury.

The rival obediences, anxious to curry favor with the powers that be, often granted to secular rulers concessions which endangered the liberties of the church and subjected it to the most shameful humiliations. Laymen were in a maze of doubt and distrust, and thousands lost all faith and fell away into utter evil living or infidelity, which, as far as the dogmas of the church were concerned, was kept very secret for fear of the Inquisition, thus engendering terrible hypocrisy.

It was no wonder that heresy spread; the church had only herself to blame for it. Indeed, the schism gave birth to all sorts of fanatical sects and to numberless false prophets. People believed everywhere that Antichrist was coming, and more than one bold preacher maintained that the Pope was Antichrist.

The most widely circulated false prophecy was that of Telesphorus, an Italian. He says the schism was a punishment for the sins and crimes of the Roman Church and clergy, and he prophesies that all that will come to an end in 1393, when the antipope would be slain in Perugia, and the church be completely renovated, renouncing all property. A new Pope and a new emperor would then appear, and that emperor would be a Frenchman. The whole bearing of this prophecy shows its author to have been a fierce French partisan. Henry of Hesse answered this wide-spread nonsense, and opposes the principle it laid down that the clergy ought to be deprived of their wealth. He shows very clearly that it would be perfect madness to teach laymen, already too grasping, that they had the right to take possession of church property under the pretext of reform.

The spoliation of the clergy was a favorite theme with all these fourteenth-century prophets, and it was not to be wondered at, when men were constantly witnessing such avarice and greed and simony in the highest church positions. Everywhere, especially in Germany, was there growing a great hatred

of the clergy, and in Mayence, in 1401, the cry
"Death to the priests!" often resounded through
the streets. Faulty as the Inquisition was, it did
good service often in shutting the mouths of blas-
phemers and revilers of all good. One sect, called
the sect of "Free Thought," taught that by a devout
contemplation of the Godhead you could come to be
one with God, absolutely perfect and incapable of
sinning. No commandments were binding on the
perfect, and this was carried into practice with a vengeance.

But the very number of sermons and treatises on
the state of morals and discipline proves that all
Christians were not sunk in sin and indifference; the
fervor of the protests shows that the wide chasm
yawning between the devout life as Christ commanded it and the life then led was deeply felt and
struggled against. Devout men drew closer together.
The mystics, as will be seen in a future chapter, were
a large and powerful body. The Brethren of the
Common Life were a very oasis in the dry and filthy
desert of the monastic orders. This century gave
birth to that immortal book, "The Imitation of
Christ." Preachers all on fire with the love of God
and man were to be found everywhere, and in many
a humble home fervent prayers went daily up from
pure hearts that God would have mercy upon His
church. There is a letter of Gerard Groot, of Deventer, in the Imperial Library of Vienna, in which he
wishes that both the popes and all the cardinals
could be transported to heaven and sing " Gloria in
Excelsis " there, and another line bring peace and

unity on earth. It is sad to think that the members
of the Council of Constance were so well aware of
the frightful state of the ordinary life of Christians,
and that they should have done so little to heal the
wounds inflicted by the sins of her sons on our common Christianity.

CHAPTER XXV.

JOHN WYCLIF.

NDOUBTEDLY one of the most famous men of the fourteenth century was John Wyclif; indeed, it was said at that time that the four greatest schoolmen of the century were Duns Scotus, Occam, Bradwardine, and Wyclif. His direct influence was, however, very transitory, and the Reformation which took place long after under Luther and Calvin bears but little trace of having drawn any inspiration from the great English protester. One great reason is that Wyclif's religious belief, similar as it was to that of the after Reformers, was so mixed up with political theories that it failed of its due spiritual effect; the dangerous tendency of some of his ideas about the state very much neutralized the noble and enlightening tendency of his creed.

He was born at a small village named Spresswell, near to old Richmond in Yorkshire, close to the Tees River; there were descendants of his name at Barnard Castle at the beginning of this century.

The exact date of his birth cannot be given, but it was between 1320 and 1324. He entered Oxford

University at the age of fifteen, and, although that classic place was by no means as beautiful or as well appointed as it is to-day, it had many more students, the numbers running up into the thousands. There were only five colleges then, and it is not accurately known to which Wyclif belonged, or who were his teachers, though thirty years of his life were mostly spent there. He undoubtedly went through the "seven arts," the usual curriculum, and studied theology and canon law. His writings show that he was familiar with Latin, but was totally ignorant of Hebrew and Greek. He devoted much of his time to logic and dialectics, which was natural, for in his time an over-valuation of logic prevailed in all the universities of Europe; and in the disputes and tourneys of logic which were constantly taking place he held the very front place, and his university was very proud of him. He was fellow of Merton College, and of course a priest, in 1356, master of Baliol in 1360, and Warden of Canterbury Hall in 1365; soon after that he was made a doctor in theology. He held several livings, and was a pluralist, like most of the prominent clergy of his time.

It was about the year 1366 that Wyclif came forward as an English statesman and patriot, and took a prominent part in opposing the usurpations of the Papacy against the rights of the crown, and the taking of so much money out of the country for the papal court at Avignon, and, as a necessary corollary to this last, the secular and worldly lives led by so many of the clergy. As an Englishman he was opposed to a French Pope, and as a Christian to the enjoyment of rich livings by men who took not the slightest interest in the spiritual welfare of their parishes. He thought these intruders ought to be dispossessed, and that the state ought to force them out. So far, so good, and most thinking Englishmen agreed with him; but the theory by which he attempted to sustain these propositions led him into much trouble and practically ruined his influence. It is called the theory of dominion, and amounts to this: "To God alone [Sheldon] belongs unqualified dominion; He alone has the unrestricted right to property. Men have only a delegated right, and this delegated right they forfeit by mortal sin. Tenure of property depends upon the state of grace in the holder."

But it will be better to give his exact words, so that the rock on which he split may be clearly seen: "God is and has dominion over all. Each man in his degree is bounden to serve God, and if he do not render this service he is no lord of goods of true title; for he that standeth in grace is the true lord of things, and whoever faileth by default of grace falleth short of the right title of that which he occupieth, and maketh himself unfit to have the gifts." Now the champions of Wyclif may try to explain this away if possible; but it seems to teach clearly a doctrine so revolutionary, so socialistic, indeed, so destructive of civil and religious order, that it is no wonder it damaged greatly Wyclif's cause; and when the English peasants, under John Ball, attempted to reduce it to practice it so disgusted the great mass of Englishmen that they disregarded generally Wyclif's teachings; and it forms a complete explanation of the entire and total neglect into which Wyclifism fell in England, however much it flourished in Bohemia, under the teaching of John Huss, who adopted in all their fulness Wyclif's political views.

To repeat somewhat the discussion already mentioned in the case of John Huss, who is to be the judge of a holder of property being in mortal sin? Suppose the state is; just think how easy it would be then for a greedy king to say to any occupant of paying church property, "You are in mortal sin, and I confiscate your goods." Suppose the democracy is (as in the John Ball insurrection the rebels assumed); if they are opposed to a ruler they have only to declare with one voice, "He is in mortal sin," and his goods will then fall to their share. Nothing could be more vague and more pernicious, and to say that Wyclif only held this as a theory is no excuse. The worst anarchism is held as a theory, and theories are very apt to develop into practice if they have a chance.

It is no wonder that Wyclif was arraigned before the church authorities; and while political friends helped him at first, and his university long stood by him, yet his opinions were condemned at last by king and clergy. It is true he died in his bed, and Fuller says so quaintly, "Admirable that a hare so often hunted with so many packs of dogs should die at last sitting quietly on his form." But that he did so die, and that he who had opposed nearly every distinctive doctrine of the Church of Rome should have remained parish priest of Latterworth until his death, gives much color to the assertion of Roman writers that he recanted his errors. If he did not,—and his Protestant biographers all vigorously deny it,—how can he be exculpated from a charge of performing duties and going through ceremonies which were in direct opposition to his published views? I do not refer to his censure of the Pope, for the very best of men then separated the Pope from the church; but the daily saying the mass, the holding property, the being known as a priest in subjection to a worldly bishop, his well-known views on transubstantiation and image-worship—how could he reconcile all these things with honor and consistency? Roman and Anglican writers have asked the question often, and as yet there has been no sufficient reply.

He seems to have entirely mistaken the nature of the church, for he taught, in direct contradiction to Scripture, that it consisted only of holy persons who were predestined to salvation, and he held that the sacraments were vitiated by the imperfections of the minister. He recognized only the two orders of priest and deacon; in fine, he was a predestinarian in religion, a Presbyterian in church government, and almost a Zwinglian in his late views of the eucharist.

But no matter what Wyclif's views on civil and ecclesiastical polity may have been, three things he did which entitle him to the enduring gratitude and memory of all English-speaking people.

One is well expressed by Green ("History of the English People") in these words:

"With an amazing industry he issued tract after tract in the tongue of the people itself. The dry syllogistic Latin was thrown aside and the schoolman transformed into the pamphleteer. If Chaucer was the father of our later English poetry, Wyclif is the father of our later English prose. The rough, clear, homely English of his tracts, the speech of the ploughman and trader of the day, though colored with the picturesque phraseology of the Bible, is in its literary use as distinctly a creation of his own as the style in which he embodied it—the terse, vehement sentences, the stinging sarcasms, the hard antitheses, which roused the dullest mind like a whip."

A second thing was a preaching order which he instituted, called " Poor Priests." They took no peculiar vows, but went about preaching in plain and even vulgar language to plain people, much after the manner of the Salvationists of our day. They totally discarded the far-fetched and forced exegesis of that time, and dwelt mainly on simple gospel truths which the commonest men could understand. They and their followers were nicknamed Lollards. The derivation of this word is uncertain. A passage of Chaucer would seem to connect it with *lolium* (" tares "):

> " This Lollere here will prechen us somewhat;
> He wolde sowen some difficulte
> Or sprengen cockle in oure clene corn."

A more probable derivation is from *lullen* (" to sing softly "), referring to the soul-lulling doctrines their enemies declared they held. The earliest official use of the word is in a mandate of the Bishop of Worcester against five priests: " Nomine seu ritu Lollardorum confœderatos."

If these preachers had confined themselves simply to the gospel of salvation and to the familiarizing the people with the Holy Bible in English, they would deserve only praise; but, being devoted followers of Wyclif, they of course adopted his political theories, and within ten years after his death those views had grown so popular that the Lollard party was strong enough to petition Parliament to reform the church on their platform. This petition, called the " Lollard Conclusions," stated that all temporal possessions ruin the church, that the priesthood of Rome was not the priesthood of Christ, that kings should possess episcopal rights, that all war was against the principles of the gospel, that such trades as goldsmith and armorer ought to be put down by law, that the principal duty of a priest was to preach, not to give sacraments, and that the worship of images is sinful. Every word of this can be found in Wyclif's writings. A popular view of Lollardy is best seen in the famous political poems called " Visio de Petro Plowman," " Visio de Do Well," " Visio de Do Better," and " Visio de Do Best." These poems go over the general subject of the greed and sensuality of the monks, and the low tone of life in both the higher and lower classes. They well deserve study for their strong and nervous English and their curious alliterative metre.

Of course such radical doctrines could not be overlooked, and when Henry IV. came to the English throne it is probable that he promised Arundel, Archbishop of Canterbury, as a reward for his valuable aid, that he would do all he could to put down Lollardy. In 1400 Parliament passed the act for which even yet Englishmen blush, " De comburendo haereticos," and an active persecution of the Lollards began. Arundel in 1408 published by order of Convocation his " Constitutions," which provide that no preacher could preach without a license from the bishop, that he must let the shortcomings of the clergy alone, and that all Lollard books and Wyclif Bibles were to be destroyed. The best-known person who suffered in this persecution was Lord Cobham, who was burned quite as much, though, for his political as his religious heresies. If it is asked why, since Lollards were so abundant, there was so little resistance made to these persecutions, it may be said that the Lollard denunciations of war, made to a people filled with the martial spirit and plunged in the fierce war with France, cooled the ardor of their partisans and made the nation indifferent to their fate. After the Council of Constance Lollards no longer preached in public, but only in concealed places, and by the end of the fifteenth century scarcely a trace of Lollardy remained. It is doubtful whether there was any connection at all between it and the Reformation under Henry VIII.

But Wyclif's greatest achievement was the translation of the Bible into English. Portions of it had been translated before, especially the Psalter and the four gospels, but his work embraced the whole Scriptures; and while, of course, his ignorance of Greek and Hebrew and his reliance upon the Vulgate were great hindrances to a thoroughly correct version, yet the effect of thus opening the whole Word of God

to the common people was tremendous; and Wyclif's
noble prayer well deserves quoting: " Help, Lord,
that Thy holy gospel may be known and held fast
by Thy simple brethren, and cause them to grow in
love and humility and patience, and with joy to suffer death for Thee and Thy law. Amen, Lord
Jesus." The indirect influence of this great work
upon subsequent translations, such as those of Tyn-
dale and Coverdale, was very great, and it moulded
wonderfully the speech of the common people; but
of course a thoroughly correct translation could not
be made by a man without knowledge of Greek and
Hebrew. Even our last revision, without really intending it, shows by frequent returns to Wyclif's text
how good it was. Out of fifty-six specimen changes
given when the revision was first published, twenty-
two were a return to Wyclif. He translated Jerome,
for he knew nothing else; yet his work was not done
slavishly, but with intelligence.

Wyclif died December 31, 1384, and in 1415, as
has been already said, the Council of Constance condemned his works and ordered his bones to be removed from consecrated ground and the ashes cast
into the neighboring stream. Wordsworth's sonnet
on it must not be forgotten:

> " As thou these ashes, little Brook, wilt bear
>   Into the Avon, Avon to the tide
>   Of Severn, Severn to the narrow seas,
>   Into main ocean they, this deed accurst
>   An emblem yields to friends and enemies,
>   How the bold teacher's doctrine, sanctified
>   By truth, shall spread, throughout the world dispersed."

CHAPTER XXVI.

CLOSE OF COUNCIL OF CONSTANCE—MARTIN V.

THO COLONNA, now Martin V., was by far the best choice that the electors could have made; his preëminent merits will explain the shortness of the conclave. He was not French, and that pleased every one but the Frenchmen. He was a prince of one of the noblest Roman houses, and that endeared him to all Italians. He had kept himself so aloof from all the squabbles and controversies in the council that Sigismund had the highest opinion of him. He was about fifty years of age, and Milman gives the following sketch of him: " Of the highest birth, irreproachable morals, with the reputation of learning in the canon law, in only two points had he departed from the calmest moderateness, in both with the full sympathies of the council. He had been strenuous for the condemnation of Huss, and he had followed Pope John in his flight, but this would find excuse as an act of generous fidelity to the ruling pontiff and a falling friend. In all other respects he had held the middle course with great dignity, no stern adversary of reformation, no alarming fanatic for change.   He was courteous in manner, short and sententious in speech, quick and dexterous, yet cautious in business, a strict and even ostentatious lover of justice.   His enemies could only assert that much craft lurked under his moderation.   Later in life his prudence degenerated into avarice.   The conduct of the Pope until the dissolution of the council without any general measure of reform, while it avoided all serious offence to the emperor or to the more formidable advocates of reform, displays the great sagacity, the consummate policy, of Martin V."

Martin, like some other cardinals of that time—and there have been examples in our own day (Cardinal Antonelli being one)—was only in minor orders. He was a cardinal deacon, but that does not imply that he was in deacon's orders ; cardinal deacons are often bishops.   He was now on three successive days ordained deacon, priest, and bishop, and on November 21st he was crowned on a platform in front of the bishop's palace.   According to ancient custom—and it still continues in our day—a heap of tow was set on fire, and as it quickly burned, a voice cried out, "So shall pass away all the glories of this world."

All were in the greatest joy over the new Pope, and there seemed rising a bright sun over the darkness of the church, when suddenly a cloud came over it before the eyes of those who were anxious for reform.   One of the first things Martin did was to approve the rules of the papal chancery, and the rules of the papal chancery were the foundation and the source of all those exactions and oppressions under which the clergy of Europe had so groaned. All these questions of annates, reservations, exemptions, etc., which had been before the reform commission, were governed by these rules, and here they were with a fresh stamp of authority. More than all, the Pope had not waited to ask the council whether he had better do this, but he had of his own motion given his sanction to this worst of all the papal abuses. This was a hard blow to all those earnest men who had so fondly hoped and so strenuously worked for reform, and it is no wonder that they rushed to Sigismund with their grievances; but he grimly said, "When I urged that reformation should come before election, you would not hear to me, but wanted first a Pope. Well, you have got one now; go and ask him to reform. My power has waned since the Pope was chosen."

This speech was well worth a reward, and the Pope gave him a very substantial one: a recognition of his position as King of the Romans, and one tenth of the church revenues of three German provinces. The emperor was in terrible straits for money, and had run up tremendous bills in Constance. His creditors wanted to see the color of their money now that the council was drawing to a close, and he offered all his silver plate in payment. They arranged to take it, when he requested that instead of it they would take all his silken hangings and tapestries. This they also agreed to, but when they got them found they were nearly useless, as they were all embroidered with the imperial arms. There was many a failure after the council among the substantial business men of Constance, on account of the emperor's unpaid bills.

The partisans of reform would not give up the struggle, and now each nation came to the Pope with separate proposals. This was just what the astute pontiff wanted; he could make separate treaties with each country, and using their divided interests to play one against the other, they would never be likely to unite against the Papacy. The Germans wanted the number of cardinals limited and more Germans appointed, and insisted strongly on the restriction of the papal power in diocesan affairs. The Pope in very wary and very guarded language agreed that there should be fewer cardinals, that they should be taken from the different nations, and that Germany should always have its share. He also consented in very many cases to give up the right of nomination, and promised to take great care that indulgences were only used in rare instances.

The "Concordat" with the English was received with silent contempt in England. The English felt themselves so protected by the statutes of premunire and provisors that they did not trouble themselves about any possible oppression from the Pope. The French Concordat met with very little more favor in France. The king, indeed, declared himself ready to obey the council, with the far-reaching proviso, "so much as God and reason would allow." The Parliament of Paris utterly refused to accept the Concordat. All this was fish to the papal net, and the Pope must have smiled inwardly and outwardly at his great success. He had acted with perfect fairness; he had said that whatever measures of reform the nations would agree upon he would carefully consider, knowing well that their differences would prevent their agreeing on anything. They had not agreed, and the Pope had all the credit of having shown great courtesy and willingness to oblige. The French tried hard to induce him to go into the Jean Petit business, and the Poles to engage him in a like controversy they were having in Poland over a John of Falkenberg; but he wisely declined to meddle with either. The Poles, always troublesome and quarrelsome churchmen, kept badgering him until the very last moment, but he parried their attacks with the greatest dexterity, and they got nothing.

There is not much more to tell about this famous council. On February 19, 1418, there arrived in Constance an embassy from the Greek emperor with propositions for a union between the Greek and Latin churches. The Turks were closing in upon the Greek empire, already shorn of its fairest provinces, and the unhappy sovereign felt that he needed the aid of Christian Europe, which could only be procured by recognition from the Pope as orthodox believers; for in those days you might as well be a heathen as a heretic. This was not the first of similar advances, for coquetting between the churches had been going on for some time. Great courtesy was shown these Greek ambassadors, and they were allowed to have the Greek mass in Constance with their own creed; but nothing came of it. The council was too worn out and feeble to take up so great a question as that.

The Pope put forth a fierce bull against Wyclif and Huss, and it was sent off to Bohemia, where a religious war was raging, with all the horrible adjuncts that usually accompany religious wars, and where it had about as much effect as whipping with a feather would have had. One thing the monks tried to force Martin to do, which with great good sense he refused, and that was to condemn the Brethren of the Common Life. This was a society which had been formed in Holland by Gerard Groot, of Deventer, a man of great spirituality of character, whose preaching and whose example drew great crowds of followers. These followers, chiefly young men, gradually formed themselves into a community whose object was the life of perfection and imitation of Christ. Every member had to work to help the society, and no begging was allowed. As they were not monks, the monks took offence at them, crying out that no perfection was attainable outside the monastic profession, that having property and living in the world barred all great spiritual advancement.

The monks' champion was Grabow, a Dominican, who laid down the proposition that "no one can meritoriously and after God's manner fulfil the duties of obedience, poverty, and chastity but true and regular monks and nuns." This proposition the Pope was asked to indorse. He submitted it to a body of theologians in the council, and they advised him to refuse to sanction it, since laymen were as able without vows to strive after perfection as any monks were. This was quite a blow to the notion, which had so long prevailed, that to become a truly devout and acceptable servant of God you must become a monk.

And now the council had finished its work, and after fixing Pavia as the seat of the next council, to be held in five years, on April 22, 1418, the last general session was held, the Pope pronounced the decree of dissolution, and prepared to leave. The French tried hard to get him to take up his residence at Avignon, and Sigismund tried equally hard to get him to stay in Germany, for he thought that perhaps he could manipulate him if he had him under his thumb; but Martin was too clever a man to be manipulated by anybody, and, returning a polite reply to each invitation, he urged that his own Pontifical States needed his presence very badly.

On the 16th of May he embarked for Schaffhausen on his way to Geneva, and his going was a splendid ceremony; just as at his enthronement, on either side his horse walked the emperor and the Elector of Brandenburg, while four counts of the empire held a canopy over him. Behind came a great train of prelates and nobles, amounting, according to Ulric von Reichenthal, who, being a Constance burgher, swelled numbers a little, to forty thousand people. The Pope and the Curia could alone of all that crowd have felt light of heart, for every earnest looker-on knew what a disappointment the whole gathering had been. To reform had been its great reason of being, and where was the reform? It had all disappeared in thin air under the dissensions of the members, the perseverance of the cardinals, and the sagacity of the Pope.

Before leaving the Council of Constance one point deserves to be noticed, which has been much dwelt upon in our day, and that is the flat contradiction between its decrees and those of the Council of the Vatican, held under Pius IX., as far as concerns the authority of the Pope as superior to that of a general council. The Council of Constance declared in explicit terms that it had from Christ immediate power over the universal church, of which it was the representative; that all were bound to obey it, of whatever state and dignity, even if papal, in all matters pertaining to the faith, the extirpation of the existing schism, or the reformation of the church in its head or members. It summoned three popes before it with full conviction that it had authority to do so.

The Council of the Vatican decreed exactly the reverse. It decreed that the Pope had from Christ immediate power over the universal church; that all were bound to obey him, of whatever rite and dignity, collectively as well as individually; that this duty of obedience extended to all matters of faith, of morals, and of the discipline and government of the church; that in all ecclesiastical cases he is judge, without appeal or the possibility of removal; that the definitions of the Pope in faith and morals, delivered ex cathedra, are irreformable, and are invested with the infallibility granted by Christ in the said subject-matter to the church.

Here, then, are two great Roman councils, both confirmed by a Pope and thus both with the stamp of infallibility, and directly in conflict. Which are men to follow? Roman Catholics know that this is a hard nut to crack, but they manfully try to crack it. Dr. O'Reilly says that Constance was a special council for special circumstances, and therefore is not of the same authority as other general councils; but every general council has been summoned for special circumstances, and the argument will not stand. Others say that Martin V. only confirmed those decrees of Constance which related to faith, and these controverted points about the chief authority were not matters of faith, but of government. The Roman Church, however, certainly makes these points matters of faith, and Martin V., in the last session, when he confirmed the acts of the council, did not make any exceptions; he did not say, "I only confirm the decrees about the faith;" he sanctioned everything that was done at Constance *conciliariter*, that is, in a general session, as opposed to *nationaliter*, that is, done in the meetings of the nations. These decrees, on which the modern controversy turns, were adopted *conciliariter*, and have just as good papal authority as any decrees ever passed; and it cannot be denied that we have here two popes and two councils in direct opposition on one of the most important points in the constitution of the church.

Martin V. certainly admitted the power of the council to decree matters of faith, for in his bull against the Hussites he says, "Every heretic shall be required to say whether he believes that what the holy Council of Constance, representing the universal church, has sanctioned and sanctions, 'in favorem fidei et salutis animarum,' is binding on all Christian

believers, and also that what that synod has condemned as contrary to the faith must be held by all
to deserve reprobation." This fact remains clear:
Martin V. adopted a decree which declares the
judgments of the Pope to be reformable, and Pius
IX. adopted a decree which declares certain judgments of the Pope in matters of faith and morals to
be infallible and irreformable. As Gladstone says,
" One oracle contradicts another, and no oracle which
contradicts itself is infallible."

And so ends the Council of Constance. It had
sat for three years and six months, and the Count
Palatine Louis, by whom the whole police and com-
missariat department was supervised, deserves more
credit than he has ever received for so managing
things that during that whole time there never was a
tumult in the streets, a rise in the price of provisions,
nor any epidemic or contagious disease, although
sometimes eighty thousand people were crowded in
the little burgh.

CHAPTER XXVII.

THE RETURN OF MARTIN V. TO ROME, AND HIS TRIUMPH.

REATLY as Martin V. longed to be in his own dominions, it was impossible for him to go directly there on leaving Constance. The Papal States, as well as other parts of Italy, were overrun at that time by large bodies of organized brigands (for they were nothing better) called the " free companies," or the " free-lances." They were regular bodies of troops collected together by some soldier of fortune, able, brave, reckless, and anxious to win for himself and his family a place among the powerful ones of the earth. They sold their swords to the highest bidder, and were ever on the lookout for some town to plunder, some province to invade.

When John XXIII. went to Constance he left the captain, or condottiere, of one of these companies in command at Bologna, one Braccio. As soon as the Pope was away, Braccio, with the utter disregard of obligations that characterized his kind, sold their liberty to the Bolognese, marched against Perugia, took it and many another papal town, and forced his

way to Rome just about the time Martin V. was
leaving Constance. Against him came the captain
of another free company, in the pay of Naples—
Sforza, one of the most famous of that desperate
band. He drove Braccio out of Rome, but that did
not make it safe for the Pope to return there, although
Sforza was on his side; for Braccio intrenched himself at Perugia. The wise Martin concluded that he
would not venture into that hornets' nest, but travel
gradually and magnificently southward while events
were developing themselves. He lingered awhile at
Geneva, then went to Turin, then to Milan, where he
was received with great pomp; then, towards the end
of October, to Mantua, where he dwelt for some
months, reaching Florence on February 26, 1419, the
Florentines having promised him their assistance.

He had several distinguished visitors there. First
came old John XXIII., who, with the assistance of
friends, had raised the money to ransom himself from
Louis of Bavaria. It was a curious sight to the
Florentines, that violent and haughty prelate on his
knees before Martin imploring his protection. Martin raised him up and put a cardinal's hat on his head.
Soon he died, and in the splendid baptistery of Florence the passing traveller can see his splendid tomb.
Then came the condottiere Sforza to get instructions from the Pope about the war for the recovery
of the Papal States. Then came Braccio, the rival
captain, who had been reconciled to the Pope.
Braccio was a very showy person, and spent so much
money in Florence, and gave the people so much
entertainment, that they could not help contrasting

his conduct with the parsimonious and quiet life led by the Pope; for Martin, not having much money to spend, could not be very lavish with entertainments. The street boys of Florence were very like their descendants of the present day, and they sang under the papal windows this doggerel:

> " Braccio the strong
> Conquers all along,
> But old Pope Martin
> Isn't worth a farden."

Silly as these words were, it is said they touched to the quick the proud Colonna.

Towards the end of September, 1420, it was considered safe for the Pope to proceed to Rome, and on the 28th of that month he made his solemn entry. It was a dreary and desolate city to which he came. The Rome that Augustus had found brick and left marble had sunk to the dimensions of a third- or fourth-rate provincial town. The houses were in ruins, the streets in frightful condition, and the churches in many cases roofless and tumbling to pieces. Gibbon gives four causes for such a state of things, each of which has some weight: 1. The ravages of time. But when we see the state of preservation of the pyramids, and the grandeur of the temples still standing at Pæstum, we are not inclined to attribute much to that. We often are told that the burning of Rome by Nero worked irreparable damage to it; but, on the contrary, it was a great advantage, and it is becoming evident now that the conflagration, so much blamed, was really a drastic but most effectual measure of the emperor in order to clear the ground for laying out broader streets, he having in vain tried to buy the property from the various owners. 2. Hostile attacks of barbarians. The barbarians, however, remained too short a time to destroy great buildings. Many of the temples the Christians destroyed from hatred of idolatry, but they destroyed no porticoes, theatres, or civic buildings. 3. The use of old material to build new houses. This was a great source of destruction; the beautiful marbles were burned for lime and cement, and the hewn stones furnished material for many a patrician palace.

The greatest cause was, however, the fourth: the domestic quarrels. For five hundred years families had been in a constant state of discord, and Colonna, Orsini, Savelli, and their fellows had turned the old classic remains, like the theatres of Marcellus and Pompey, into fortresses. Even the churches, not excepting St. Peter's, were garrisoned; the engines of war grinned from their battlements. In all these feuds the whole city, ancient and mediæval, suffered greatly. The Romans of the fourteenth century cared little about classic remains, and Petrarch was surprised that he, a stranger from the Rhone, knew more about Roman antiquities than the Romans themselves. When the famous group called " The Nile," which now graces the Vatican, was discovered, the owners covered it up again as of no importance; a fortunate stupidity, for by that means it and many other noble statues were preserved for more enlightened times. The damage to the antiquities would have been much greater if the population had been larger.

It is to the credit of Martin V. that he set himself immediately to work to bring order out of this disorder, to restore the ruined buildings and clear the streets of obstructions. Two years after he returned, his labors were arrested by a great flood that came up to the high altar of the Pantheon; but before he died he had the satisfaction of seeing almost a new city, old buildings protected, and new ones of great beauty everywhere going up. Much more than the buildings had to be changed. The constant state of war, the public distress, the want and penury, had robbed the citizens of all refinement and gentleness; they were a set of rough boors. Robbers swarmed up to the very gates of the city, and one of Martin's first undertakings was the clearing out of the nests of brigands, and making it safe for pilgrims again to approach the Eternal City.

Time soon brought around a troublesome subject for the Pope, and one which he much disliked, and that was the assembling of the Council of Pavia, which had been arranged at Constance to convene in five years; and the great University of Paris took care to remind the Pope that the hour of its meeting had struck. He did not want any council, for it was only too evident that the first subject it would take up would be papal reform; but it was impossible for him to go back on his plighted word that it should be summoned.

The times were not very favorable for general councils. England and France had been so long at each other's throats that both were completely exhausted, and Sigismund was plunged in the Hussite wars. Very few appeared at Pavia, and, the plague soon breaking out there, the Pope transferred the council to Siena; but even there only five German prelates appeared, six French, and not one Spanish. The council, small as it was, showed such very democratic tendencies in the way of arranging the votes, and such a determination to reform the Curia, that the Pope took alarm, and after the council had passed the stock resolutions condemning Huss and Wyclif, those who still held to old Benedict at Peniscola, and all heretics wherever they might be, and had approved of union with the Greek Church, a thing Martin was very anxious to bring about, the Pope took advantage of the very small attendance to declare the council a failure, and ordered his legates to publish a decree of dissolution, which every one was surprised to see posted on the door of the cathedral, March 7, 1424. The legates hurried out of town, and the reformers, though very angry, felt that they would only make themselves ridiculous by trying to carry on a shadowy council; so after proroguing it for seven years, to meet at Basel, all went home.

The Pope felt now that for seven years at least he could breathe free, and that same year he breathed even freer; for both the condottieri generals, Sforza and Braccio, bade farewell to life, and old Benedict XIII., aged ninety-four, and a constant bugbear to Martin, for Spain threatened more than once to go back to his obedience, breathed his last. The two or three cardinals he had left behind did indeed elect a phantom Pope; but the wise Martin soon got him to exchange his empty honor for a fat bishopric, and this ghost was now effectually laid.

Now that the Italian sky had cleared up a little, the Pope turned his attention to church affairs in other lands. He did not mean to abate one jot of the pretensions of his predecessors, and he resolved to secure everything he could by a full use of those weapons which many former popes had found so effectual, but which did not now cut as sharply as they once did. In France he met with good success. Charles VI. was dead, and his firm resistance to papal exactions was not to be carried out by his weak and hardly pressed successor, Charles VII., the unworthy hero of Joan d'Arc. He yielded speedily to Martin's demands, and gave orders that the Pope's nomination to benefices and collection of annates, etc., should be enforced by the state officials. The Parliament rebelled, but the deed was done.

In England Martin did not carry things with so high a hand. Premunire and provisors were two statutes right across the papal path; no wonder that popes hated them with deadly hatred and lavished on them every imaginable papal curse. Henry V. paid no attention to the passionate entreaties of the Pope that they might be abolished. The Pope tried, in the reign of Henry VI., to stir up the Archbishop of Canterbury, Chichele, reminding him that Becket, when he occupied the see, had not hesitated a moment to sacrifice his life to save the church's rights; but Chichele was a weak spirit, and not at all of the Becket type, though he did strongly hint that all the Pope wanted was money.

Chichele felt that his dignity had been touched by the appointment of Henry Beaufort, uncle of Henry V., legate *a latere*, and the people of England sympathized with him, and they refused to recognize Beaufort in that capacity. The king was opposed even to his being made a cardinal. He was most unpopular, and Shakespeare, in the death scene in the third part of " Henry VI.," expresses the common opinion of him by his contemporaries. The unfortunate Chichele's was the head on which all the vials of papal wrath were poured out. The Pope wrote him to calmly ignore premunire and provisors, as if Englishmen would be likely to stand any such attempt against their liberties. He went before the Parliament and pleaded with it to give up these obnoxious laws, or else he feared an interdict; but this did not frighten the Parliament in the least, and all that they would do for the primate was to agree to write and ask the Pope to treat him more kindly. Martin had to give up the contest, and the statutes remained to be Henry VIII.'s most powerful weapons in breaking off all supremacy of the Pope in England.

Martin V. was now drawing near the end of his career. He just missed being ranked among the great popes, and he deserves more credit than has been generally accorded to him by historians. He did not, indeed, possess any noble, lofty traits of character, had very little spirituality and very little generosity, though his life was free from any stains of evil living; but he possessed in an eminent degree that immensely valuable trait called " common sense." He had great wisdom and great self-control. When one thinks of the mire and filth out of which he raised the Papacy, which had become a scorn and byword to all Christendom, and which the Council of Constance had endeavored to make its creature, we cannot help admiring him.

He bullied and tyrannized over bishops and cardinals, and is as much responsible as any one for the present crouching attitude of the Roman episcopate; but he was very careful about his appointments, and, much as he loved money, never received it in exchange for rich preferments, to be enjoyed by some shameless and utterly incompetent ecclesiastic. He answered perfectly to the American definition of " smart," and never lost an opportunity, when a country had a young king or a weak government, or was disturbed by internal or foreign troubles, of inserting a fresh wedge of papal encroachment, and riveting more closely the fetters of papal exaction. Like most popes, and as was to have been expected of a Colonna with many needy relatives and a great family name to keep up, he was guilty of the most barefaced nepotism, and heaped on his family vast treasures and splendid preferments. If he had lived the Council of Basel would not have been the discordant and little-credited body it proved to be; but he died immediately after convoking it and appointing Cardinal Cesarini to preside over it. Apoplexy carried him off February 20, 1431, and his tomb of brass can be seen now in the baptistery of St. John Lateran.

CHAPTER XXVIII.

THE HUSSITE WAR.

EFORE entering on the pontificate of Martin's successor, it is necessary to review the terrible state of affairs in Bohemia, which had gone on deepening in horror ever since the close of the Council of Constance. The executions of Huss and Jerome of Prague lit a fire in that land which was not extinguished for many a year, and not without the pouring out of oceans of blood, the ruin of many a fair town and many a stately cathedral.

After the burning of Huss, in September, 1415, there was held a great meeting in Bohemia, where four hundred and fifty-two nobles addressed a letter to the Council of Constance, signed by those who could write, and sealed by those who could not, expressing their full trust in Huss, and their conviction of the iniquity of his condemnation, and also affirming themselves to be good Catholics. A few days after they entered into a solemn compact to maintain for six years the doctrine which they thought, and which really was, so important, namely, the allowing the laity to receive the chalice. Their devotion to this doctrine gave them the name of Calixtines, from *calix* ("a chalice"), and more commonly Utraquists, from the Latin words, *sub utraque specie* ("the sacrament under both kinds"). A chalice also formed the device upon their banners. They did not at that time, nor did many of them ever, differ in any other point from the received Roman doctrine.

In March, 1417, the University of Prague communicated to the Council of Constance their decision that the laity should be allowed the chalice; but the council paid no attention to it, and in 1418 Pope Martin launched the bull heretofore noticed against Hussites and Wyclifites, and he then chose precisely the worst man he could have chosen, the Cardinal of Ragusa, to be his legate in Bohemia. This legate began his stupid career by burning a priest and a layman for their Calixtine views, and such foolish and cruel acts roused the Bohemians to fury.

The King of Bohemia, Wenceslas, a drunkard and a laggard, but very popular, now became alarmed, and threw in his lot with the papal party, taking away from the Utraquists all the churches in Prague but two. This only infuriated them more, and, under Nicolas of Hussinetz, and John, commonly called Ziska, either from his having one eye (*ziska* meaning "one-eyed" in Bohemian), or from its being his family name, large bands of Utraquists roamed over the land, enforcing everywhere the use of the sacrament in both kinds. The partisans of that opinion held on July 22, 1419, a vast open-air meeting on a hill, and, from the tents in which the multitude lived and which are called in Bohemian *tabor*, got the name of Taborites. This,

however, was not the origin of the name of the Calixtine town afterwards founded, for the names of the
mountains in Scripture—Tabor, Horeb, Sinai, etc.—
were favorite appellatives with the Taborites. Forty
thousand people were present at this meeting, and
all received the communion in both kinds, no previous
confession, as is the rule in the Church of Rome,
being enforced. The priests celebrated in their civil
costumes, and the strict rule of the Roman Church
about having the communion vessels of metal was
broken, wooden chalices being used, and plain wooden
altars without a cover. The Roman doctrine of the
sacrament was, however, carefully maintained.

This meeting created great enthusiasm among the
Utraquists, and, headed by Ziska, they marched to
Prague, and commenced that series of riots and kill-
ings which were to mark this war, even among the
usual horrors of religious wars, as bloodier and crueller
than any other. How could it be otherwise when we
consider the convictions of the two parties? The
papal party held that no faith was to be kept and no
quarter shown to heretics; heresy being the most
awful of crimes, nothing was to be neglected, no
matter how violent, that could put it down. The
Taborites held that the righteous must be the avengers
of God, and root out all His enemies, and that all in
mortal sin must be put to the sword; and they made
the sweeping statement that all priests and nuns were
ex officio in mortal sin, and therefore must be exter-
minated. It is not meant to say that all Hussites
thought this; but the extreme and fanatical party,
which obtained the ascendency, held these views, and

many others more fanatical, and bitter was the outcome. We see yet the effect, for of the magnificent churches with which Bohemia was filled, no other European country, Eneas Sylvius says, being able in this respect to compete with it, all were destroyed except the chapel of the Hradschin, and we have now only the rococo and tasteless creations of the Jesuits.

The riots at Prague threw the old King Wenceslas into an apoplexy, and in August, 1419, he died, and the crown fell to his brother, the German emperor, Sigismund, who played so important a part at Constance. It was unfortunate, just at this juncture, for Sigismund's conduct towards Huss had set the whole Bohemian nation against him, and the extremists were determined not to recognize him as their sovereign. His first acts of sovereignty were not at all calculated to allay the feeling against him, for he beheaded twenty-three Utraquists at Breslau, and authorized a crusade against the Hussites. This infuriated even the moderate party, and both Utraquists and Taborites (as the extremists were now called) joined to resist the emperor by an appeal to arms. Prague declared for them, and Ziska, with comparatively few fanatical but patriotic partisans, besieged the citadel, which still held for the emperor. Sigismund attempted to relieve it, but the savage peasants, burning with religious zeal, beat to death with their flails four hundred of the attacking nobles, and the emperor fled in disgrace.

The people of Prague now sent Sigismund their ultimatum, which is called " the four articles," and which seems reasonable and fair enough; so fair that the Archbishop of Prague was willing to accept it. These articles were: 1. Freedom for the Hussite preachers, and the Scriptures free to all. 2. Communion in both kinds. 3. The clergy not to hold estates or to meddle with secular affairs. 4. Christianity to be the rule and the appeal in social and civil life. The papalists would, however, hear to none of these things, and nothing came of it.

More unfortunate than all was the fact that the Hussites did not agree among themselves. There was the conservative party, who wished to remain Catholics if they could have the cup, which all on every side acknowledged was a regulation within the power of the church to alter, and not at all a matter of faith; then there was the Ziska party, who wanted to throw off the German rule and do away with the Roman priests and nuns; then came the extreme Taborites, who held that every person was directly inspired by the Holy Ghost, and who rejected transubstantiation; then there was a large party of Millenarians, and even a sect of Adamites, who went about stark naked and practised the most shameless lust. All these parties killed, burned, murdered one another without the slightest compunction, and all joined to hate Sigismund, and they opposed him to some purpose.

His first crusade, in 1421, consisted of an army of two hundred thousand men, which fled before even the rumor of John Ziska's approach. Ziska was a most able general, and one novel mode of warfare instituted by him conveyed terror by its strangeness to every foe. He had the wagons of the country, drawn

by swift horses, arranged according to a certain numbering and lettering, and the drivers so drilled that
each man knew his place; and when a battle began,
these wagons would come thundering down, draw up
in squares, and make throughout the field a hundred
fortified camps to which the hard-pressed Hussites
could retreat behind an impregnable rampart.

A second attempt of Sigismund, in December,
1421, was just as adverse to his fortunes as the first,
and he lost twelve thousand men before Kuttenberg,
January 6, 1422. It is not germane to this book to
follow the Bohemians in their different schemes for
independent government, since all were rendered abor-
tive by their intestine quarrels. Fiercer and more
fierce grew the strife between the moderates and the
extremists, and in 1424 the fury of Ziska was un-
bounded; he harried and burned and killed his fellow-
countrymen without stint. The plague carried him
off that autumn, and his bereaved followers called
themselves "the Orphans." A new leader arose,
called Procopius the Great to distinguish him, Procopius being a very common name in Bohemia. He
was a priest and a noble, and was not such a narrow
type of man as Ziska. He invaded Saxony and laid
siege to Aussitz, and on June 16, 1426, a battle was
fought under the walls of that town, seventy thousand Germans against twenty-five thousand Taborites,
and yet the latter once more prevailed, and ten thousand Germans were left dead on the field.

Once more Procopius, now the idol of Bohemia,
invaded Austria and Silesia; and this time Germany,
thoroughly alarmed, summoned men-at-arms from

every German principality to meet the foe, and two
hundred thousand men were gathered together,
Henry Beaufort, Cardinal of Winchester, among them
as leader and papal legate. He, though a priest, was
a valiant man-at-arms, and when that whole splendid
array fled in dire confusion before the wild shouts of
the oncoming Procopius, he alone tried to rally the
terrified soldiery. This was in 1427, and in 1429
Sigismund endeavored by a conference to bring about
peace, and the Bohemians gave as their ultimatum
the holding of a general council, which should include
deputies from the Greek and Armenian churches (they
both teaching communion in both kinds), and that the
Holy Scriptures, and not the Pope, should be the final
appeal.

Of course this came to naught, and Martin V.
urged Sigismund to undertake another crusade. It
was time, for even Coburg and Baireuth had been
burned by the victorious Procopius. One hundred
thousand men were gathered, and Henry of Winchester brought five thousand English horsemen; but he
could not tarry long, for the victorious career of Joan
of Arc in France forced him to hurry his forces back
to the help of his flying countrymen. All Europe
was now intensely interested in the Hussite question,
and priests bewailed everywhere the fact that their
parishioners were discussing the religious questions
involved, and showing their sympathy with the
Bohemians. Even as far as Spain this trend of popular feeling was noticed.

Martin V. was now urged on every hand to summon the Council of Basel to consider these pressing

questions, and, much as he hated the very name of council, he felt he could not much longer delay. On February 1, 1431, the bull was issued for its convening, and Cardinal Cesarini, charming, popular, able, and conscientious, was appointed to preside over it, with full power to change the place of meeting if necessary, and to confirm its decisions, just as if the Pope were present. Cesarini had before this been sent as legate to Germany, and the news of his appointment to the presidency of the council reached him at Nuremberg. He was at that time plunged in the preparations for a new Bohemian crusade, and he could give but little attention to anything else. This was the state of Bohemian affairs on the 20th of February, 1431, when Martin V. closed his earthly account, and was laid to rest in Rome amid great and very sincere mourning on the part of the Roman citizens, which tribute he had well deserved.

CHAPTER XXIX.

EUGENIUS IV. AND THE COUNCIL OF BASEL.

HERE were fourteen cardinals present in Rome when the hour came to enter into conclave for the election of a new Pope, and the conclave did not meet in the usual place, the Vatican, but in the well-known church of St. Maria sopra Minerva. One strong determination possessed them all, and that was, no longer to permit themselves to be trampled upon as they had been by the late Pope. Martin had been severe with his cardinals, and his manner was so stern that they trembled when he spoke to them; often, when at his country palaces, he would not suffer one to come near him. He was too much of a gentleman to follow the example of Urban VI., and say " Shut your mouth " to them; but he had been a hard master, and the Sacred College was resolved to give itself an easier one. As a prelude to this, they drew up a paper, which every one took oath he would embody in a bull if he were elected Pope. This compact bound the new Pope to engage seriously in the reform of the papal court and the Curia and of the whole church, especially the monastic part of it; not to remove the papal throne from Rome, except with the consent of the cardinals; to do all he could to help on the approaching council at Basel; to make no cardinals except according to the rules laid down at Constance, unless the college requested him to do so; and to be ready always to take the advice of the cardinals and uphold their privileges. They also were vain enough to make a point that whenever the Pope wrote letters to princes, announcing decisions in church matters, the names of the cardinals who had advised the course should be mentioned.

The college, small as it was, had a majority of Italians,—twelve Italians to eight of all other nations, —and an Italian was likely to be chosen. They went into conclave March 1st, and on March 3d took the first vote, which elected Gabriel Condolmieri, a Venetian and Cardinal of St. Clemente, who took the name of Eugenius IV. The reason for choosing him was very evident: he was the least important and the most insignificant of their number; he had no learning and no strength of character, and could, they thought, be easily manipulated.

They repented at their leisure. Eugenius seemed so unfit for his office that the Holy Ghost, as usual, was supposed to have overruled the whole matter, and the Pope had a stock anecdote which he told so often that people ran away when he began again to tell it. He said he was acting as porter when he was a monk at Venice, and a hermit appeared, whom he accompanied to the monastery chapel, and with whom he prayed. When the hermit was leaving, he turned to Eugenius and said,

" You will be made cardinal, and then Pope, and you will suffer great adversity."

The Pope was a handsome man, forty-eight years old, and graced well the papal ceremonies; and he was a man of unblemished character, and passed much of his time at his devotions. He was a thorough type of the true monk, austere, narrow, and with the extremest notions of the power of a Pope and the duty of a Pope. His one absorbing thought was to put down heresy and root out heretics, no matter how; if mild measures could not do it, kill, burn, behead. He had not one tenth part of the wisdom of Martin, as the Romans soon found out, and his very first acts showed his hardness towards his enemies, or rather the enemies of the church; for Eugenius had no personal ambition and no personal ends to serve.

Martin V., as was natural, had shown every favor possible to the Colonna family, and he left behind him vast sums of money in the hands of his nephews. This money had ostensibly been collected for a crusade against the Turks, and Eugenius was right in thinking that it ought to be paid over to him. Part was paid, but he knew there was much more kept back, and he pressed for it. The Colonnas hated to disgorge, and Stephen, the head of the house, attacked Rome, believing the people would rise to his support. He was mistaken; they rose on the Pope's side, and he laid hands on all the Colonnas in Rome. Dire was his vengeance: he took off the heads of two hundred of their partisans, tore down their palaces, Martin's included, and chiselled out the late Pope's arms wherever they occurred. He also issued a decree taking away every rood of ground and every cent of income from every Colonna. This brought that haughty family to their senses, and a peace was made, by which Antonio Colonna paid seventy-five thousand ducats to the Pope, and gave up all his castles in the Romagna. Eugenius had then leisure to turn his attention to the States of the Church, which were in a flame of revolt, for the chief cities, as soon as Martin's strong hand was removed, had refused to pay taxes or acknowledge the Pope's officers. The free companies who were hired by the Pope soon brought them to terms, and, this being all arranged, Eugenius now occupied himself with arranging the Council of Basel.

Wealthy and important as Basel now is among the Swiss cities, it is not as populous as it was in the fourteenth century, before the Black Death raged in it with peculiar ferocity. The classic Romans had important fortifications there, and it was, as all cities were in the middle ages, surrounded by walls which have now been turned into shady boulevards. The Rhine divides it into two parts; it is well built, but beyond the cathedral there is no building of any great beauty or of much historical importance. The cathedral was founded in the beginning of the eleventh century by Henry II. of Germany. Calvinistic sternness has deprived it of all internal beauty, and it doubtless presented a very different appearance when the council gathered for its opening ceremonies. The hall in which the council met is still shown in Basel. It was a free, imperial city, and it ruled over much of the adjacent country with an iron hand. It did not formally join the Swiss confederacy until 1501.

As has been said, the appointed president, Cardinal Cesarini, was too busy with the Hussite difficulties to be present at the opening; but he sent two deputies, John of Paloman and John of Ragusa, who came and went through the regular ceremonial of opening on the 23d of July, 1431. It was a sorry contrast to the crowded splendor of the Council of Constance, for only three bishops, seven abbots, and a few doctors were present. The roads were unsafe, the times very unsettled, and the bishops very doubtful about leaving their dioceses. There were too few to attempt anything, and things dragged along until Cesarini arrived, September 9th. His first step was to drum up recruits, and letters were sent in all directions begging the attendance of bishops and doctors.

Discussions then commenced as to what work they would undertake, and the opinion was that they could put down heresy, reform the church, unite the Greeks, and institute a crusade against the Turks—a large contract for so few men. It was considered unwise as yet to arrange the way of voting, although, as events proved, they gained no wisdom by waiting, for it was to the injudicious arrangement of votes that the council owes the small credit it has ever received. Cesarini's letters to the Bohemians and to the Pope are models of prudence, keen foresight, Christian charity, and noble aspiration. The Bohemians were begged to send to the council representatives of all parties, taking care that they were men of learning, of piety, and of wisdom. They were promised a free hearing and perfect personal safety, and the letter roused no sleeping dogs.

But this mild letter to those whom the Pope chose to call heretics aroused the suspicions of Eugenius, who, moreover, did not at all like the democratic spirit shown at Basel. It was very evident from the beginning that the voting would not be done by cardinals alone, and that was enough to set the Pope against the council, which he plainly hated from the beginning. He wrote to Cesarini, empowering him to dissolve the council and call another at Bologna in a year and a half. The reasons given were plausible enough: that so few had come; that war between Austria and Burgundy would hinder travel; that the Greek emperor had promised to come to a council held in an Italian city, but would not cross the Alps. He sent on a bull of dissolution to Basel by his treasurer, but the latter found that such a hornets' nest was raised by the mere knowledge that he had such a document that he thought it wise to vanish and leave his bulls behind, to get published as best they might.

It was then Cesarini wrote his famous letter to the Pope, which is one of the most interesting documents among the abundant literature of the Council of Basel. Milman gives an excellent résumé of it, taken from Eneas Sylvius, and the following is taken from Milman. " This council," Cesarini says, " is the only hope of union and success, and I receive an order to dissolve it. Your reasons do not hold water. Bishops are gathering from all quarters, the emperor has taken the council under his protection, and Austria and Burgundy have proclaimed a truce. We have tried arms in vain ; if you really wish to reconcile the Bohemians, this council is the only way. If this be dissolved, all heretics will laugh in our faces and say that the Catholic Church is afraid of them. Is your Holiness aware of the deep, unquenchable feeling in the minds of all about reform? Its long delay is working like a ferment in men's minds. Magdeburg has expelled her archbishop and clergy, Passau has expelled hers, and Bamberg is likely to follow suit. Indeed, all over Germany, in Aix, Cologne, Spires, Strasburg, and elsewhere, the burghers are struggling to throw off the ecclesiastical rule. Something must be done, and we will lose our temporalities, as well as our souls, if this council be dissolved. The Germans especially will not stand it, and there will be another great schism in the church if this council is closed. Wait until July at least; wait until we have done something."

The letter was all very well, but the council, which had now greatly increased, seemed to care very little what the Pope did, and, without waiting for any answer to the cardinal's letter, held its first session December 14th, when the Bishop of Constance said mass. This session directed that the three subjects for discussion should be the extinction of heresy, the restoration of the unity of the church, and the reformation of the clergy. The system of voting was also arranged, and this was the fountain and the origin of all the errors of the council. It will be remembered that at Constance the voting was by " nations." It was resolved not to continue this for two reasons: one was the jealousy it had created, and the other

was that by that system the cardinals all voted together as a separate nation and always supported
the Pope. It was resolved now to create four " deputations," or committees, to take charge of (1) faith,
(2) unity, (3) reformation, (4) general business. These
four committees were chosen out of every " nation "
and of every rank—bishops, parish priests, doctors
of law, monks. These committees were reconstructed
every four months, and they chose a new president
every month. A committee of twelve, chosen from
the five great countries, decided who should belong
to the deputations, and through them to the council.
The reports of the deputations were submitted to a
general congregation, which promulgated the decrees.

This looks fair enough, and many of its features
are in general and efficient use now in deliberative
assemblies; but it did not work well at Basel, for the
reason that the influence of the prelates and high
dignitaries of the church was entirely swamped in the
number of inferior clergy who were allowed to vote.
Men of learning and position shrank from the fierce
democracy, got out of the way, quietly left Basel.
The personnel was all the time changing, and the
thread of business was lost. Eneas Sylvius says that
cooks and stable-boys got in to vote, but this is beyond doubt a gross exaggeration. It shows, however,
that there was great looseness in this most important
matter.

While, then, it is true that the Council of Basel
passed many wise and judicious measures for the
reform of the church, and showed a toleration but
rarely exhibited in a general council, it is also true

that the way in which its measures were passed, and the hasty and inconsiderate action often shown, have greatly discredited the council, especially with the Roman and Anglican communions. Another point which makes against the council is the too great predominance of Germans and French. Spaniards, Italians, and English could not in any numbers undertake the long journey. The small account taken of this council in the Roman communion was very evident in the matter of the dogma of the immaculate conception. Basel had declared favorably for that, but its declaration counted for nothing in the council of 1854, which decided the question without any reference to it.

CHAPTER XXX.

CONTINUATION OF THE COUNCIL OF BASEL.

HE coldness that the Pope had shown towards the council was somewhat counteracted by the news from France that, at a large meeting of the clergy at Bourges, the course of the Basel fathers had been enthusiastically commended; and the Calixtines sent the council word that they were willing to negotiate on the basis of the four articles. It was resolved to send representatives to Eger, that the preliminaries of a meeting might be arranged. Sigismund also endeavored to induce the Pope to take a more favorable view of the council, but Eugenius answered his letters sarcastically, saying, "You had better let canons and councils alone, and stick to fighting, in which you have been so successful." This cut deep, for Sigismund's success in the field had not been very remarkable. The history of Sigismund's visit to Rome to be crowned, and all his troubles and vexations in Italian affairs, will not be considered in this book. He advised the council not to pay any attention to the Pope's reiterated order to dissolve, but to invite him to Basel. They took his advice, and on April 29, 1432, the council summoned the Pope either to come in person or to send representatives within three months.

This was not calculated to mollify Eugenius, who proceeded to heap upon the assembled fathers a choice vocabulary of papal epithets, among which "synagogue of Satan" was the least objectionable. He insinuated that any person who would put an end to these rebels would be well pleasing to God. His curses, however, acted as blessings to the council, for it increased in numbers every day, and daily received letters of commendation from the powers of Europe. Cardinals began to slip away from the Pope to the council, and one of them, Capranica, brought with him as secretary a young man of brilliant parts, to whose literary labors we are very much indebted for a great deal of information about the council, and of whom much was to be heard in the future; for his name was Eneas Sylvius, afterwards Pope Pius II. His youth had been most dissolute, and his morals were never very severe, but his great ability rapidly advanced him.

At the second session of the council, February 15, 1432, the celebrated and much-discussed decree of Constance was renewed, declaring general councils to derive their authority direct from Christ, and to be superior even to the authority of the Pope. It was in the third session that the summons to the Pope was decided upon. At the fourth session, June 20, 1432, it was decreed that if during the council the Pope should die, the election of his successor must take place wherever the council was meeting. It was also decreed that the Pope should make no cardinals while the council lasted. The fathers took the great liberty of appointing a governor for the Avignon territory over the head of Eugenius's own nephew, appointed by himself. At the fifth session the council met the objections of the Pope to Basel, and stated that if he interfered with their work he would be grieving the Holy Spirit. At the sixth session the council came near pronouncing the Pope contumacious, but his legates interceded and obtained for him further time. On December 18th sixty days' further time was given Eugenius to revoke the bull of dissolution and approve the council.

On the 4th of January, 1433, the Bohemian representatives, seven nobles and eight priests, with Procopius at their head, entered Basel. The citizens had been lectured severely as to their behavior while the Bohemians were there, for it was reported that they were great Puritans and would be shocked at the light behavior of the Balese. These deputies, strangely dressed and savage-looking, were a great show; but Cesarini set the example of treating them with the utmost courtesy.

On the Epiphany, January 6th, they celebrated the festival in their own lodgings, for no church was allowed them. Their simple forms were objects of great curiosity, and such crowds flocked to see them that Cesarini was afraid they might alienate people from the ordinary mass; but the excitement did not last long; very few persisted in going.

The discussion on the Bohemian question commenced on January 16, 1433, and was one of the most interminable, wordiest, and most wearying ever heard, although many of the speakers were eminent men. Some of the speeches were eight days long, and the whole subject consumed fifty days. The Bohemian Rokyczana was the most eloquent and one of the longest winded; but John of Ragusa, on the part of the council, held forth steadily from January 31st to February 12th. The weary council found that nothing would come of this unending oratory, and they appointed fifteen members to endeavor to arrange matters in private with the fifteen Bohemians. The tact and the Christian courtesy and charity of Cesarini prevented any violent language, though the discussions were often very heated, and the tolerance and good temper of the council are to be commended in the highest degree.

The council could not be brought to accept the four articles, though they were willing to tolerate much in the Bohemian church not allowable elsewhere. With the hope of peace, they sent a deputation to Prague with the returning Bohemians, who left Basel amid the kindest feelings and with a deep sense of the courtesy shown them. This deputation could bring about no conclusion, and returned to the council to report that the Bohemians differed so among themselves that any union seemed improbable. Another embassy was sent, and after oceans of words and much diplomacy and wire-pulling, on November 30, 1433, the Bohemian Diet accepted the following propositions from the council: 1. Those who so desired could receive the holy eucharist in both kinds, but the clergy must explain that our Lord is perfectly present in each kind. 2. Private persons have no right to punish sins or crimes; it belongs to those whose duty it lawfully was, clergy over clergy, and laity over laity. 3. For the sake of order, preachers must be authorized by their superiors, namely, the bishops and deans. 4. Individual priests might inherit fortunes and the churches might possess temporalities, with the understanding always that such property was faithfully administered. Around this " compact," as it was called, all the moderate Bohemians rallied, for the land was weary of war and stricken with plague; but the Orphans and the extreme Taborites would not hear to it, and each side again had to resort to arms. The great battle of Lepan, where thirteen thousand Taborites fell, settled the question in favor of the adherents of the council. Fanaticism no longer had the upper hand in Bohemia, and gradually moderate views and temperate counsels prevailed.

After the Bohemian debate at Basel the council turned its attention to the burning question of the relations between it and the Pope. In February, 1433, the Pope had word that the council was about to proceed with his impeachment, and, finding that Sigismund was now strongly on the Basel side, felt that he could not longer, with any safety to himself, keep up the high-handed course he had hitherto pursued. He tried every way to move the council to some other place; suggested Bologna, then any city in Italy, and at last any city in Germany; but the sturdy fathers of Basel would not be transferred, and at last, driven to the wall, he issued a bull agreeing that the council should be held at Basel, and naming (March 1st) four cardinals as legates and presidents. The bull, however, struck the council as very vague. It agreed that a council could be held at Basel, but it ignored the existing council, and it did not mention the reform of the church as one of the points for discussion. The members of the council saw through this transparency, and on April 27th they decreed that general councils should be held every tenth year, and could get together at the appointed time, Pope or no Pope consenting; that a Pope trying to impede a council laid himself open to deposition or suspension; and that the present council could not be transferred unless two thirds of each deputation wished it, and two thirds of a general session approved it. Every cardinal was to take oath that if he were promoted to be Pope he would obey the Constance decrees. These were noble decisions, and great would have been the change in the Western Church if they had been carried out; but they were, for the most part, mere waste words.

When the papal legates arrived, they expected to share the presidency of the council with Cesarini, but the council demurred. They feared the " Greeks bringing gifts," and above all they feared the evident understanding going on between the emperor and the Pope, who was dangling a coronation before Sigismund's eager eyes. The emperor, as fortune favored or repelled him, was now on this side, now on that, but he tried hard to keep the fathers from indicting the Pope. He secured sixty days' extension of time for him in which to answer the charges against him, and the emperor, really anxious to avoid another

schism, strained every nerve to get the whole indictment quashed. He induced the Pope, August 1st,
to issue another bull, acquiescing in the council from
the beginning, and asking that his legates be admitted
and his trial abandoned. This bull did not satisfy
any more than the other. The men at Basel did not
intend to be merely tolerated; they insisted that the
Pope should decree that Basel from the first had been
a valid council. Sympathy, however, now turned
towards the Pope, and several governments notified
Basel that it ought to be satisfied with the bull.
Thirty days more were then granted the Pope; before they had expired Sigismund came in person,
October 11th. He pleaded hard for the Pope, who
was busily engaged, he said, in the work of reformation; and after endless talk he procured from the
council, on November 7th, a further extension of
ninety days.

The Pope was having a hard time at home. The
Duke of Milan and other Italian princelets were arrayed against him, and he had alienated all his friends.
He was obliged most unwillingly to fully clear himself with the council, for there could be no peace for
him unless he made peace with it. Hard necessity
then forced from him a bull, on January 30, 1434,
without any reservations whatever. The council was
valid from the beginning, it said, and had the full
adhesion of the Pope. Great was the joy of the
fathers over their triumph, and with much ceremony,
on February 3d, they expressed themselves satisfied,
and admitted the papal legates to the co-presidency,
they swearing to the Constance decrees about the

supremacy of a council to the Pope. Certainly this would seem to carry the papal sanction of that council with it. Everybody at Basel thought so, and Sigismund, while disappointed at the small figure he had cut in the transaction, felt that he need no longer remain at Basel, which he left with much pomp on May 19, 1434.

The great concessions of Eugenius did not bring him the peace he expected. The popes at that time slept on a volcano, and on the 29th of May the Roman populace flew to arms on account of the haughty manner of the Pope's nephew in receiving some requests from them. Once again the old cry of " Roman republic " echoed through the streets, and the Pope, seeing a prison looming up before him, managed, as his predecessors had done and his successors would do, to escape in disguise. He embarked in a little fishing-boat, and was rowed swiftly down the Tiber; not swiftly enough, however, to prevent discovery, and stones and arrows rained upon the boat from angry Romans on either bank. But the little craft passed safely through; Eugenius reached Ostia in safety, sailed thence to Pisa, and so to Florence, where he found refuge in the monastery of St. Maria Novella.

CHAPTER XXXI.

CONTINUATION OF THE COUNCIL.

EFORE the emperor left Basel, he brought to the notice of the council, by the mouth of the Bishop of Lübeck, a most important matter, viz., the celibacy of the clergy. The bishop laid before each deputation a weighty arraignment of the morals of the clergy, which, he justly said, nothing would remedy but the permission to marry. He made the sweeping charge that the whole body of the clergy was living in concubinage or adultery. Laymen, he said, would not allow their wives to go to confession, and public odium everywhere rested on the priestly caste. There was a general fear that the property of the church would be alienated to the children of priests. Greek priests married, the Jewish priests always married; why could not Catholic priests do the same, and avoid this awful scandal? His plea found many supporters, and it is worth while to recall the words of the aged Cardinal of St. Peter's: " Although I am an old man, and have no inclination to matrimony, yet I think it would be a holy act to ' restore ' their wives to the clergy, for the grace of being able to resist the law

of the flesh is not given to all men." Pity it was
that the fierce opposition of the monks caused this
question to be smothered as being untimely and not
properly to be considered then.

The council was now much more frequented, and
the year 1434 was its most prosperous time. The
most prominent men in it were Louis of Arles, who
was afterwards its president, the Archbishop of Palermo, Cesarini, and, above all, Eneas Sylvius, and
Nicolas of Cusa, a Hollander, much interested in the
reform of the clergy and the success of the council,
until his sense of loyalty to the Pope induced him to
leave it and go over to the Pope's council at Florence.

It must not be thought, because so much has been
said about the Bohemian difficulties and the quarrel
with the Pope, that the council did not devote much
time to the crying evils in the church, which it had
been summoned to reform. Its subsequent conduct
nullified much of the good which the decrees it passed
might have effected, but that they were passed shows
how strong a party there was in the church for reformation. Robertson sums up as follows the questions which it decided : " Decrees were passed for the
entire freedom of elections in churches, against simony,
expectations, usurpations of patronage, reservations,
and, above all, annates ; against frivolous appeals, the
abuse of interdicts, the concubinage of the clergy,
and the burlesque festivals held in churches. Rules
were laid down as to the election of popes and their
conduct. Each Pope was to profess his allegiance to
the Constance decrees, and every year, at his anni-
versary mass, this profession was to be read over to

him.   There were to be but twenty-four cardinals, taken from all countries, none to be admitted without the consent of the others, and the nephew of a Pope was not eligible to the cardinalate."

Let us turn now to a subject long uppermost in men's minds, and one of the subjects for the consideration of which the council had met: the reunion of the Greek and Latin churches.   Ambassadors from Greece arrived in Basel July 12, 1434, and proposed a conference.   Their terms were, all expenses paid, and the place of meeting to be in Italy, or, anyway, a city on the other side of the Alps, as they would not consent to cross them.   After the manner of Greeks, they were dickering with the Pope at the same time, and each party was most anxious to obtain the feather for its cap of having brought about the meeting.   The Pope was willing to let it take place in Constantinople, but the fathers at Basel were determined not to allow it to be held beyond the Alps. The Pope saw his opportunity; he saw that he could make it appear that he, and not the council, was anxious about this matter, and that they would make no concessions, while he was willing to accommodate the Greeks.   This would give him immense preponderance with both Greeks and Latins.

The council, after a good deal of huckstering with different cities which were trying to secure the place, had agreed, by a vote of two hundred and forty-two out of three hundred and fifty-five, to adjourn to Avignon; but this vote had not been fairly obtained.   It had only been made possible by calling in every parish priest around Basel who could possibly be procured, and allowing every one to vote. This most unwise and unusual proceeding much disgusted Cesarini and the more moderate and conservative prelates. The Pope did not lose the chance; he sent the Archbishop of Tarentum as a new legate to accompany the Greek ambassadors who had been with him in Bologna. Avignon had failed to fulfil its contract about the money necessary for the expenses of the Greek embassy, and the time stipulated being up, April 12, 1437, Cesarini pleaded that another place should be chosen. The new legate supported him. The papal party could only muster seventy votes, while their opponents could count on two hundred; but the minority was resolved not to submit.

No agreement could be reached, and on May 7th the conflict came to a head in one of the most shameful scenes of disorder a council had ever witnessed. The decree of the majority adjourning to Avignon was to be read by the Bishop of Albienza from the pulpit of the cathedral. The moment he began to read, the Bishop of Porto, in another part of the church, jumped on a table, armed men closing in around him, and began to read the minority decree for Bologna. One reader strove to outyell the other, and the poor Cardinal of Arles shouted vainly for order. First one side sang Te Deum, then the other, and the service ended in the wildest confusion. The next thing was to affix the seal of the council to the document; but the seal, which had three custodians, was stolen out of its box, and was found to be affixed to both majority and minority decrees. Amid the wildest confusion, the Archbishop of Tarentum avowed himself to be the thief, and justified his act by his duty to the church and the Pope. After this avowal he thought it wise to vanish from Basel as soon as possible. He forwarded the minority decree to the Pope, who accepted it as the true decision of the council, and on September 8th published a bull allowing that body to remain thirty days at Basel, and then transferring it to Ferrara, where those of Basel who adhered to him, and all other prelates whom he could induce to attend, met and opened a council January 8, 1438.

This council will be separately considered. Let us return to the Council of Basel, which, however much it might decree and storm and assert itself, lost ground from the beginning of the proceedings at Ferrara. Naturally the action of the minority had greatly angered the majority, already very hostile to the Pope, and determined to humble him, as they had already shown by depriving him of that large part of his income called " annates." On the 31st of July new charges were made against Eugenius, among which was one that he intended to sell Avignon to pay for the Greek expenses. He was cited to appear in person or by proctor within sixty days. At the twenty-eighth session, October 1, 1437, his neglect to answer was formally reported, and he was pronounced in contumacy. In vain Sigismund wrote and protested, but in December of that year his voice was closed by death, and, whatever his faults, it must be said of him that he had labored hard and earnestly to prevent schism.

Cesarini felt that he could no longer countenance

the irregular and anarchical doings at Basel, and, full
of bitter disappointment that the six years he had
spent there in the interests of peace and reform had
been spent in vain, he left Basel January 9, 1438, and
Louis d'Allemand, Cardinal of Arles, was elected
president in his place. The legates, of course, had
retired long before. The council received some crumbs
of comfort from the Synod of Bourges, July, 1448,
which put forth a celebrated document called the
"pragmatic sanction," interesting not only because
it accepted the reforming decrees of Basel, but because it asserted boldly the independence of a national church, and its right to review the decisions
of a general council. A German diet at Mayence in
March, 1439, also indorsed the Basel reforms, but
did not commit itself to the quarrel between Pope
and council. Apart from these, it was evident that
the council aroused but a lukewarm interest in kings
and senates.

Now that the greater part of the moderate members had withdrawn, the council went on with its attack on the Pope with renewed fierceness. The charges
against him were one hundred and fifty in number,
most of them repetitions, and many of them absurd.
It was, however, after much talking agreed, about
the middle of April, 1439, to discuss and vote upon
eight propositions: (1) that it is a truth that a general
council has power over a Pope; (2) also a truth that
a Pope cannot *proprio motu* transfer or dissolve a
general council; (3) any one who says these things
are not so is a heretic; (4) Eugenius IV. implicitly
denied these things when he first attempted to dis-

solve this council; (5) but he withdrew his denial when the council remonstrated; (6) his second attempt, however, to dissolve the council contravenes the truth of the first two propositions; (7) his persistence in this act shows him a lapsed heretic; (8) by calling a new council he shows himself a persistent schismatic.

Then came days of heated discussion on these points, the Pope's side being led by the Archbishop of Palermo, and the other side by the Cardinal of Arles, who was far more than a match for his opponent, and as a speaker and party leader has rarely been surpassed. When the time came to vote, there was the wildest confusion, and at last, in the most arbitrary manner, raising his voice above all the din, D'Allemand cried out, " I declare the first three propositions passed," and closed the session. At the next session there was more confusion and greater noise, the Archbishop of Palermo protesting and complaining bitterly that he had been outwitted. He and a number of others then left the room. The general session for publishing the decree was held May 16th, but the merest fragment of the episcopacy was present—no Spaniards, one Italian, and from all other kingdoms only twenty. The president did a thing which, even to those believing in the inherent efficacy of relics, must appear ridiculous. He gathered together all the relics, leg-bones of saints, etc., which could be found in Basel, and put them in the vacant seats of the bishops. It was a curious substitute, but history records that the great crowd wept over it as a most moving spectacle. There was one comfort: the relics could not vote; D'Allemand had it all his own way, and the decree was passed.

On June 23d the other five propositions were passed, and on June 25th there was another session, at which a small number of bishops were present, and between three and four hundred of the lower clergy. The Pope was deposed, and all the usual epithets of contumely were heaped upon him. He was declared to be guilty of simony and perjury, a schismatic, a damnable heretic, etc. All Christians were released from their oath of fealty to him, and he was styled Gabriel Condolmieri. Nothing that he did or said was to be counted of any authority. This, of course, was principally aimed against the proceedings at Ferrara and Florence.

The next step was the election of a new Pope; but the plague was raging violently in Basel; five thousand of its citizens, and many of the attendants on the council, died of it that summer, and the sittings of that body had to be abandoned. It met again in October, Eugenius in the meantime having cursed its adherents in the choicest language. They were a "horde of robbers, and an assemblage of all the devils in the universe" to consummate their work of iniquity in desolating the church of God. The first business was, of course, the election of a Pope, and the first question, Who should vote? There was only one cardinal now left in the council, D'Allemand of Arles, and, as the choice of a Pope could not be left solely to him (although he really did choose him), it was necessary to arrange a body of electors. The number was fixed at thirty-three, and a nominating committee was chosen, empowered to select twenty-nine others besides themselves. The committee showed the greatest wisdom, as was demonstrated by the approval with which their choice was received.

The electors were twelve bishops, the Cardinal of Arles being one, seven abbots, five theologians, and nine doctors, all these being in priest's orders. The conclave was fixed for October 30, 1439. The Cardinal of Arles, as has been already said, had a candidate in his mind who, he felt tolerably sure, would be elected. He knew that some one of some political weight must be chosen, and there was one man eligible, who was both a person of exalted political position and a sort of ecclesiastic—Amadeus VIII., Duke of Savoy, ancestor of King Humbert, who, overcome with grief at the death of his eldest son, had resigned his dukedom and retired with seven of his friends to a quasi-hermitage at Ripaille. The life they led there was probably not a very ascetic one, or we would scarcely have had the French phrase "faire ripaille," meaning to make extraordinary good cheer; but there is no good reason to suppose that it was marked by any low or unworthy conditions. Much that was uncharitably said against it was said by bitter enemies of the antipope, and from them also sprang the report that Amadeus had given up the dukedom and put on this semblance of hermit life so that he would stand a better chance of being chosen Pope when the time came. When one thinks how heavy and thankless a charge the place of rival Pope was likely to be, it does not seem probable that a man would give up the dukedom of Savoy for it.

That point, however, cannot well be settled; suffice it to say that on the sixth day of the conclave the choice of the electors fell on the Duke of Savoy, who, when he was notified of his election, professed great unwillingness to accept the office. He stipulated that he should retain his name and his beard; but he yielded the first point, and was called Felix, and when he saw how odd he looked amid all the clean-shaven bishops and priests, he consented to be shaved. He was not in holy orders at the time of his election, but neither was Martin V. That defect was readily remedied, and he was crowned at Basel July 23, 1440, with great pomp, the Cardinal of Arles officiating, and the duke's two sons assisting at the mass, a strange sight indeed. One reason for choosing him had been his wealth, for no one knew where to raise any income for another Pope, since Eugenius held all the papal territory. Amadeus, however, did not much relish the idea of being expected to support himself, and said indignantly, " You have abolished annates; on what do you expect the Pope to live ? I cannot use up all my patrimony and leave my sons penniless." The council then put the tax of a fifth-penny on all benefices for the Pope's maintenance; but it was an empty decree, for the tax never could be collected, and the new Pope had to pay his own expenses.

It is needless to say that both popes now fired volleys of anathemas and curses at each other, and Eugenius even went the length of pronouncing the degradation of the archbishops of Cologne and Treves, who adhered to Felix; but nobody paid much attention to him. Indeed, the changed state of things was very evident in the apathetic way with which the question of the two popes was treated by the kings of Christendom. France called Felix " Monsieur de Savoie," and the German emperor was very careful not to say " your Holiness " to him. The important kingdoms either adhered to Eugenius or played fast and loose.

At the forty-third session of the council, July 1, 1441, the feast of the Visitation of the Blessed Virgin, July 2d, was decreed, but nothing more of any importance took place at Basel. Fewer and fewer became its members, especially among prelates of any standing. It dragged along until June 16, 1443, when it fixed on Lyons as the place of meeting of the next general council; and this may practically be counted its last session, although it pretended to live a few years longer. It is not proposed to trace further the history of either Eugenius or the antipope Felix, who amounted to nothing. The scope of this volume extends no further than the Council of Basel, although the story of the Pope's council at Ferrara and Florence will be given in a separate chapter.

While some Protestant writers consider Basel of great authority, it is generally discredited throughout the Roman communion, and has but little weight with Anglican historians. It began well, and many of its acts were of the highest importance; but it killed itself by its own loose methods of admitting members, and by the confusion and quarrels which marked its closing years. It falls far below Constance or Pisa in that great trio of reforming councils. Many of the principles for which the reforming party contended in these three councils have become, the Vatican Council to the contrary notwithstanding, the working principles of the modern Roman Church. Popes no longer depose princes and absolve subjects from their allegiance; cardinals can no longer hold a dozen sees and pocket their revenues; heretics cannot be burned or beheaded. The law of libel will soon clap in prison an over-zealous bishop who excommunicates, and indulgences, while still granted, are not now hawked about the country. The same dogmas may be held by Leo XIII. as by Eugenius IV., but they are often held only as a theory, not as possible to be put in practice; and day by day, in spite of the constant cry of Rome that only by entire submission to her can there be any union of the faithful, facts show that the differences are being softened and the distances lessened.

CHAPTER XXXII.

THE COUNCIL OF FERRARA AND FLORENCE.

HE Council of Basel and Pope Eugenius bid against each other for the Greek deputies, coming to the West to beg for aid against the ever-encroaching Turk, who had gradually snatched from them their vast empire and left them very little more than the city of Constantinople. The price of the aid was to be submission to the Bishop of Rome, and an abjuration of certain points in the Greek dogma and discipline. The Pope had the most money and the most flattering tongue, and he captured the prize. He hired galleys from the Venetians to transport the embassy, and on the 29th of November, 1437, the Emperor of Constantinople, John Palæologus, the Patriarch Joasaph, twenty-two bishops, and a great train of priests and nobles, five hundred in all, all furnished with splendid clothes, and the theologians armed with ponderous tomes of Greek theology, set sail for Venice, where they were received with a pomp which dazzled even their eyes, accustomed as they were to Oriental splendor. This was February 8, 1438. The Pope was to meet them at Ferrara, and early in March the Emperor John reached there, passing the patriarch on the road, very much nettled at being left behind. The Pope met him at the palace gate and prevented him from kneeling, kissed him, and gave him a seat at his right. The Pope's chamberlains lifted up the papal cassock and got the Pope's foot all ready to kiss; but the Greeks played they did not see it.

A day or two afterwards came the patriarch, who was told that he would be expected to kiss the Pope's foot. He absolutely refused. "If the Pope be the successor of St. Peter," he said, "we are successors of the other apostles. Did they kiss Peter's foot?" He threatened to turn about and go home, and would have done so if Eugenius had not compromised. The foot-kissing was given up, and the Pope received him with a chaste salute, seating him, very much to his annoyance, on a level with the cardinals. As neither Pope nor patriarch could understand each other an interpreter had to be called in. The thin-skinned Greeks were determined not to see their patriarch put down, and when they went to inspect the church where the council was to be held, and saw the high-placed throne for the Pope alone, they vowed, emperor and all, that they would not go near it unless different arrangements were made. The Pope's chair was then lowered several pegs; on his right was a vacant chair for the Emperor of the West and the Latins, on his left a chair for the Eastern emperor, and next him the patriarch and the other Greek dignitaries. The Greek emperor declined to begin business until some of the Western potentates, who were conspicuous by their absence, should appear, and a long time was wasted waiting for them; but the Duke of Burgundy alone was represented.

At last the persuasive tongue of Cardinal Cesarini induced the Greeks to consent to the opening of the discussions, and they began June 4, 1438. The leaders on the Latin side were Cesarini and John of Montenegro, and on the Greek side Bessarion, Bishop of Nicea, and Mark of Ephesus. Four points were considered the most important, and these only were to be discussed: (1) the procession of the Holy Spirit; (2) purgatory; (3) leavened bread in the holy communion; (4) the supremacy of the Pope. The doctrine of purgatory was first taken up. The Latin doctrine was that sins not repented of during life are purged by material fire; but the Greek doctrine taught that they are purged by pain and grief, but by no physical torment. The Greeks taught also that neither punishment nor reward is complete until after the resurrection. The Latins admitted this about punishment, but held that the blessed enjoyed perfect happiness in heaven, though it could not be deemed eternal happiness until after the judgment. These first conferences showed plainly that, while the Latins were perfectly agreed on their doctrine, the Greeks differed greatly among themselves; but a long discussion did not disclose very much important difference between the two churches.

The conferences were now interrupted by the breaking out of the plague in Ferrara, and of the one hundred and fifty bishops present at the opening scarce fifty remained. The Greeks were very much frightened, and many ran away, but were caught and brought back. Some few did get away and reached Constantinople, where, by the orders of the patriarch, they were flogged for cowardice. It was October before another session of the council could be held, and the question then was the doctrine of the procession of the Holy Ghost.

The Nicene Creed in its original form read, " We believe in the Holy Ghost, who proceedeth from the Father;" but in the Western Church it had been thought that this expression was not clear, and derogated from the dignity of the Son; so the words had been added, at times and places not necessary to note here, " Filioque " ("and from the Son "). The Greeks, great metaphysicians, thought this threw into dispute the doctrine of the Trinity. The modern opinion in the Western Church seems to be that, while the addition was unfortunate, it does not teach any heresy or change any doctrine, and its being there is not important. Of course there are theologians who fiercely deny this and battle for its removal from the creed; and if there is ever to be a union between the Greek and Latin churches the " Filioque " will probably have to be dropped; not that the two churches really hold any different doctrine about the Holy Spirit, but because the Greek Church holds that without a universal council no words ought to be added to or taken away from the creeds. There is no doubt that political feeling and ecclesiastical jealousy between the two churches had magnified this difference until it came to have, and still has, an importance it little deserves. One party of the Greeks wanted to discuss first the question, " Ought an addition ever to be made to the creeds?" and then to come to the discussion of the Double Procession. This course was chosen, and an interminable talk took place upon it, which very evidently would lead to no result. The astute Cesarini, with immense difficulty, and only successful because the news came that Constantinople was dangerously threatened by the Turks, at last extorted from the Greeks a consent to discuss the doctrine.

The Pope was anxious to transfer the council to Florence, for the plague was raging at Ferrara, the Duke of Milan's general was plundering the neighborhood, so that no money reached the papal coffers, and the Florentines had promised him a good round sum if he would move the council there. The Greeks were very loath to go, for they dreaded the mountain crossing, and they did not wish to go any farther from their own land. The all-powerful argument was, however, brought to bear upon them, " Unless you come you get no money, and we are all going; what will you do then?" So they yielded, and by February 16, 1439, all parties were safe in Florence and ready to begin the weary controversy. The Emperor John was much cast down, for, subtle Greek that he was, he had hoped to play off the Council of Basel against the Pope, and by holding out hopes to both sides to get money out of both; but he found that nobody cared much about the Council of Basel, and that it could do him no good. His only hope, he saw, was in the Pope, who was going to be a hard taskmaster and make hard terms, which the emperor, as it afterwards proved, would find much difficulty in carrying out on his return.

On the 2d of March, 1439, the public discussion on the doctrine of the Double Procession was begun, the principal speakers, and very long-winded ones they were, being, on the papal side John of Montenegro, and on the Greek side Mark of Ephesus. Only Greek manuscripts were to be used as authorities. It is useless to consider in detail the controversy; but at last a statement of John that "the Latin Church recognized the Father as the only source of the Son and of the Holy Ghost" was accepted by the Greeks as of the same meaning as the language of St. Maximus, a celebrated Greek theologian of the seventh century. This was the initial point of agreement, though the extreme Greek party fought long and desperately. Bessarion was probably nearest the truth when he argued that the Latin dogma expressed by εξ ("from the Son") and the Greek δια ("through the Son") were synonymous, if both agreed that there could be but one cause of the procession.

The sudden death of the patriarch seemed likely to put a stop to all proceedings, and Pope and emperor were almost in despair; but it was found that he had left a paper agreeing under certain conditions to accept the supremacy of the Roman Church. At last, after infinite diplomacy and halts and advances beyond number, on July 4th the final decree was finished, running in the Pope's name, " with the consent of our dear son, the Emperor of the East," and on July 5th it was signed by one hundred and fifteen

Latins and thirty-three Greeks, the latter protesting much and assenting most reluctantly.

The conclusions reached on the four points were these: 1. The question of the double procession was compromised (Robertson) on the ground that the Greeks, by speaking of the Spirit as proceeding from the Father, did not exclude the Son, but only intended to guard against the idea that the Spirit proceeded from two principles; and since the Latins disavowed this, the two churches really held the same truth. 2. The holy eucharist may be celebrated either with leavened or unleavened bread, each church to retain its own custom. 3. Souls whose sins have not been fully expiated in this life are purified by purgatorial fires, each church retaining its view of the nature of purgatory. Souls in purgatory can be helped by masses and good works. 4. (Creighton) The Pope is recognized as the sovereign pontiff, Vicegerent and Vicar of Christ, shepherd and teacher of all Christians, and ruler of the church of God, saving the privileges and rights of the patriarchs of the East.

On July 6th a splendid service was held to celebrate the long-wished-for and now seemingly accomplished union between the Eastern and Western churches. The Greeks had the finest clothes, but mass was sung with the " Filioque " in the creed. The Pope had triumphed, and he intended to make the most of it. The Greeks were paid up, and a treaty was signed by the Pope and emperor as follows: 1. The Pope to send back in a handsome manner and at his own expense all the Greeks. 2. The Pope to furnish every year two galleys and three hundred men-at-arms for the defence of Constantinople. 3. All ships going to the Holy Land to touch at Constantinople. 4. In any case of great extremity there, the Pope to furnish twenty galleys for six months, or ten for a year. 5. The Pope to use his influence with Western princes to induce them to help the Greek emperor.

With these arrangements the Greeks at last departed, and after many trials by sea and land reached the Golden Horn. Their reception was a disheartening one indeed; so far from being welcomed as the promoters of union in the church of God, they heard on all sides the cry of " Traitor! renegade! apostate! " The churches and the clergy which favored the union were boycotted by the populace, and a rebellion against the emperor broke out. The whole scheme of union vanished into thin air, and before twenty years were over Constantinople was a Turkish city, the Greeks preferring to be slaves of the Moslem rather than subscribe to what they considered the heresies of the Latin Church. While we smile at their obstinate magnifying of trifles, we must greatly admire their constancy and courage; they truly sacrificed themselves for their religious belief.

It is not worth while to say more of the Council of Florence, for this was its principal work. It was never of any authority outside the Roman communion; its members were nearly all Italians apart from the Greek contingent, and the powers of Europe took no part in it. Yet it subserved two purposes: It introduced a large number of the best Greek scholars into Western intellectual life, and quickened greatly the study of the Greek classics, and it also restored the dignity of the Papacy. Through the obstinacy and narrowness of Eugenius that power had been much humbled; but now Europe rejoiced with Eugenius that he had been able to heal the Greek schism, for so it then appeared. The papal power was again on the upward path, and the two succeeding popes, Nicolas V. and Pius II., devoted their great abilities, with much success, to the consolidating and strengthening of this wonderful system, even yet the most powerful of the religious forces which move the Christian world.

CHAPTER XXXIII.

THE GERMAN MYSTICS.

IT may be well to begin by defining what is meant by mystics and mysticism. It refers to a craving to get away from low and unspiritual levels, to break away from the formality and perfunctoriness of the average religious life,—and it was perhaps never much lower or more perfunctory than in the fourteenth century,—a desire to find a union with God which should be as real as the common relationships of daily life. It will be better understood by mentioning some historical characters to whom the word "mystic" would apply: Gautama in India, Confucius in China, Fénelon in France, John Bunyan and John Wesley in England, the Fratricelli, the Brethren of the Free Spirit, the many divisions of the Spiritual Franciscans. While these differed much in views, their teaching all partook of that quietism, that renunciation of the will, which characterizes mysticism in one or other of its forms.

The fourteenth century was the golden age of mysticism. Germany was its peculiar home, and its great promoter was undoubtedly Master Eckhart, a

Dominican. Though no mean scholastic, he threw away all scholastic modes of expression, and appealed, not to the understanding, but directly to the hearts of the people by pithy sermons and short tracts, not in Latin, but in the vernacular. His great idea of absorption with God he carried so far that it exposed him to the charge of pantheism. He used the expression, " All things are in God and all things are God." This would seem to connect him with the licentious doctrines of the Brethren of the Free Spirit, but he abhorred them, and taught only purity and an ardent desire after God. His expressions were, however, unguarded enough to expose him to the charge of heterodoxy, and the very year he died Pope John XXII. condemned him as having held twenty-eight false ideas; but the Dominicans manfully stood up for him, and his writings influenced greatly the more religious of his time.

It would be impossible to trace all the different shades of mysticism. Many of its teachers, especially the Beghards and the Brethren of the Free Spirit, were rank pantheists, and taught that the supreme end of existence was the absorption of the individual into the infinite substance of God. It will be sufficient to follow the career of one who is better known than any other, whose sermons, dull though they are, are still read, and who did not fall into the pantheistic snare which seemed to entrap so many of his brethren.

John Tauler was born of wealthy parents in Strasburg in 1290 or 1294, and at the age of eighteen entered upon the religious life in the Order of St.

Dominic. He studied in Paris, and on his return to his native city fell under the influence of Eckhart; he never was, however, so great a quietist, but taught that true piety is the application of religious principles to real life. " One can spin," he said, " another can make shoes; and all these are gifts of the Holy Ghost. If I were not a priest I would esteem it a great gift that I was able to make shoes, and would try to make them so well as to be a pattern to all. The measure with which we shall be measured is the faculty of love in the soul; by the submission of the will of a man shall all his life and works be measured." Vaughan in his work on the mystics says: " The memorable step of progress made by Tauler and his companions is briefly indicated by saying that they substituted the idea of the immanence of God in the world for the idea of the emanation of the world from God; an idea familiar to us, but at that time liable to be misunderstood."

Tauler lived during that weary strife between Frederic of Austria and Louis of Bavaria. His native city, Strasburg, declared for Louis, and on that account was put under the ban by the Pope, which involved, of course, the stopping of all spiritual ministrations by the clergy. Tauler, however, paid no attention to the ban, but spent his time in consoling the sick and dying, and burying the dead. He addressed a letter to his brother priests, and no braver words were ever spoken in the height of the Reformation, two hundred years later. He said: " You are bound to visit and console the sick, remembering the bitter pain and death of Christ, who hath made sat-

isfaction not for your sins only, but also for those of
the whole world; who doth represent us all before
God, so that if one falleth innocently under the ban,
no Pope can shut him out of heaven. You should
give absolution to such as wish, therefore giving heed
rather to the teaching of Christ and His apostles than
to the ban, which is issued only out of malice and
avarice. " Those who hold the true Christian faith and
sin only against the person of the Pope are no heretics.
Those rather are the real heretics who obstinately
refuse to repent and forsake their sins; for let a man
have been what he may, if he will so do he cannot
be cast out of the true church. Through Christ the
truly penitent thief, murderer, adulterer, all may have
forgiveness. When Christ beholdeth such under an
unrighteous ban, He will turn for them the curse into
a blessing." During the awful ravage of the Black
Death in Strasburg, Tauler was most devoted to the
sick and dying.

A curious crisis occurred in Tauler's life in 1340.
He was then a noted preacher, and with vast influence far beyond Strasburg, and was about fifty years
of age. One day a mysterious stranger, who is sometimes called Nicolas of Basel, though without much
authority for so doing, called on him, and asked to
confess. Several times he came to confession, and
his conduct and conversation made a great impression
on Tauler. He then asked Tauler to preach a sermon
on the way of reaching the highest spiritual attainment, and after the sermon said to the preacher,
" You preach to others, but you do not know the

sinfulness of your own heart, for you have never yet surrendered yourself completely to God."

These words seemed to go to Tauler's very heart, and to throw him into an agony of sorrow and suspense. For two whole years he never once preached, and was ever seeking and praying for light and peace. At last peace came, and with the peace a greater power of preaching than ever before; for so lit up with spiritual glow were his sermons that the men of his time called him the "Doctor Illuminatus."

This mysterious stranger figures largely in Tauler's life, and in the religious life of that period. His mission seemed to be the founding, secretly and quietly, of a society called the "Friends of God," of whom Tauler became one of the chief. It was not very numerous, for the members could only be those who willed what God willed, and disliked what He disliked; but they were to be found scattered all over Europe, from Holland to Italy. The renunciation of the will was their great doctrine. This, they taught, brought about freedom from all passions and desires, even that of salvation, and so it was possible to arrive at absolute sinlessness, and at death go direct to heaven without passing through purgatory. The Friends of God never broke with the church, and their unchanging loyalty to Rome enabled them to escape much condemnation. Gregory XI. had interviews at Avignon with the mysterious founder of the sect, and saw nothing objectionable in his allegorical warnings, and even threatenings, of him if he did not reform the church. The popes of those days heard a great deal of plain speaking, and the Gregory in question was much badgered by St. Catherine of Siena.

The Friends of God held the, at that time, unusually tolerant view that many Jews and Moslems were saved; for God, they said, abandons none who seek Him, and, though such could not enjoy Christian baptism, yet they held that God Himself baptized them spiritually in their death-agony. In the same spirit, they refused to denounce a heretic to human justice, for fear of anticipating divine justice. They felt that they could tolerate him in the world as long as God saw fit to do so.

There is no doubt that the mystic theology was well known to Luther, and greatly influenced him, so far as it urged men to forbear trusting in outward observances, and to seek spiritual and inward life; but the Lutheran doctrine lays far more stress on sacraments than the mystics ever did, for, with their views, all external usages and ceremonies were of little importance compared with the inner union of the soul with God.

CHAPTER XXXIV.

THE INQUISITION IN THE FOURTEENTH CENTURY.

HE Inquisition was an institution which was gradually formed, and grew out of the impossibility of stopping heresy by eloquent sermons, or by examples of the most devoted piety and unselfishness. These the Western Church employed lavishly, but heresy still grew; and, as the doctrine of the age was that of all crimes heresy was the worst, and as every Christian endangered his own soul's salvation by not doing all he could to root it out, there only remained the use of organized and forcible means. It was to perfect such organization, and bring to bear most effectively such force, that the Inquisition began.

The friars of the mendicant orders were naturally the most available inquisitors and the most interested, and of those orders the Dominicans proved the most serviceable and undertook the most of the work. It never was a showy organization; the dress of its officials was plain and simple, and it avoided in every way attracting public attention. The chief town of each province was the chief seat of the Inquisition, and there also were its prisons; but the inquisitor was bound to make a personal examination of a case of heresy on the spot where it was reported.

It must not be thought that the Inquisition never pardoned, that it was certain death even to be accused by it. It very often pardoned. The men conducting it were not monsters who loved to kill; they were ordinary Christians, with the same feelings of pity and tenderness that other men have; they often were of eminent spirituality, devout and spotless in character; but they were imbued with the firm conviction that heresy sent a soul to hell, and that it was infinitely more merciful to torture the body if by that means the soul could be saved from eternal torture. Doubtless they often found their duty very hard to do, and prayed that the cup might be taken from them. We sometimes forget this, and judge harshly men who were only the creatures of their age. It was the horrible system, the utterly perverted doctrine, that worked such terrible havoc.

One of the worst abuses of the Inquisition was the encouragement it gave to slander and calumny. No one knew what tales an enemy might be carrying to an inquisitor, and often a man's arrest was the first intimation he had that he was even suspected. Then, it made every one suspicious of his neighbor. Men hesitated to speak freely of the commonest topics— and at that time religion was the most common—for fear lest it might give color to some accusation of heresy, and be worked up into a case against them. A constant mass of papers was accumulating in the archives of the Inquisition, and when least expected some damaging item against some one would be brought out. Thus, in 1306 (Lea), the Inquisition took umbrage at the royal governor of Albi, and brought out letters showing that the governor's grandfather had been a heretic, and therefore, according to law, the grandson could not hold office.

Although the Inquisition avoided publicity, there was one event connected with it which was made as public and splendid as possible, and that was the *auto da fé,* or " act of faith," as the ceremony was called which settled the fate of the accused. At one held in Toulouse, April, 1310, twenty were condemned to wear crosses and go on pilgrimages, sixty-five were imprisoned, and eighteen were burned then and there in the public square. Two years after, in the same place, fifty-one were sentenced to wear crosses, eighty-one to imprisonment, the bones of thirty-six were ordered to be dug up and burned (this certainly harmed nobody), five were burned, and five more would have been if they could have been caught.

The methods of the Inquisition, its questionings, its tortures, are too well known to render it necessary to describe them here. Its influence on the civil courts was most deplorable; for they, owing to the great preponderance of the church, adopted its tortures and its perfectly unjust manner of dealing with criminals. Lea, in his " History of the Inquisition," well says: " It would be impossible to compute the amount of misery and wrong, inflicted on the defenceless up to the present century, which may be directly traced to the arbitrary and unrestricted methods introduced by the Inquisition, and adopted by the jurists who fashioned the criminal jurisprudence of the Continent. It was a system which might well seem the invention of demons, and was fitly characterized by Sir John Fortescue as ' the road to hell.' "

The Inquisition in France during the fourteenth century sank into great decadence. The royal authority overruled it in so many instances that gradually its officials and its methods fell into contempt. Thus in Carcassonne, a very paradise for Dominican inquisitors, they were unable, in 1314, to put down a simple blacksmith who carried on his noisy trade too near their convent; the royal authority had to be called in. The University of Paris took up the business of heresy-hunting and thus superseded the Inquisition; and while it still existed, its teeth were drawn and its claws pared. The fiercest inquisitorial hatred in France was lavished on the Waldenses. These were sectaries resembling in many respects the Lollards. They held their distinguishing tenet that the sinfulness of the minister invalidated the sacrament. They professed to hold to episcopal ordination and to transubstantiation, but any good man, priest or lay, could consecrate. They did not believe in purgatory, nor in the invocation of saints, and theoretically they were non-resistant, though they often fought desperately. The names of Waldenses often appear in the lists of burnings in the fourteenth century; but gradually we lose trace of them, and in the troubles of the schism and of the kingdom of France there was too much other important business going to allow much attention to be given to them.

In Spain the Inquisition was fully established about the middle of the thirteenth century, and it worked on languidly through the fourteenth; but it was not until the fifteenth century, and under Ferdinand and Isabella, that it became the cruel, blood-sucking octopus so well known in history.

The Inquisition in Italy in the fourteenth century, like that in France, showed great signs of weakness and decay. There were arrests and burnings of Waldenses in Piedmont and Savoy, and the few Cathari who remained were hunted down; but there was great indifference about the Holy Office, and when heretics were to be attacked, even popes, as Martin V. (1417), disregarded the regular officials of the Inquisition, and appointed specials to manage the campaign.

Germany long resisted the Inquisition, but it was brought in at last by Urban V., in 1367, who appointed two inquisitors, and they went to work with considerable success at crushing the Beghards. Charles IV. was a great friend of the Inquisition, and under him it raised its serpent head proudly in the land, and large numbers of burnings and torturings took place. There were plenty of heretics to work upon, but after the death of Charles IV. it lost its power, and gradually, as in almost all other European lands, it grew more and more out of date. It cuts a small figure in the Reformation under Luther.

Sorcery grew to vast proportions in the fourteenth century, and the Inquisition devoted itself to putting it down; but it had to struggle against great odds, for the very edicts, such as John XXII., a firm believer in magic, put out, forbidding Christians to enter into a compact with hell, or to imprison devils in rings or mirrors, made people believe that such things really could take place, and increased the number of dupes. All over Europe, in the fourteenth, fifteenth, and even sixteenth centuries, sorcery and witchcraft played a prominent part, and the efforts of the Inquisition to put down these superstitions were well meant, and, while drastic, were often efficient.

Lea, at the close of the third volume on the " History of the Inquisition," summarizes its career in the middle ages: " It infected and distorted secular justice, and gave the popes a terrible weapon to use in political aggrandizement. It stimulated the morbid sensitiveness to doctrinal aberrations, until the most trifling dissidence roused men to fury. In its long career of blood and fire, the only credit it can claim is the suppression of the pernicious dogmas of the Cathari and the Brethren of the Free Spirit, and these dogmas carried in themselves the seeds of self-destruction. The judgment of impartial history must be that the Inquisition was the monstrous offspring of mistaken zeal, utilized by selfish greed and lust of power to smother the higher aspirations of humanity and stimulate its baser appetites."

CHAPTER XXXV.

LITERATURE AND ARTS IN THE FOURTEENTH CENTURY.

T is true that the ecclesiastical history of the fourteenth century was a troubled and a shameful time; that has been shown in the preceding pages; but in spite of all the abuses, the frightful immorality, the destroying pestilence, there has not often been since the time of Christ a period of greater advance in many important points. The fourteenth century was marked by wonderful activity in architecture, in commerce, in the arts, in the study of the classics, in the softening of the harsh features of feudalism, in the rise of the class of great lawyers who took a bold stand in the contest between church and state, and in the founding of great universities and the spread of their influence far wider than ever before or since.

But it was in the development of national literature, and in the perfecting of the vernacular in place of the stately Latin, which had so long been the only vehicle for expressing thought, that this century was particularly distinguished.

The Italian language was the one most quickly

and perfectly developed, and it owes this distinction to one man, who still stands in the very front rank of the world's great intellects, Dante Alighieri (1265–1321). He wrote his immortal poem, the " Divine Comedy," in Italian, and not in Latin, adopting that course after the most serious reflection; not that he was not perfect master of Latin, but from motives of the loftiest patriotism. This poem is a whole epitome of the middle ages, and no one can understand them who does not familiarize himself with its lofty strains. Then, after Dante came Petrarch, who brought out more completely the softer and tenderer parts of the language in his love-sonnets, and also in his pathetic canzone over the unhappy lot of Rome. Then came Boccaccio (1313–1375), who brilliantly illustrated the wit and humor of his native language. He was coarse, even obscene, but his clear and finished prose still marks him as one of the classics of his tongue.

These three men thoroughly transformed the Italian language, and left it, even at that early date, so perfect that even now their works need no polishing to fit them for the use of the scholars of to-day, which cannot be said of the writings of any one in England, France, or Germany. These men also did much to arouse that interest in the treasures of ancient literature, the Greek and Roman classics, which blossomed and bore full fruitage in the Renaissance.

The great natural ability of the Italian people is shown by the contrast between the condition of Italy and that of other European countries during this century. It is true that the States of the Church were in wretched condition, and the city of Rome in ruins;

but that was not the case in other parts of Italy. Amalfi, Pisa, Venice, Genoa, were all the seats of a splendid commerce. Milan had two hundred thousand people, and possessed great manufactories of armor, saddlery, and " Milanery " (from whence our word " millinery ") of all sorts. Lombardy was a vast garden from the effects of the irrigating canals, and the Lombard and Florentine bankers were woven in with the commerce of all Europe.

Let us not forget that, amid all the wars and squabbles of Pope and Kaiser, it was in the fourteenth century that Gian Galeazzo built the wondrous cathedral of Milan, which still stands, like some dream in marble, and that painting then burst its swaddling-clothes under Masaccio, Cimabue, and Giotto. The morals were low, but the civilization was high—a lesson to us that this modern idea about the refining and elevating influence of splendor and wealth is not at all a sure sign of corresponding wealth of virtue and prudence, of high morality and patriotic self-renunciation.

The French language made great progress in the fourteenth century, though not as rapid nor as far-reaching as the Italian. Its most conspicuous example is Froissart, the chronicler (1326–1400). He writes in a clear, pointed, spicy, delightful way, which makes him even yet a favorite with every lover of stories of adventure. He was a born traveller and gossip, and spent his whole life wandering from castle to castle, from tournament to tournament, from siege to siege, listening and noting, weaving it all, much as any skilled modern reporter would do, into a series of

papers which would have commanded instant attention if the press had existed at that time. It is
germane to this book to quote his remarks on the
church troubles of his time. "This I well know," he
says, "that some day people will be astonished that
the church should have become involved in such difficulties, and so long have been unable to free herself
from them. It was a plague sent by God to warn
the clergy, and make them consider what a great
estate and superfluity they held and managed; but
many did not take that into consideration, for they
were so blinded by overweening pride that each one
wanted to be like every one else, and because of that
things went badly. If our faith had not been confirmed by the hand and the grace of the Holy Spirit,
it would have wavered and given way; for the great
nobles did nothing but laugh and play at the time I
write, providing neither a remedy nor a plan."

Vernacular French was also greatly assisted in its
development by the dialogues from the Bible called
"mysteries," spoken in rude booths, with rough stage
accessories. All the parables and miracles were thus
brought home in the most realistic way to the beholders. The foolish virgins wake up on the stage
and cry, "Unhappy wretches! we have slept too
long." Charles VI., in 1402, licensed a company
which every Sunday presented in the vernacular the
leading events in our Lord's life.

England was one of the last countries to form an
idiom, a fact which is easily understood when one
thinks of the many different races which had conquered and overrun her, each with its own language,

thus checking the growth of a common tongue. In the fourteenth century, the Normans and the Saxons getting closer together, the two languages, French and English, blended and made a mixed language, in which Saxon had the preëminence and gave the dominant tone. A writer of the time says that, after the Black Death (1385, Richard II.), in all the grammar schools of England children began to leave off French, and construe and study in English. Edward III., in 1362, decreed that all the law pleadings should be in English. It was Chaucer, however, who fixed the floating elements of the English tongue, and gave us the first work we can really call English. Then came Wyclif's nervous and vivid translation of the Scriptures, and that charming and piquant book of travels of Sir John Mandeville.

The German language was already in form. The brilliant poets under the Hohenstaufen dynasty had given it much distinction and power, and during this century Tauler and other preachers made a most skilful use of it. The collection of laws published at that time shows also the great progress German had made towards its present copious, and even over-rich, vocabulary.

Already, in the thirteenth century, the code of Alfonso the Wise shows the stateliness of the Spanish idiom, and from that time that language slowly displaced the Latin and the Arabic in the courts of the petty Spanish princes, and in the fourteenth century we have "El Conde Lucanor" and the "Chronicle of Ayala." The "Romancero of the Cid" is too varied and by too many different authors to be easily classified.

YORK COLLEGE LIBRARY

Many universities were founded in the fourteenth century: Heidelberg, 1386; Cologne, 1389; Prague, 1348; Vienna, 1386; Erfurt, 1392. In England the great schools of Winchester and Eton were founded, the first in 1387, the latter in 1440. The University of Paris had been founded in 1200, but it was during this century that it attained the height of its power and exercised so astonishing an influence in the current controversies. It is probably a great exaggeration, that which attributes to it twenty thousand pupils, but no less than seven popes and a vast number of cardinals called it their alma mater.

INDEX.

YORK COLLEGE LIBRARY

28168

YORK COLLEGE
Library No. 22808

WESTMAR COLLEGE LIBRARY
LE MARS, IOWA